G000257701

Inventing Future Cities

Inventing Future Cities

Michael Batty

The MIT Press
Cambridge, Massachusetts
London, England

© 2018 Massachusetts Institute of Technology

All rights reserved. No part of this book may be reproduced in any form by any electronic or mechanical means (including photocopying, recording, or information storage and retrieval) without permission in writing from the publisher.

This book was set in Stone Serif by Westchester Publishing Services. Printed and bound in the United States of America.

Library of Congress Cataloging-in-Publication Data

Names: Batty, Michael, author.
Title: Inventing future cities / Michael Batty.
Description: Cambridge, MA : MIT Press, [2018] | Includes bibliographical
   references and index.
Identifiers: LCCN 2018011623 | ISBN 9780262038959 (hardcover : alk. paper)
Subjects: LCSH: Cities and towns--Growth. | City planning--Technological
   innovations. | Sustainable development. | Technological innovations--
   Economic aspects.
Classification: LCC HT371 .B38 2018 | DDC 307.76--dc23
   LC record available at https://lccn.loc.gov/2018011623

10 9 8 7 6 5 4 3 2 1

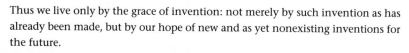

Thus we live only by the grace of invention: not merely by such invention as has already been made, but by our hope of new and as yet nonexisting inventions for the future.

—Norbert Wiener, *Inventions*, 3

Contents

Preface

Most of us would agree we cannot predict the future. But until quite recently, this was not the case. Little seemed to change from generation to generation. People rose in the morning and worked until dusk, engaging in many social pursuits that remained unchanged throughout their lives. When cities finally emerged some 5,000 years ago, they mirrored this relative stability, and it was entirely logical for those who thought about urban futures to assume cities' future physical form and the functions reflected within would change very little over hundreds of years. Only in the last 500 years, since the Renaissance in Europe—and perhaps really only in the last 200, since the beginning of the Industrial Revolution—has our long-lived certainty about the future come under scrutiny.

In this book, I argue that we now stand at a threshold with respect to what we are able to predict (or rather not predict). We are living through a time when our view of science is fast maturing to a state in which prediction is no longer the only major determinant in judging its applicability and relevance. For hundreds of years, cities have manifested a simple spatial structure based on a well-defined central core embodying the power and wealth cities are designed to process and transform. This image of the city as a high-density core with different land uses and activities arrayed concentrically about it, organized so that the richest are able to bid out the poorest to occupy the most accessible locations, is one that has been perpetuated since the first cities emerged during the Agricultural Revolution.

All this is changing. What is now happening is that a massive disconnect is emerging between what the city looks like and what goes on "under the hood," so to speak. We can no longer assume form follows function, and the old certainties that have dominated city planning since classical times are disappearing. Cities are getting more complex at a faster rate than our understanding is able to keep up with, and the theories that we held dear not half a century ago are no longer appropriate. Predictability has been a victim in this transition—this is one of the main themes around which this book is organized. Invention is another, and I will argue time and again here that the future is one we invent. Yet although this might seem a plausible alternative to prediction, we will never be able to predict what we invent. So we are in a double bind when it comes to what we might imagine the future city to be like. In fact, the future city may look quite similar to what cities look like now, but everything within them may be arranged differently from what we see at present. This, I will argue, will be the usual condition henceforth.

This book does not set out a final program for inventing future cities, for this will take a sea change in the way all of us need to think about cities. What I have tried to do is assemble a series of snapshots or views of the terrain needed to think about this future. Much of the material I introduce comes from general reflections on how various scholars have sought to think about this future, but I have been helped enormously by my own research group, who have developed many perspectives on the contemporary city that I point to here. In 2010, I was rather lucky to gain a European Research Council Advanced Grant, which brought together many of the colleagues who have helped me with this work in my center, also keeping me at University College London (UCL). I acknowledge their individual contributions in the material introduced below, but I also need to spell out how they have helped me. During this period, computers have scaled down to the point where they are being embedded into the most detailed fabric of our lives, enabling us to develop new responses to the world and capture massive amounts of data about our own behaviors. Social media is perhaps the most obvious example of this evolution. The fact that my research is deeply informed by colleagues who do not come to this world of cities like I do, with the intellectual baggage of the last half-century, has been massively influential in the perspectives I have attempted to adopt here. At the same time, the development of a science of cities has proceeded apace as new waves of thinking from statistical physics and economics have begun to invade our world, enriching, extending, and questioning our theories about how cities form and evolve. Complexity theory lies in the vanguard of these developments, and in and of itself has led to some of our newfound skepticism over our abilities to predict.

In my group, Elsa Arcaute has done a remarkable job running our research program in the science of cities and, with Clementine Cottineau, has been responsible for resurrecting our interests in city size, diffusion, percolation, and innovation. Carlos Molineros has been key to the work noted here on hierarchy and percolation defining the regions and cities of Britain and neighborhoods in London. Duncan Smith's efforts at visualizing the form of megacities and urban sprawl complements much of this work. In terms of the real-time city, Jon Reades, following his thesis on information flows in southeast England with Peter Hall and myself, initiated our work on the functioning of transit systems using smart card data in London, while Chen Zhong and Ed Manley continued and enriched this once Jon had decamped to Kings. Richard Milton supplemented much of this work from the real-time streaming of actual traffic on various transport modes in London. Steven Gray began our work on packaging much of this real-time data through his city dashboards, with Ollie O'Brien extending these ideas through various portals, such as his London Panopticon. Fabian Neuhaus first began mapping Twitter data in 2009, while Joan Serras initiated our work on visualizing transport flows, extending this to visualizing flows using credit card data in Madrid and Barcelona. Yao Shen helped in developing algorithms for aggregating London into contiguous areas of commuting intensity. All these applications are noted below at appropriate points.

I first began to think seriously about urban form and function many years ago, but received a major push when I retooled myself in computer graphics in the early 1980s. This led quite quickly to my work with Paul Longley on fractal cities, which set us on the road to the kind of science implicit in much of this book. Paul has continued to work tangentially with us in developing the geodemographics of the contemporary city, and in social media both of our research groups at UCL function together. Two of my mentors from earlier days, Peter Hall and Lionel March, focused my interest on the socioeconomic structure and growth of cities as well as their geometry. Their contributions, which will be remembered for years to come, are reflected in many of the themes that run through this book. Peter's contribution to thinking about future cities is legendary. I think he would be surprised that I embarked on this kind of book, but I hope he would be pleased, because several of the themes I reference here—long waves, singularities, sprawl and compactness, and the massive impact of cities on generating innovations in science and technology as well as culture—were ideas he wrote about throughout his life. Lionel's passion for urban form and function runs deep in these pages, and the research directions that he established in the geometry of environment continue to enrich our views about the future of cities. In my previous book, *The New Science of Cities* (MIT Press, 2013), Lionel argued that I should have given a lot more weight to Benton Mackaye's ideas about how urban flows define the forces pushing and pulling the city in myriad ways. I have tried to take his advice here when I discuss the way future cities will continue to expand and contract outward, inward, and upward.

I think there is much more we need to say about cities as we come to terms with a world that is intricately connected and where information underpins our every act. In fact, this has been the case since cities first emerged, but only quite recently, in the last 25 years or so, have we begun to embark on a world where our every action is mediated by instant communications. What this will mean for a world where we all live in globally connected cities is another of the great challenges I pose in this book. In this sense, this book, like all such books, is unfinished business. As I argue throughout, the message is that we will never know what the future city will look like, just as we will never know how we and other species might evolve. But we can engage in an informed discussion about this future, elucidating key issues and how these are likely to change. What cities will look like physically in the future is interesting, but it is only one of many features of this future.

This book would not have been possible had not Beth Clevenger, my editor at MIT Press, been so enthusiastic about its publication. I also need to thank Anthony Zannino and Virginia Crossman of the press for their work on editing the manuscript. My wife Sue, as always, has supported me in this endeavor, and her wit and tolerance in dealing with my idiosyncrasies and foibles turned this idea for the book into a reality.

Michael Batty
Little Britain,
London EC1A 7BX
March 2018

Image Credits

Figures 2.1–2.8: Author's own.

Figure 3.1: Redrawn from C. Alexander, "A City Is Not a Tree." *Architectural Forum* 122, no. 1 (1965): 58–62.

Figure 3.2: Duncan Smith, Centre for Advanced Spatial Analysis, University College London, http://luminocity3d.org/WorldPopDen.

Figure 3.3: Yao Shen, Centre for Advanced Spatial Analysis, University College London.

Figure 3.4: Author's own.

Figure 3.5: Carlos Molineros, Centre for Advanced Spatial Analysis, University College London. Published in E. Arcaute et al., "Cities and Regions in Britain through Hierarchical Percolation," *Royal Society Open Science* 3, no. 4 (2016), doi:10.1098/rsos.150691.

Figure 3.6(a): J. Cary, "Survey of the High Roads from London to Hampton Court … Richmond," 1790, p. 10, https://archive.org/details/caryssurvey ofhig00cary.

Figure 3.6(b): P. Abercrombie, "Greater London Plan 1944," 1945, His Majesty's Stationery Office, London. Reproduced in M. Batty and P. Longley, *Fractal Cities: A Geometry of Form and Function* (London: Academic Press, 1994), 50, from http://www.rtpi.org.uk/media/882342/london_plan ning_history._february_2014.pdf.

Figure 3.6(c): Carlos Molineros, Centre for Advanced Spatial Analysis, University College London.

Figure 4.1(a): Town plan of Nippur, Babylonian, 1300 BCE, https://www.pin terest.co.uk/pin/488359153314169881.

Figure 4.1(b): Babylon, 600 BCE, https://geekydementia.wordpress.com/2014 /11/27/babylonian-map-of-the-world.

Figure 4.1(c): Ga Sur, abstracted, near Catal Hyuk, 2500 BCE, https://semra bayraktar.blogspot.co.uk/2013/03/maps-from-beginning-catalhoyukten -piri.html.

Figure 4.1(d): Ur, 4000 BCE, https://www.realmofhistory.com/2017/07/27 /reconstruction-ur-city-sumerian.

Figure 4.1(e): Ur, redrawn from http://www.worldhistory.biz/ancient-history /71457-ur-the-royal-tombs.html.

Figure 4.2(a): Miletus, https://quadralectics.wordpress.com/4-representation /4-1-form/4-1-3-design-in-city-building/4-1-3-4-the-grid-model/4-1-3 -4-2-the-greek-grid-towns.

Figure 4.2(b): Platner's Map of Ancient Rome, 200 CE, 1911, https://commons .wikimedia.org/w/index.php?search=Platner%27s+map+of+Rome +&title=Special:Search&profile=default&fulltext=1&searchToken=56e 9nhfe8hhx16ujg0o4rej7t#/media/File:The_Topography_and_Monu ments_of_Ancient_Rome.jpg.

Figure 4.2(c): Roman castra, after http://www.daviddarling.info/encyclope dia_of_history/R/Roman_camp.html.

Figure 4.3(a): Leonardo da Vinci—Plan of Imola, https://commons.wikimedia .org/wiki/File:Leonardo_da_Vinci_-_Plan_of_Imola_-_Google_Art_Project .jpg.

Figure 4.3(b): Urbino, https://en.wikipedia.org/wiki/Filarete.

Figure 4.3(c): Palladian villa, https://www.pinterest.co.uk/pin/42763092710785 1462.

Figure 4.3(d): Palmanova, https://commons.wikimedia.org/wiki/File:Palmano va1600.jpg.

Figures 4.4(a) and (b): Author's own.

Figure 4.5(a): J. Cary, "Survey of the High Roads from London to Hampton Court … Richmond," 1790, p. 10, https://archive.org/details/caryssurvey ofhig00cary.

Figure 4.5(b): J. Kohl, *Der Verkehr und die Ansiedelung der Menschen in ihrer Abhangigkeit uon der Gestaltung der Eudoberflache*, 1841. Reproduced from M. Batty, *The New Science of Cities* (Cambridge, MA: The MIT Press, 2013).

Figure 4.5(c): C Minard, *Des Tableaux Graphiques et des Cartes Figuratives*, 1861, https://sandrarendgen.files.wordpress.com/2013/06/bestiaux1.jpg.

Figure 4.5(d): R. Unwin, *Town Planning in Practice: An Introduction to the Art of Designing Cities and Suburbs* (London: T. Fisher Unwin, 1909), https:// archive.org/details/townplanninginp00unwigoog.

Figure 4.5(e): A. Rae, "Work Journey Flow Visualizations," 2017, by permission, http://www.undertheraedar.com/2010/09/flow-map-layout
.html.

Figure 4.6(a) and (b): Richard Milton, Centre for Advanced Spatial Analysis,
University College London, http://quant.casa.ucl.ac.uk.

Figure 4.7(a) and (b): "Inflows and Outflows," from B. MacKaye, *The New
Exploration* (New York: Harcourt and Brace, 1928), 77.

Figure 4.8(a): Frank Lloyd Wright, Illinois Building, copyright © 2018
Frank Lloyd Wright Foundation, Scottsdale, AZ. All rights reserved.
The Frank Lloyd Wright Foundation Archives 5617.002 (The Museum
of Modern Art | Avery Architectural & Fine Arts Library, Columbia
University, New York), https://artblart.files.wordpress.com/2014/05/the
-mile-high-illinois-web.jpg.

Figure 4.8(b): Frank Lloyd Wright, Broadacre City, copyright © 2018 Frank
Lloyd Wright Foundation, Scottsdale, AZ. All rights reserved. The
Frank Lloyd Wright Foundation Archives 5617.002 (The Museum of
Modern Art | Avery Architectural & Fine Arts Library, Columbia Uni-
versity, New York), https://www.mnn.com/green-tech/transportation
/stories/why-the-google-car-could-change-everything.

Figure 4.8(c): Ebenezer Howard, Garden City of Tomorrow, 1898, http://2014
-2015.nclurbandesign.org/sustainability/rebuilding-neighborhood.

Figure 4.8(d): Le Corbusier, by permission, copyright of FLC/Société Des
Auteurs Dans Les Arts Graphiques Et Plastiques, Paris and DACS (Design
and Artists Copyright Society) London, 2018, at https://www.archdaily
.com/411878/ad-classics-ville-radieuse-le-corbusier/.

Figure 4.8(e): redrawn from G. B. Dantzig and T. L. Saaty, *Compact City:
A Plan for a Liveable Urban Environment* (San Francisco, CA: W. H. Freeman and Company, 1973), 176.

Figure 5.1(a): Steven Gray, Centre for Advanced Spatial Analysis, University
College London, http://www.citydashboard.org.

Figure 5.1(b): Oliver O'Brien, Consumer Data Research Centre, Department
of Geography, University College London, http://vis.oobrien.com/pan
opticon.

Figure 5.2(a) and (b): Author's own.

Figure 5.3: Richard Milton, "Geospatial Computing: Architectures and Algorithms for Mapping Applications," unpublished PhD thesis, 2018, Centre
for Advanced Spatial Analysis, University College London.

Figures 5.4(a), (b), (c), and (d) and Figures 5.5(a), (b), (c), and (d): Jon Reades, Geocomputation Group, King's College London, and M. Batty, Centre for Advanced Spatial Analysis, University College London.

Figure 5.6(a), (b), and (c): Joan Serras, from the EUNOIA and INSIGHT projects, http://eunoia-project.eu/publications/ and https://www.insight-fp7.eu/publications.

Figure 5.6(d) and Figure 5.7(a), (b), (c), and (d): Fabian Neuhaus, "Urban Rhythms: Habitus and Emergent Spatio-Temporal Dimensions of the City," 2012, unpublished PhD thesis, Centre for Advanced Spatial Analysis, University College London.

Figure 5.7(e) and (f): Shi Zeng, Centre for Advanced Spatial Analysis, University College London.

Figure 5.8(a) and (b): Eric Fischer, by permission, https://www.flickr.com/photos/walkingsf/6755911359/in/set-72157629014750905, https://www.flickr.com/photos/walkingsf/4621770253/sizes/l.

Figure 5.8(c): Maxime Lenormand, Institute for Cross-Disciplinary Physics and Complex Systems, Palma, Spain, by permission, https://ifisc.uib-csic.es/humanmobility/tweetsontheroad.

Figure 5.8(d): Paul Butler, "Visualizing Friendships," Monday, December 13, 2010, by permission, https://www.facebook.com/notes/facebook-engineering/visualizingfriendships/469716398919.

Figure 6.1: P. G. Geddes, *Cities in Evolution* (London: Norgate and Williams, 1915), 97, https://openlibrary.org/books/OL7136247M/Cities_in_evolution.

Figure 6.2(a): "Los Angeles," by permission, M. Davis, *Ecology of Fear: Los Angeles and the Imagination of Disaster* (New York: Vintage Books, 1999), 78.

Figure 6.2(b): Levittown, NY, by permission, Levittown History Collection, The Levittown Public Library, https://www.flickr.com/photos/markgregory/8087087647.

Figure 6.3(a) and (b): Duncan Smith, Centre for Advanced Spatial Analysis, University College London, http://luminocity3d.org/WorldPopDen.

Figure 6.4: NASA Earth Observatory, by permission, https://earthobservatory.nasa.gov/Features/CitiesAtNight.

Figure 6.5: Redrawn from Jeff Desjardins, "Sizing Up the Tallest Skyscraper of 2015," Visual Capitalist blog, February 11, 2016, http://www.visualcapitalist.com/sizing-up-the-tallest-skyscraper-of-2015.

Figures 6.6(a) and (b), 6.7(a) and (b), and 6.8(a), (b) and (c): Author's own.

Figure 6.8(d): by permission, J. Barr and J. Cohen, "Why are Skyscrapers so Tall? Land Use and the Spatial Location of Buildings in New York," American Economic Association Meeting, January 2011, Denver, CO, https://www.aeaweb.org/conference/2011.

Figure 7.1: Author's own.

Figure 7.2: Redrawn with permission from H. J. Naumer, D. Nacken, and S. Scheurer, "The Sixth Kondratieff—Long Waves of Prosperity," 2010, https://www.allianz.com/v_1339501901000/media/press/document /kondratieff_en.pdf.

Figure 7.3: Hannah Fry, Centre for Advanced Spatial Analysis, University College London, after a sketch from MATLAB.

Figure 8.1: Based on and redrawn from Rick Reider, "The Topic We Should All Be Paying Attention To (in 3 Charts)," Blackrock Blog, December 11, 2015, https://www.blackrockblog.com/2015/12/11/economic-trends-in -charts.

Figure 8.2(a): author's own, from M. Batty and P. Longley, *Fractal Cities: A Geometry of Form and Function* (London: Academic Press, 1994), 63.

Figure 8.2(b): Naarden, Amsterdam, Holland, tourist web site, with permission, https://www.iamsterdam.com/en/plan-your-trip/day-trips/castles -and-gardens/naarden.

Figure 8.3(a), (b) and (c): Ebenezer Howard, *Garden Cities of To-Morrow*, 1902 (reprint edited by F. J. Osborn, London: Faber and Faber, 1946), http:// urbanplanning.library.cornell.edu/DOCS/howard.htm.

Figure 8.3(d) and (e): Urbed, with permission, http://urbed.coop/wolfson -economic-prize.

Figure 8.3(f) and (g): "Behind the Façade of Prince Charles's Poundbury," December 3, 2013, with permission, http://www.architectmagazine.com /design/behind-the-facade-of-prince-charless-poundbury_o; and L. Krier, *The Architecture of Community* (Washington DC: Island Press, 2011).

Figure 8.4(a): A. Soria y Mata, Ciudad Lineal, 1882, http://arqui-2.blogspot .co.uk/2014/07/ciudad-lineal-la-utopia-construida-de.html.

Figure 8.4(b): J. R. Gold, "The MARS Plans for London, 1933–1942: Plurality and Experimentation in the City Plans of the Early British Modern Movement," *Town Planning Review* 66 (1995): 243–267.

Figure 8.4(c): Llewelyn-Davies, Weeks, Forestier-Walker, and Bor, "Milton Keynes Planning Study, 1969," *Architects' Journal*, January 23, 2017,

https://www.architectsjournal.co.uk/news/culture/aj-archive-milton
-keynes-planning-study-1969/10016661.article.

Figure 8.4(d): R. Müller, 1908, http://urbanplanning.library.cornell.edu/DOCS
/muller.htm.

Figure 8.4(e): C. R. Lamb, 1904, http://urbanplanning.library.cornell.edu
/DOCS/lamb.htm.

Figure 8.4(f): Author's own.

Figure 8.4(g): W. Christaller, 1933, from M. Batty and P. Longley, *Fractal Cities:
A Geometry of Form and Function* (London: Academic Press, 1994), 53; and
https://blogs.ethz.ch/prespecific/2013/05/01/diagrams-christaller-central
-place-theory.

Figure 8.5(a) and (b): Author's own.

Figure 8.5(c): J. Miller, by permission, http://unequalscenes.com/masiphu
melele-lake-michelle.

Figure 8.5(d): Scottsdale and the Salt River Indian Reservation, Arizona,
https://www.reddit.com/r/CityPorn/comments/71c7w4/the_boundary
_between_scottsdale_arizona_usa_and.

1 Predictability, Complexity, and Inventing the Future

We cannot predict, by rational or scientific methods, the future growth of our scientific knowledge. ... We cannot, therefore, predict the course of human history.

—K. R. Popper, *The Poverty of Historicism*, v–vi

In the middle of the last century, Karl Popper, one of the great philosophers of science, demonstrated conclusively in an inspired essay that there was no such thing as a predictable future.[1] As the quote above dramatically highlights, there is no possibility that we can predict the course of future history. His argument is based on a very simple premise: that there are always extraneous events—outside our experience, control, or context—that will discount the validity of any such predictions. Moreover, as human agents with self-will, we ourselves will always be able to invent such extraneous events—invent the future, so to speak—but we do not know from one moment to the next what this future might be. This notion of the future as being one of invention rather than prediction has been articulated in many commentaries. In 1963, the Nobel prizewinner Denis Gabor said: "The future cannot be predicted, but futures can be invented," while Alan Kay, chief scientist at Xerox PARC in the 1970s, always remarked:[2] "The only way to predict the future is to invent it." If this is so—and many now ascribe to Popper's view—then there is no such thing as prediction, despite the continued reinforcement of the power of prediction in the science we teach to our children.

This is a very hard lesson to learn. Since we know something of the past, our natural inclination is to consider that the future is at least as knowable as this past. But this is where logic always fails us, and our intuition no longer wins out. Moreover, we also tend to think that the short-term or immediate future is more predictable than the long term, that we have

ˈrol and can better anticipate events over short periods than over
ₒ. ᴆut Popper's argument is uncompromising. Short-term prediction is
no more possible than long-term prediction, although there is a sense in
many contexts that the near future will be closer to the present than to the
far future. The idea that the passage of time influences predictability is based
on the notion that it is likely more extreme events will occur over longer
time periods. But a moment's reflection will convince us that the very notion
of an extreme event is such that we have no idea when it will occur. Events
like this do not come as a steady stream of disruptions, thus destroying any
notion that the world is predictable. For all intents and purposes, the future
is a series of events that are random in their occurrence in size and scale in
space and time. From this perspective, no single event is any more probable
at any one time than any other when conceived over the very long term.

In fact, the ultimate insight Popper first articulated was not that the
future was unpredictable, per se, but that the predictions from any theory could never be proven true. In somewhat perverse fashion, following
Popper, just as we can say that the future is unknowable and inherently
unpredictable, we can also say that we do not know if this assumption
of unpredictability will ever be overthrown. All that we can say about a
particular theory is that it can be falsified, and Popper's real contributions
and insights were to extend and define the conditions for such falsification. Science generally proceeds by assuming that a good theory withstands
attempts at falsification and that the logic of good theory is continually reinforced as more and more observations—predictions about the future, if you
like—are generated. This is the inductive method, as it is called, but it is
merely a working template, which, at some point, will always be demon-
strably wrong as Popper vividly argued.

Induction was first laid bare by philosophers such as Hume during the
Enlightenment, which was in the vanguard of the Industrial Revolution. But
as Popper argued in terms of the scientific method, no amount of new facts
that confirm a hypothesis could lead to the truth, for there is always the
possibility that a new fact will emerge that refutes the theory or hypothesis
under consideration. Thus induction is fatally flawed. Continuous induction
cannot lead to truth, for there is always the possibility that a contradictory
fact will emerge. This notion is encapsulated in the idea of the black swan
discussed recently and popularized by Nicholas Taleb.[3] "All swans are white"
was the empirical law until Australia was discovered, where there were black

swans. Bertrand Russell's concept of the inductivist turkey is even more graphic. The turkey woke each morning, day after day, and at 9am was fed. Being a good inductivist, the turkey assumed that this would always be the case until the day before Christmas when it woke and its throat was cut! The turkey did not consider, could not consider, the wider context.[4]

In short, what this means is that all one can ever do is falsify a hypothesis. One cannot confirm it. But the wider question relates to why this is so, and in the case of our swans and turkeys, it is because the system of interest onto which the hypothesis or theory is anchored, is bounded. If we had known of Australia before its discovery (which is a contradiction in terms), then we would already have observed black swans. Had the turkey been able to stand back and look at what happened to successive generations of its kind, it would have realized that the good life always ends. In short, by broadening the frame of reference, the context changes and what was considered impossible becomes possible, and vice versa. This, as we shall see, in this book is absolutely critical to our thinking about cities, for in many respects our entire argument is premised on the notion that there are multiple definitions with no one definition being "correct," no one theory being "right." This realization has to an extent always been part of science, but Popper, who first laid all this out formally in *The Logic of Scientific Discovery*, argued vociferously that all science could ever do was to falsify a hypothesis, not confirm it.[5] He popularized the notion that good science should seek conjectures that could be refuted, with progress in science being measured by the extent to which a hypothesis resisted falsification, but set against a background where any hypothesis could always be wrong.

Can Anything About Cities Be Predictable?

There is, however, a major qualification to this notion of the future being unpredictable, and this relates to the context in which prediction is sought. Sometimes we can abstract a system to the point where we close it completely from its wider environment—thus, in theory, removing the possibility of the occurrence of various extraneous events. In such a case, it might be possible to demonstrate certain simplified models that are sufficiently stable to generate what appear at first sight to be completely determined predictions. Popper himself argued that Newton demonstrated the determinism of his laws of motion on the obvious closed system available to him at the time—the solar system. With such predictability and simplicity, we can thus apply the complete laws of Newtonian mechanics which we do so routinely in launching satellites which orbit the earth and unmanned probes to the planets. In short, we can use Newton's equations to compute the trajectories of rockets within this system with complete certainty, but once we scale to the universe, all this breaks down and we are forced to consider relativities. When we move to the social world and the world of cities, no such closure is possible. The edifice of economic theory constructed over the last two centuries, to an extent in the shadow of physics, has been refuted time and again. At the present time in the global world we have invented for ourselves, where it seems that everything is related to everything else, no such closure necessary to robust prediction is possible.

To an extent, what is predictable depends on the system or object under our scrutiny. Cities as we perceive them here are aggregates of multiple decision-making processes that generate designs and decisions pertaining to the way we organize our social and economic activities in space and time. It is these aggregates we find difficult to predict, but they are composed of elements, some of which are more predictable than others. Many of these are highly routine decisions with a high degree of predictability, but in aggregate, this degree of predictability is confounded. When these events that compose cities are examined over the short term, then the more routine the events, the higher the degree of predictability. This undermines Popper's argument that events of any duration are unpredictable. Philip Tetlock and Dan Gardner make the point time and again that there is much that is predictable in terms of our own behaviors, but that this predictability is not well understood. Certainly, so far, there has been little effort to figure out an evidence base that discriminates what might be predictable from that which is not. The conditions under which prediction might take place are still largely unknown.[6]

Our views of prediction are continuing to change, and it is very likely that the great transition we are living through will change them further. Popper's argument that prediction is impossible for complex systems is unassailable, but what we might have considered predictable with respect to routine behavior in the past is also changing. Slowly but surely our knowledge about prediction is growing, and we are beginning to assemble evidence about what kinds of routine prediction might be possible. At the same time, routine behavior in cities is changing as shifting technologies provide new opportunities in the space of possible actions and interactions. In one sense, our ability to make predictions for some events is getting better, while for others it is getting worse as the general environment for decision making is becoming more volatile. In much of this book, we will be dealing with what we consider to be largely unpredictable issues, but when we come to examine more detailed forms of routine behavior and their urban dynamics, we will introduce ideas about how we can think of future cities through short-term prediction. Still, the kinds of inventions we have in mind for future cities involve deep-seated changes that are intrinsically unpredictable, and these will continue to dominate our notions about how the future will enfold.

It is now widely accepted that social systems and cities are more like organisms than they are like machines. In this sense, they are the product of countless individual and group decisions that do not conform to any grand plan. These actions lead to structures that are self-organizing and exhibit emergent behavior, of which we will have much more to say in later chapters. This notion of cities evolving is quite consistent with the idea that they are unpredictable, the product of our inventions. Closing one city off from another or from its wider environment is thus fraught with difficulty, as we will soon repeatedly show. Moreover, cities are getting more and more complex as new technologies are being invented, adding yet another nail in the coffin of a predictable urban future. This question of closure will pervade many of the ideas in this book. But before we launch into the great kaleidoscope of attributes that characterize the contemporary city, we need to tack back a little and explore what Jane Jacobs phrased as "the kind of problem a city is," thus introducing the notion that cities are systems, but systems with very different structures and dynamics from those we are familiar with in the machines we use in everyday life.[7]

Complexity: "The Kind of Problem a City Is"

Jacobs drew her inspiration from two sources. The first were the tightly knit, well-defined neighborhoods where she lived in midtown Manhattan, which were under threat from a zealous municipality that sought to demolish extensive areas of 19th-century high-density housing and replace it this with high-rise public housing in the name of progress. At the same time, an extensive network of freeways to cater for the rapid growth of the automobile was proposed for the city, thus hastening a flight to the suburbs in accord with the prevailing view that low-density living was part of the American dream.[8] The second influence on her thinking was an address to the Rockefeller Foundation by Warren Weaver, its then-director of natural sciences, whose all-embracing description of the sciences raised the prospect that a theory appropriate for a wide range of systems should be based on notions that most systems were self-organizing, built and managed from the bottom up; in short, he articulated what has since come to be called "complexity theory."[9]

These two rather disparate sources of inspiration were merged in that she saw cities as being constructed from the bottom up, full of diversity that can only come from individuals acting both separately and together in concert, adapting their ideas to the problems of building livable and sustainable environments. She argued throughout the book that cities were built in such a manner. She drew extensively from her experiences of living in Manhattan to illustrate this thesis, a thesis that she demonstrated largely in practice, but also one that she gave strong theoretical power to in her last chapter, which drew on Weaver's address. Sixty years on, the world of urban planning is slowly but surely coming around to her view as we continue to amass experiences of how difficult it is to try and build cities from the top down, imposing inflexible master plans that always run out of steam due to our inability to provide the organization to implement them and the control to ensure individuals do not undermine them.

The notion that cities are complex systems is entirely resonant with the notion that we cannot predict their future. But the origins of these ideas in fact assume, like most of science prior to the late 20th century, that the world is ultimately predictable. Complexity theory is fast changing this perception, but its origins lie in a different kind of systems theory that relies more on systems that are "designed" from the top down rather then "evolve" from the bottom up. The critical point of such a "general system theory," which emerged from biology and physics in the 1930s, is best summed up in the phrase "the whole is greater than the sum of its parts." Credited to Ludwig von Bertalanffy,[10] the idea that you cannot assemble the complete object by merely adding up the bits was the watchword of those who sought to counter science's long-standing quest to reduce everything to fundamental indivisible units like atoms. Biology was the natural focus of this movement, for clearly no one knew then or knows now how sentient activity can be produced from the basic chemistry of life.

Merely adopting this viewpoint, however, although revolutionary and controversial at the time, is no guarantee that we can devise new and practical theories of how "wholes" might be synthesized from "parts." Indeed, during the 1960s, when general system theory was in full swing, discussion was dominated by how logical the idea was to so many of the more ill-defined sciences and social sciences, but little was ultimately achieved in showing how wholes could be derived from parts. Cities, of course, are the classic exemplar, both with respect to how buildings add up to urban forms and how we as individuals aggregate into urban collectives.

Take economics, for example. Its history had been structured around theories based on describing how a prototypical rational economic man might allocate resources to optimize some personal utility. This microeconomics was shown to be consistent with the way markets formed, for such individual interactions could generate fixed prices that remained stable. But a quite different theory was required for showing how entire economies allocate their resources. Macroeconomics shifted the focus to aggregations of individuals and their interaction, without ever showing how microeconomic theory might be consistent with the way the macroeconomy worked. These two levels were not necessarily inconsistent; they were simply different. Some worried about the aggregation problem, but in general it has not proved possible to integrate these two perspectives.

In the study of cities, a similar difference exists. Theories of the micro-urban and macro-urban economy were developed from the 1950s on—the micro-urban based on showing how individuals locate in space, specifically consumers in particular markets such as housing, whereas the macro-urban focused on interactions between aggregate populations, which appealed to physical analogies based on defining potentials, as in physics. In fact, one of the great triumphs of the 1960s in this field was the clear demonstration that disaggregate models of individual resource allocation in space in which individuals maximize their utility are consistent with macro physical models based on gravitation and potential. Consistency of a kind between spatial scales was thus established.

Yet this was somewhat of a hollow triumph. The real issue of how parts could produce wholes was sidestepped, for—although showing the consistency of theory between hierarchical levels was an achievement in reconciling differences—the essential mechanisms for showing how actual systems developed from their parts were impossible to fathom. What had been demonstrated for city systems was that at a cross-section in time, local decision making could be added to aggregate decision making. But how the city grew, prospered, diversified, developed, and changed was simply not on the agenda. In short, systems theories of the city were structured around parts adding up to wholes via an equilibrium that could not cope with any form of change other than that with the most local impacts. John Holland, one of the founders of complexity theory, sums up the problem rather well when he writes:[11] "A city is a pattern in time. No single constituent remains in place, but the city persists. ... It is suggestive to say that Adam Smith's invisible hand, or commerce, or custom, maintains the city's coherence, but we are still left asking How?"

The contemporary embodiment of general system theory is, in fact, complexity theory. But there has been a sea change since its inception in the early and middle years of the 20th century. Dynamics in the temporal sense has become significantly more important than structure in providing essential drivers, and the notion that cities and all other applicable systems are always in disequilibrium—ranging from periodic to catastrophic and chaotic change—has become the "normal" mode in which systems in general operate. The idea that systems can be "explained" in static terms now seems nonsensical, notwithstanding the fact that most systems can and continue to be described in this way. Ideas about city planning have remained in this frozen state in which time is generally disregarded until quite recently, and that was certainly the case when Jacobs wrote her classic book.

Complexity theory, however, has begun to grapple with ways in which systems manifest qualitative differences as they evolve, how they become locked in to certain behaviors that reveal a kind of path dependence, and how feedback contributes to growth and decline in surprising and novel ways. "History matters" has become the catchphrase of this kind of thinking. Philip Anderson, one of the early proponents, demonstrated that physics—despite its reductionist program—is full of examples that can only be characterized in these terms. In particular, when simple systems with symmetry are broken, he says:[12] "We can see how the whole becomes not only more but very different from the sum of the parts."

In one sense, complexity theory deals with systems whose structure is emergent. This property is clearly a feature of cities, economies, and ecologies within which new and surprising elements evolve. This newness and surprise may only be in terms of positioning within the system, but, nonetheless, it is usual enough to be characteristic of what we know but unusual enough to be largely inexplicable using traditional approaches. So far in our understanding of cities, we can only point to the most obvious examples. For a long time, the similarities between different spatial levels of the urban hierarchy have been known, and it is now possible to show how little cities scale to big cities via simple models that illustrate how local processes generate global patterns. We will introduce some of these ideas in later chapters, but fractal morphologies are a good example. Yet, in some sense, these are too obvious; and even in fractal geometry the focus has been on static structures, not upon the ways in which fractal structures actually emerge.

Dynamics, of course, holds the key to all this. As architects and planners and urban theorists, we delight in approaching the city in terms of its morphology. But morphology is not enough. It must be unpacked, and the only way to unpack it is through dynamics. We require good theories and models that show how positive feedbacks can generate new and surprising structures in situations where the conditions for growth are "right." Although we know how incremental change feeds on past change to generate its own momentum through the realization of scale economies, we still have little clue why such change takes place in the locations it actually does. Of course, we know in generic terms why new clusters of activity, such as edge cities, emerge, but we do not know why such change takes place in particular locations. We can track the development process and articulate such change in terms of locational economics, but we never know where or when such phenomena are likely to take place. Emergence, then, is the key. Holland once again defines it as "much coming from little,"[13] echoing Philip Anderson's inversion of Ludwig Mies van der Rohe's famous cliché: less is more and "more is less"! This is a good oblique riddle of what complex systems are all about, and implicit in this thinking is the notion that such systems are inherently unpredictable, in comparison with traditional views of classical machine systems.

Decisions and Designs

Building and using cities involves a continuous stream of decisions that involve all aspects of human problem solving, from simple tasks that are routinely implemented to major changes in the way we respond to new problems that emerge with little warning. Many of these problems involve us in developing new solutions that need to be designed according to our ingenuity, and many involve responses to new technologies that threaten to disrupt any sense we have of the city being in an equilibrium or steady state. The hallmark of a complex system involves unforeseen repercussions we find hard to anticipate in advance and that are often motivated by attempted solutions which, once implemented, become as much part of the problem as the original conditions that motivated us to attack the problem in the first place. This is very typical of systems whose boundaries we find hard to define and whose interactions with their wider environment are impossible to measure. Horst Rittel, many years ago, defined such problems as "wicked," portraying them rather colorfully as being problems that fight back,[14] often becoming even more severe once attempts at solutions to them are implemented. In fact, this is simply another way of seeing complex systems, such as cities, getting ever more complex with the passage of time as we invent new technologies and adopt new forms of behavior that change the very nature of the system itself.

The problem of dealing with systems that are not well defined (with respect to the existence of a hard boundary between the system and its environment) is that the causal loops that define interactions between the elements of the system spill out into the wider environment in such a way that it is impossible to trace their ultimate impact. To alleviate this, the boundary of the system has to be pushed out further and further, until it might appear as though the entire planet or, in more abstract terms, the entire "universe" has to be embraced. This is certainly the case with global cities, and in a world where everyone can communicate with everyone else, at least in principle, using network devices such as smartphones, cities become almost impossible to define. We will explore this boundary problem in some detail in later chapters, but there is another boundary that we need to note here, and that is the one associated with time. One of the more perverse features of complex systems is that the impacts of feedbacks and interactions often die away at first, but then restore and reinvigorate themselves and blow up through time, leading to all kinds of perverse dynamics that are impossible to even define, never mind track. These are wicked problems with a vengeance. The classic example is that introduced to illustrate chaotic systems by Edward Lorenz,[15] who in 1966 illustrated that very small changes in climatic conditions could set off major events. His colorful example of predictability, or lack of it, is contained in the question that is the subtitle of his paper: "Does the flap of a butterfly's wings in Brazil cause a tornado in Texas?" His illustration that it does with respect to simple climate models is yet another nail in the coffin of a predictable future.

Our perspective on prediction has evolved, certainly, since the 17th and 18th century Enlightenment and the first Industrial Revolution. This is largely because, as the world has become more complex, our certainty that the future is in some sense predictable, or at least could be predictable if we worked hard enough at inventing appropriate scientific forecasting mechanisms, has slowly retreated. Up until the Machine Age, when we built cities, most development was slow but sure, with individuals and small groups adapting their designs to the prevailing conditions, which changed slowly enough to embrace new innovations that could be easily absorbed into the fabric of our building and the location of urban activities. Christopher Alexander[16] portrays the way cities were designed in past eras as unselfconscious processes of evolution and adaptation from the bottom up, in which good design emerged by continual tinkering with the object in question and users acting as builders continually refining their products. When too much changed, there was not enough time for buildings and builders to adapt to these changed circumstances, and cities thus became dysfunctional in countless ways. Cities that are built more slowly thus appear to grow and change more like biological systems than machine systems. This, of course, is the message of complexity theory—design and development from the bottom up—and it is somewhat ironic that these deep-seated evolutionary processes have been largely destroyed by the way we build cities in the modern era. In short, our cities are no longer well adapted to our needs, largely because the rate of change is too fast for those involved in building to respond quickly enough to our changing needs and the innovations that seem to pile up and into one other at an ever-faster pace.

In terms of design, no standard process exists that everyone follows when they make changes to their urban environments. Design involves elements of problem solving, with flashes of inspiration, insight, discovery, and innovation pursued individually and in group contexts. Design is also set in social and political contexts that involve all kinds of speculation, intrigue, one-upmanship, bluff, and every other sentiment that occurs when decisions are made. In short, there is no standard process, nor will there ever be. Context is all-important, and so many discoveries depend upon being in the right place at the right time. In fact, inventing the future can be cast in different ways—as decision making, problem solving, design—but the key issue is that such inventions are impossible to predict. There may be elements that are predictable in a limited sense, but, in general, such futures are unknowable.

It is easy to think of cities in history, particularly those that evolved prior to the Industrial Age, as being well adapted to their wider context. We will argue in this book that the great transition taking place will change the concept of the city as a physical, and perhaps even a spatial, entity quite radically. Even the notion that cities followed a more organic process of change in the past than the contemporary city has in the last 200 years could well change in the next century and beyond. In fact, until the modern era, towns were planned in parts, but most top-down planning was relatively benign and most development slowly adapted to its context—hence the terminology of "vernacular" design. The Industrial Revolution changed all this, and from the mid-19th century, housing, industry, and transportation were all infected by new technologies and new organizational processes that took local decision making away from user-builders on behalf of corporations and agencies whose mission and impact on the built environment has been very different from anything hitherto. The mass public housing programs of the early and mid-20th century are the best examples of this, associated as they were with high-rise buildings. This represents in terms of city building a clean break with the pre-industrial past, with cities being conceived according to Le Corbusier's hallowed phrase:[17] "A house is a machine for living in." We could easily substitute the term "city" for "house" in this phrase, but complexity theory implies that cities are more like organisms, adapting as they do to changing conditions rather than imposing top-down models of strictly designed environments where every building block and occupant knows their place.

Thinking About Future Cities

Since one of our working hypotheses here is that the future is inherently unpredictable, this is not a book about visions for what future cities might "look like," nor is it a set of recipes for designing future cities. It is much more about how we should *think* about future cities based on the argument that we invent these futures. But just as we cannot predict the future, we cannot predict how we might invent it, especially as the future, particularly with respect to cities, is composed of a multiplicity—indeed, almost an infinity—of decisions predominantly generated from the bottom up by all of us. Nevertheless, the world of cities is not random. What we will do here is elucidate certain themes, principles even, that we consider apply to all cities through all time and which we consider must lie at the basis of our invention of the future as well as the past.[18]

In what follows, we introduce examples of city forms invented by visionaries, but these, we will argue, are invariably wide of the mark when it comes to how cities actually grow and evolve. Those looking for new, straightforward, visually appealing pictures of future cities will not find them here. Although we introduce examples taken from the past, these, despite their obvious relevance as "thought experiments," only constitute a tiny fraction of what might emerge as future cities. In fact, the inventions that we will allude to here are hardly inventions of artifacts, per se, but of processes that we argue should lie at the basis of all our thinking about the future. This difference between popular visions of future cities and future realities has been summed up rather well by Peter Thiel, the iconoclastic entrepreneur. In commenting in 2011 on the evolution of information technologies, he said:[19] "We wanted flying cars—instead we got 140 characters". The future will not be about mile-high buildings or extensive urban sprawl. It will not be about driverless cars, nor will it be about us all living in "electronic cottages," places connected wirelessly but physically remote. It may, in fact, be about all of these things, but it is inherently unknowable, and the only way we can second guess it is to define an approach we believe is generic to all cities and their future form. In this approach, we will emphasis invention, not prediction, but an invention very different from the notion of invention and inventors popularized by the contemporary media and the press. In short, our focus will be on inventive processes, on "inventing" rather than inventions per se.

To anticipate what we will say in the following pages, we will begin with some speculations about growth and change in the world's population during the rest of this century. We will argue that the dire predictions concerning overpopulation in a runaway world of depleting resources first made by Thomas Malthus in *An Essay on the Principle of Population* in 1798 and repeated again some 200 years later in the Club of Rome's 1972 report *The Limits to Growth* are never likely to be borne out. It looks as though the demographic transition, as pictured in the familiar logistic or S-shaped curve, will occur across all populations as the growth of world population slows and enters a very different regime, perhaps even a steady state, by the end of this century. But at the same time, by the end of the century, most if not all of us will live in cities. Not in one big city, but in a wide range of cities of different sizes that will follow the first law or principle that we introduce here—the iron law of size distributions, Zipf's law—which predicts that there are many more small cities than big.[20] In short, the coming century will see a great transition from a world where most do not live in cities, which was the case some 200 or more years ago, to a world where everyone lives in cities: not from "City 1.0" to "City 2.0" but from "no city" to "city."

If we are all to live in cities by the end of this century, then the very concept of a city becomes problematic, and a more generic descriptor would be what we would call "urban." The great transition might thus be pictured as one from "nonurban" (even rural) to "urban." As we will never know the future, the prospect of there being massive decentralization in terms of the way we organize urban society is a possibility too. In fact, George Gilder[21] suggests, "big cities are the leftover baggage from the industrial era ... largely due to the fact that new information technologies are continually breaking down ... cities and all other concentrations of power ... implying ... that small, cheap, distributed organizations and technologies will prevail." His vision of the future is one in which the electronic cottage is writ large. Such is our uncertainty about how we will invent this future that these speculations are as significant as any other.

In a global world where everything affects everything else, cities will merge into one another as well as relate to each other across vast distances in space and time. Moreover, their definition, certainly in physical terms, is ever more problematic. Where they begin and where they end is increasingly uncertain. This dilemma is writ large in the many estimates of the population of the biggest cities—but it goes for cities of whatever size. This problem has become severe since cities lost their hard edge—their city walls—over 250 years ago, beginning in Europe, as part of the move to the nation-state. Technological change has accelerated this blurring, as well as the fusion of originally free-standing towns and cities as they have grown together. In characterizing cities, we will invoke the idea that cities are clusters where the cement that binds their components together into networks provides a useful model for their definition. Cities exist as part of a hierarchy of settlements, and this provides us with a way of examining the range of city types, from the hamlet and the village up to the metropolis and megalopolis. To an extent, the physical definition of cities is not breaking down because the cement that ties their components together is dissolving—quite the opposite, for the cement is becoming stronger and more extensive as cities become part of a global network. Only in the last decade have we all come to appreciate this with the rapid spread of smartphones, by which we can be in contact with anything and anybody, anywhere and at any time. This implies our second principle, originally attributed to Edward Glaeser, which we will refer to as the "paradox of the modern metropolis." This suggests that proximity or nearness is becoming more important as the cost and time of connecting across distance is becoming less.[22]

This revolution in information technologies will continue apace during this century. It is this, however, that is forcing a major disconnect in the long-standing notion, first articulated at the end of the 19th century by Louis Sullivan[23] but evident at least from classical times, in the mantra "form follows function." To progress this idea, we first introduce a set of principles—what we call the "standard model," from Johann Heinrich von Thünen,[24] who articulated its essential form nearly 200 years ago. This is the economic logic that suggests cities are structured around their central business districts, usually the origin of settlement or the original market where barter and exchange first took place. Land in such a system is used in such a way that the prices or rents that different land uses are able to command for being nearer and nearer the market center determine concentric bands of similar land use around the center in which those uses will locate. Thus, distance plays a key role in structuring what goes on at different locations in cities. As land near the center is more and more valuable, rents and densities increase as one gets closer to the center. Traffic volumes increase too, as does congestion, which is the price of proximity. But in a world where more and more of us are communicating through the "ether," so to speak—using email and social media via access to the network of networks called the web, while also storing our information remotely in the so-called cloud—the traditional glue that constrains what we do in any place forcing us to cluster and agglomerate is losing its effect. The glue is dissolving, while the cement that enables us to build ever-denser networks between ourselves using information is strengthening: this, in a nutshell, is Glaeser's paradox—proximity becomes more important as the deterrent effect of distance is of lesser significance.

It is information technology that is also changing and extending our perspectives on the structure of the city. In the past, certainly for the last 100 years, we have looked at how cities evolve, change, and can be planned primarily in physical terms in a large-scale, long-term manner. Plans for the future have been phrased in terms of years or decades, and our access to information about how cities function in the very short term—over minutes or hours or days—has been extremely restricted. In fact, our appreciation of the short term has been somewhat casual, where our focus on what happens on a day-to-day basis has only been of relevance insofar as, over longer periods, the days add to months and then to years from which we can generate large-scale, long-term change. However, since the millennium and the rise of the smartphone, which embodies the ultimate culmination or convergence of computers and telecommunications, these technologies are enabling us to get access to, influence, sense, and control the 24-hour city. In parallel guise, we have known for a while that cities are more like organisms than machines, evolving from the bottom up rather than being planned from the top down.[25] They exert "pulses" that are now accessible using the recently developed massive proliferation of sensors, all part and parcel of what has somewhat euphemistically been called the "smart city." In fact, the city is many times more complex than a single organism in that it is a collective of many pulses all firing at different rates but that are ultimately coordinated by our own human life cycles and rhythms. This we might think of as the "high-frequency city," in contrast to our traditional model of cities whose dynamics evolve and change over much longer time scales and at lower frequencies.

Until the Industrial Revolution, there was little prospect of cities growing to populations of more than a million or so, and it took enormous resources—entire empires, in fact—to hold their components together. Rome, a city which grew to a million or slightly more, fell largely because its center could not hold, while the Chinese empire of the Ming (and earlier dynasties) with its capital at Nanjing housing a similar level of population, befell a similar fate. It took mechanical technologies to be invented for city populations to rise much above a million, enabling suburbs to become established through new forms of transportation—especially those based on the internal combustion engine—and it took elevators and phones to make possible the construction of skyscrapers in the search upward for more proximate space. We attribute our fourth principle to H. G. Wells, who in 1902 suggested that the distribution of population must always depend on the kind of transport that ties the population together.[26]

In all of this, a fifth principle, which has been called Tobler's first law of geography,[27] suggests that near locations exert a stronger pull than locations farther away. This is another of our collective ideas that can be found in everything from the standard model to the height of a skyscraper, as well as the extent of the city itself and its hinterland. Our principles suggest that as the physical bonds loosen and the ethereal ones tighten, form will no longer follow function. If we apply these principles to speculations about the future city, we will go some way to thinking about what this future might be like.

Our arguments here are in the nature of a long essay that is both speculative, technically focused, and grounded in a well-versed philosophy of modern science that treats prediction as being contingent. In the last part of this book, we focus on how we might think about inventing this future, and we survey the rapid development of information technologies as being one of its critical features. One of the most profound and deep-seated forces in this revolution in technologies is what Cairncross called the "death of distance"; although she used this to point out the impact of the Internet and all that has subsequently flowed from it,[28] we will argue that despite everything being connected to everything else, Tobler's law also suggests that distance in cities will still remain the great arbiter. All of this is part and parcel of the emergence of the smart city, which we argue is transforming a society based on energy to one based on information—a transition from atoms to bits, in Negroponte's terms,[29] from a world in which cities are the exception to one where cities are the rule, from "no-city" to "city," from nonurban to urban.

When we examine these cycles, they appear to be getting faster and more intense. As they merge, they suggest a continuous process of creative destruction in which the rate of change appears to be coming so fast that things seem out of control. This implies we are heading toward a singularity, and although we only hint here that this might be the case, we seem to have entered a period when the intensity of invention makes even the most cautious "what if" scenario seem dated before it can be properly articulated. That we are at the start of an inventive century and a disruptive one—of that there can be little doubt. A global world where cities are connected ever more closely to one another, where physical migrations between cities at all levels of the hierarchy will be the dominant force in patterns of growth and decline, and where the traditional ways in which we produce, procure, and consume goods will be affected by enormous strides in automation: these are the portents for these future years.

2 The Great Transition

Clearly the present exponential growth cannot continue indefinitely. So what will happen? One possibility is that we wipe ourselves out completely by some disaster such as a nuclear war.

—Stephen Hawking, "Science in the Next Millennium"

As we have been at pains to impress on you so far, the future is unknowable, and the question concerning the future growth of world population that Stephen Hawking poses is unanswerable. How you react to it, however, depends on whether you see yourself as an optimist or a pessimist. I do not believe we will destroy ourselves—we will always be able to invent structures and organizations to cope with exponential growth. But can we do it fast enough? Hawking himself is of similar mind.[1] In the same speech, he continues by saying: "But I'm an optimist. I think we have a good chance of avoiding both Armageddon and a new Dark Ages." In fact, it now looks as though world population growth is rapidly decreasing, and we have entered a transition from superexponential growth to what could even be imagined as a steady state, something akin to zero population growth, whose trajectory is much more reminiscent of the demographic transition[2] that many developed nations have experienced during the last 100 years. Of course, our forecasts are always wrong, but there appears little doubt now that the exponential growth of the world population will end and a new regime will set in. This is what we refer to as the "great transition"—but, as we will see, this era will not be simply one of rapidly decreasing population growth, but one where the exponential or even superexponential growth of information comes to take its place, with all the consequences this kind of automation will bring.

Here we will start by discussing the great transition from a nonurban to an urban world while predicting that the world's population will stabilize, or at least change its trajectory quite radically, over this (the 21st) century. This will be our first foray into the city of the future, and it depends on closing our system in the simplest and most obvious way: by examining how cities are organized on a global scale without worrying for the moment about their spatial extent. In the rest of this chapter, we will examine the demographic transition and the rapid pace at which the global population is urbanizing. We will then explore the distribution of cities by their size, making the rather basic point that in the future, we will not live in one giant city, as some popular accounts seem to suggest, but in cities of all sizes, in much the same way we do now. This belies another very obvious point: to be a big city, you have to be a small city first, and this asymmetry will continue to dominate our world. Despite the fact that all our cities are now connected to one another, at least in a minimal sense through the fact that we can communicate globally on our smartphones and draw information from anywhere on the planet, our cities are likely to remain distinct. As a preface to all of this, we will explore the great transition, which began in earnest with the invention of industrial technologies some 250 years ago and will play itself out over the next century and beyond. It will provide a useful framework for all our speculation about the future city, how that future might evolve, and how it might be invented.

Singularities and Tipping Points

We can just about imagine what the earth was like some 10,000 years ago, in the period after the end of the last ice age when man was moving from a nomadic existence to settled agriculture. We have images of tribes and primitive villages, and there are cave paintings that suggest what life was like. But try and imagine what life will be like 10,000 years from now, in the far distant future. This is beyond our wildest dreams, even the dreams of extreme science fiction. Narrow the timeframe to 5,000 years in the past, when the first cities were emerging, and we have reasonably good pictures of that world from our archaeologies—but 5,000 years in the future remains as much a mystery. If we then refocus our lens further, zooming in to 500 years, we have quite a clear picture of the past from numerous writings and paintings and perhaps a better chance of glimpsing our future, but even then we can only speculate. This far ahead, our technologies may have propelled us well beyond our planet—or into oblivion, as Stephen Hawking remarked[3]—and the closed system that we have inhabited since life on earth emerged from the primeval soup is no longer likely to constrain us. Or at the very least, it will constrain us in quite different ways.

There is one thing, however, that we can be sure of when looking back from the vantage point of 10 millennia in the future. Across this 20,000-year sweep of human history, somewhere in the middle, round about now, we would see a dramatic transition—a tipping point—from a world where there were no cities to one where everyone will be in cities. This is a transition from a rural world to an urban world, from a world of highly local interactions to a world of global interactions, from a world based on physical technologies to one based on information technologies; and from a world based on atoms to one of bits, as Nicholas Negroponte so presciently observed.[4] Almost as a corollary to these changes, it is very likely that we would also see a demographic transition in which an exponentially rising population quite quickly gives way to one much more stable. Total population would not be restricted by resource limits, but by birth control and changes in behavior associated with a more prosperous world that had learned to live within its limits.

Go back to the middle of the 20th century, though, and the picture painted was a very different one. In 1970, the world's population growth rate reached the highest it had ever been. In that year, the population was growing at an annual rate of just over 2 percent. If this had persisted, the population would double in 30 years, double again in another 20, and so on. It was no surprise that the vision of declining resources in the face of population increase, first raised in the late 18th century by Thomas Malthus, took hold, leading to various speculations about an apocalyptic collapse suggested, for example, in the Club of Rome's report[5] on *The Limits to Growth* in 1972. This kind of collapse was given dramatic effect in a paper some 10 years earlier by Heinz von Foerster and his colleagues. They suggested that the population growth rate was in fact "hyperbolic" and, in the future, the human population would to all intents and purposes increase to infinity. This "singularity," as it is called in mathematics, was an event horizon they referred to as "Doomsday." They even predicted an exact date when this would happen: November 13th, 2026.

We need to be a little clearer about what all this means. In figure 2.1, we illustrate the growth in world population from 70,000 BCE—the early Stone Age—to the present day. Without worrying about the precise equation that

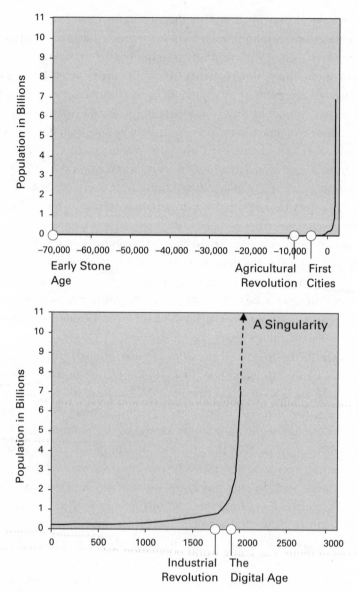

Figure 2.1
Superexponential growth of the world's population.

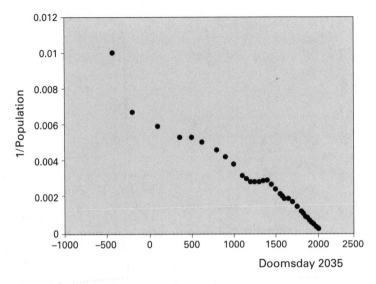

Figure 2.2
Predicting Doomsday.

fits this trend, it is clear that the population for the most part is growing much faster than its rate of change, meaning that population growth is more than exponential: it is, in fact, superexponential. What von Foerster did in 1960 was to examine this population growth and suggest that if there was a point in time when the population would essentially become infinite, then this trend could be approximated by a very simple equation where population was a simple linear function of the difference between this point in time—Doomsday—and the time already reached.[6] Turning this around, it is easier to see this if we plot the reciprocal of population against time. We can fit a straight line to this and project it to the time where the reciprocal becomes zero, which is the same as the population becoming infinite. This we show in figure 2.2. Using world population data up until 1990 from a variety of sources,[7] it is clear that with this more recent data, von Foerster's Doomsday is postponed until around 2035, which means that the rate of change is now somewhat less than when von Foerster published his paper. Therein, of course, lies the message: a world population heading to infinity is simply impossible. Something has to give, as Stephen Hawking observed in our introductory quote; the rate must fall or apocalypse will be upon us. It is this falling rate that will dominate growth during our current century.

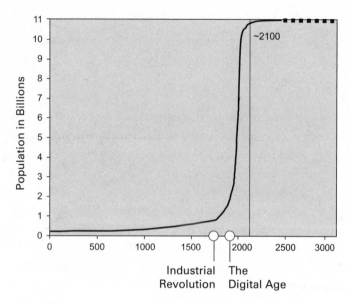

Figure 2.3
The likely demographic transition.

If we keep zooming in on the population in figure 2.1, it becomes clear that the growth rate has fallen by one-half since the 1960s. In short, our superexponential curve is beginning to slow the kind of growth we have been accustomed to for at least the last 1,000 years. The growth rate has been systematically falling for the last 50 years, and it is easy enough to predict that this will continue if the global population follows the same kind of demographic transition that has characterized many developed countries during the last century. In short, future population growth is likely to follow a logistic or S-shaped curve. The turning point, however, on this trajectory does not really become significant until well after 2050, and then there is a very rapid convergence to a "steady state," when the population becomes stable, in the early 22nd century. As the growth rate falls, von Foerster's Doomsday is pushed ever further back.[8]

To produce an informed speculation regarding the total world population at the end of this century, we map out the most likely population scenario in figure 2.3 using growth rates from the last 50 years. These, we assume, will fall toward zero by the end of this century. Of course, we have no idea if this kind of stability in population will occur, but it does appear plausible. There is, of course, the prospect of an oscillating population if various extreme events such as climate change, ever more serious economic crises, rapid progress to artificial intelligence, and dramatic changes in our aging processes take place. There is even the possibility of complete collapse as envisaged by the Club of Rome nearly half a century ago and hinted at, at least, by Hawking. But what is very certain is that the chaos of super-exponential growth, which looked so likely then, will not happen now. Exponential growth in various technologies, however, will not disappear. Indeed, growth in these technologies appears to be accelerating, and various other singularities might occur based on artificial intelligence and medical advances such as those suggested by Ray Kurzweil,[9] the prophet of the "singularity." But population growth will not be one of these. Of course, when we engage in this kind of informed speculation, there is also the nagging doubt that none of this will happen. Karl Popper's warning that the future is inherently unpredictable will always cast a shadow over any discussion of the future,[10] and will always be at the back of our minds in our continued discussion of these issues.

When All the World's a City

Our strategy for exploring future cities in terms of their form and function requires us to put some bounds on what is likely to happen. We have already limited our perspective to the next 100 years; beyond this, we see little sense in speculating. We have begun by suggesting that world population is likely to follow a logistic growth trajectory more than any other, providing us with one very strong limit, but it is now clear that the rate at which this population is becoming urban marks another transition that will work itself to completion in this century. In 2008, the UN Population Division reported that 50 percent of the world's population had become urban for the first time, and predictions until 2050 imply that by then some 66 percent will be living in cities.[11] We will assume for the moment that being urban means living in one sort of city or another, although there is considerable debate about the coincidence of the terms "city" and "urban," which we will return to in due course.[12] To anticipate this, our argument will turn on the point that defining a city physically (or, for that matter, in any other way) will always be ambiguous, for the concept of the city is ill-defined, no matter how it be construed.

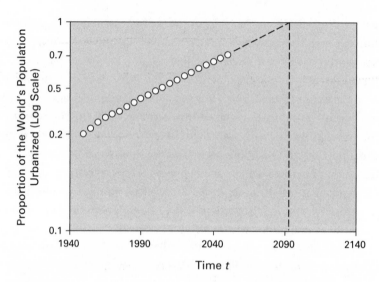

Figure 2.4
Increasing urbanization.

Nevertheless, the UN Population Division defines urban via local considerations that largely relate to the concentration or density of interconnected populations. Those defined as urban have shown an inexorable rise over the last 100 years. The increase is largely proportional to total population, as shown in the graph in figure 2.4. Assuming that urbanization is a phenomenon that is intrinsically related to the economies of scale associated with cities, then it is safe to assume the urban population will continue to grow at the same proportionate rate. Looking at figure 2.4, the simplest straight-line forecast is that the entire global population will be urbanized by 2090. We might qualify this by saying there will probably be failed states and urban-rural anomalies—pockets of poverty—that might stop this proportion becoming absolute; but for all intents and purposes, by the year 2100, the world will be entirely urbanized. In this sense, by that date everybody will be living in cities of one size or another.

Putting the logistic growth of population together with the increasing proportion of the world's population living in urban areas suggests that these transitions will feed off one another, moving the world toward zero-population growth and making it entirely urban by the end of this century. This scenario implies that as population growth slows, the proportion of those living in cities will rise. The implications of this will be profound. During this century, we are likely to see a big shift from absolute growth to relative growth, where much, if not all, of the growth in cities will be through in-migration outweighing out-migration. This implies a near zero-sum world when it comes to population change, with dramatic shifts taking place and some cities growing dramatically, while some decline by equal measure. These implosions and explosions will be quite unlike traditional migrations, such as those during the Industrial Revolution's shift from rural to urban, since this time, they will be from urban to urban and from one size of city to another. In fact, these will be much more like the migrations to the new world during the latter half of the 19th century, when people moved primarily in search of jobs and a better quality of life. To an extent this is already beginning to happen, as major waves of migration are hitting Europe and North America, with the inevitable prospect that these waves will turn back on themselves, eventually overwhelming East Asia, Australasia, and South America. These currents thus herald a century of shifting urban frontiers as populations mix and remix geographically in ways we can barely imagine.

If we now begin to zoom back to our initial focus on the years between the last ice age and some 10,000 years in the future, then the two transitions we are considering, based on population growth and urbanization, become an ever-tinier fragment of this timeframe. Over 20,000 years, the period of transition is not much more than 1 percent of this frame, and if we widen it by another order of magnitude, the transition becomes a spike, a switch from nonurban to urban, a world without cities to one composed entirely of cities. We will not draw this trajectory, for it can be easily imagined as a step function where population in the past is essentially near zero (or very small) and, in the future, it is a stable value, which is at the carrying capacity of the earth. In fact, it is this carrying capacity that is all-important in thinking about this new urban future, for although we cannot say very much about what is likely to occur, continued progress in technological development, itself superexponential, shows little sign of slowing, and this will clearly dictate the kind of urban future we will have. Whatever world emerges, this will be a world of cities, and it is this we now need to explore to give us some sense of what is likely in the next 100 years and beyond.

A Planet of Cities: Distribution of City Sizes

As the world becomes more urban, cities are becoming ever more prominent as sources of wealth and power in contemporary society. Because the biggest cities, which are often called "global cities," are feted as the most vibrant and economically advantaged places to live in,[13] there is often a sense that we will all live in ever-bigger cities. The evidence for this so far is mixed. If we take the top 50 cities in terms of their population and plot their total growth from Chandler's ancient cities database, which starts in 430 BCE, it is clear that this growth will eventually outstrip the world's population but only from the start of the Industrial Revolution. This is illustrated in figure 2.5, where we show this growth trajectory alongside world population. This trajectory looks as though it is also headed for a singularity when the population of the top 50 cities eventually exceeds the world's population, but, as we have argued, this is a physical impossibility.

There is still some uncertainty about whether the average size of cities is getting bigger or not. The total population of the top 50 cities, shown in figure 2.5, constitutes about 2.5 percent of world population round about the time of Christ at the height of Roman Empire, but over the next 1,000

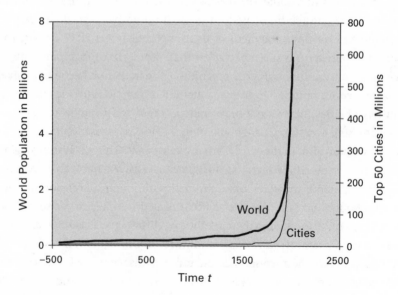

Figure 2.5
The top 50 cities as a proportion of world population, 430 BCE to 2010.

years, this proportion fell by about half through the Dark Ages, until reaching its nadir in the Middle Ages during the Black Death. This then rose slightly to about 1.7 percent as the Enlightenment began, but fell slightly to about 1.3 percent in 1825, when it suddenly started its inexorable rise as the industrial city emerged and the great transition began. This had risen to a high of almost 10 percent by the millennium, but now we detect a slight decline. The data set, however, is problematic, for it is constructed from many sources, notwithstanding the recent admirable efforts to clean up the Chandler-Modelski data, making it more consistent with information on contemporary urban populations.[14] The pattern is clear from figure 2.5, where if we divide the total city population by the world population, the dramatic increase in this proportion for the biggest 50 cities is immediately evident.

To support the claim that the biggest cities are taking an increasing proportion of the total world population, we need to examine larger and more consistent data sets. Recently, the Joint Research Council (JRC) of the European Commission generated a much-expanded world data set for urban agglomerations, where these are defined according to the density of small area population units at the kilometer grid scale while adding morphological contiguities and adjacencies from remote sensing data and moderating these by administrative and political audits.[15] This data is available for over 13,000 urban clusters whose size is greater than 50,000 persons at the baseline year of 2015. Data for 1975, 1990, and 2000 for the same set of physical clusters enables us to examine more authoritatively this question of whether the largest cities have and will continue to contain an increasing proportion of world population. If we look at different numbers of the top cities—10, 20, 50, 100, 500, and 1,000—measured by the sum of their populations, at all four dates over the last 40 years, we find their proportion of world population does indeed increase. In fact, for the top 1,000 cities, this proportion increases by over 2 percent, from 27.3 percent to 29.4 percent, while for the top 50—which is comparable to our ancient cities database—this proportion rises from 9.1 percent to 10.5 percent. If these secular increases continue to take place at the same rate as in the last 40 years, at some point in the far-distant future, the largest cities will overwhelm the world population. A casual projection suggests that the top 50 cities will reach this limit in about 2,000 years' time, if existing trends persist, but this is so far in the distant future that it is wild speculation. It takes no account of the kind of mixing and remixing of urban populations and the explosions and implosions of migration streams that are likely to dominate the future form of cities once the world has been entirely urbanized.

There is a major question at issue in all our speculations: how many cities have there been, are there, and will there be as we cross the great transition? As we will argue a little later, this is a question that depends intimately on how we define a city. Most definitions start with a minimum threshold in terms of population size—in the case of the data just examined, the minimum is some 50,000, and thus we would expect the proportion of cities as a percentage of world population to be dependent on this. To push our argument a little further, we will examine one last set of urban populations. Denise Pumain and her colleagues have put together a large database of over 20,000 cities with populations of more than 10,000.[16] When we ask about the population in cities of different sizes as a proportion of world population in this data set, we generate a slightly firmer perspective on the growth of ever-larger cities. Examining the largest 50 cities from 1980 to 2010, this proportion increases from some 8.8 percent to 10.8 percent, roughly comparable with the JRC data, but indicating that the largest cities are indeed getting larger.

Before we broaden our conversation to embrace wider issues of transition involving new technologies, there are three important questions about the future of cities that we need to pose and attempt to answer. The first concerns the distribution of city sizes, which we have already implicitly noted in our discussion of how the largest cities are changing as a proportion of world population. Since we will still be living in cities of different sizes, we need to have some sense of how many big cities there will be and how many small. We need to know whether the sizes of cities are converging (becoming more even), or diverging (becoming more unequal), given that the number of cities of different sizes is likely to increase as world population continues to grow and as more and more populations become urbanized. The second question—more fundamental and much harder to answer—concerns the total number of cities the world has supported in the past and how many it will continue to in the future. This, of course, depends on what a city is, and we can only answer it with respect to the number of cities greater than a given size. In fact, the question is best approached by defining the number of urban clusters, where the focus is on different minimum sizes of cluster. We might assume an extreme, where a cluster of one person defines the absolute minimum bound on the number of cities that can exist or are possible. The third question pertains to the smallest and biggest cities. At the bottom end, there needs to be a certain critical mass of population before city-like functions can be generated, so we will need to explore this threshold. This is likely to be greater than a single individual. At the top end, there are physical limits posed by transportation and density, but some cities become primate. We will conclude with a discussion of how the largest cities distort the baseline city-size distribution.

Stability of City-Size Distributions

The first question with respect to the distribution of city sizes is more straightforward. The most recent projections[17] suggest that world population is likely to flatten out at something a little above 10 billion by the end of this century, notwithstanding the inexorable increase in urbanization demonstrated above. This prospect, however, still conjures up very different scenarios—ranging from a world where most of us will live in very large cities, to one where we are spread out much more thinly across the planet but connected using all the instruments of transport and communication we now have at our disposal. This was Gilder's speculation, recounted in the first chapter.[18] Both prospects are in fact unlikely, for the notion of cities getting ever bigger is simply not possible. Limits on density and technologies that move people physically will continue to constrain the physical city, while a complete decentralization of populations into very small clusters would also require a very dramatic but somewhat unlikely loosening of the effects of geometry and distance.

Although we have implied that the biggest cities appear to be getting bigger and more polarized, it appears their densities are still falling. As far as we know, there is no good source of data on the density of towns and cities worldwide from which we could test this speculation (apart perhaps as a by-product of the JRC data used here), but casual evidence suggests this is the case. However, we are still able to examine the size distribution of cities, for their distribution appears to have remained quite stable for at least two centuries, if not longer.[19] This distribution is formed from a small number of large cities all the way to a large number of small cities. In its crudest form (although a gross simplification), the largest cities in the distribution appear to follow a power law, but with an overall frequency that is probably log-normal. This means that at the lowest end of the distribution where towns and cities are the smallest, there are fewer of these than there are of slightly larger places: in fact, at the lowest end, these might be hamlets and villages, with some debate as to whether or not these qualify as urban areas at all. In this sense, all we can say about the future distribution of cities by size is that it will follow a particular form or shape with respect to cities above a certain size—and there does not appear to be any absolute metric defining this shape for all cities.

What all this implies, in a completely urbanized world, is that the distribution of cities will remain roughly the same as it has been for millennia: there will be many small towns, a lesser number of larger cities, and a tiny number of really large mega-cities. That is, a completely urbanized world implies most of us will be living in small towns rather than big cities. To get a sense of this, we need another data set so that we can examine the distribution of the largest cities—those over, say, 750,000. We can explore this for the past 65 years; for example, the smallest city in our latest (2015) set of 590 cities in 1950 was at a population of just 10,000. This is, to an extent, a relative analysis, because we are not simply taking the cities over 750,000 in 1950 and comparing these over time; we are excluding cities that were greater than 10,000 in 1950 but had not reached 750,000 in 2015. However, this is the best data we can get— derived from the UN Population Division—for the distribution of world cities over the last half-century.[20]

We show these 14 distributions, one for each five-year period, in figure 2.6. The frequencies are graphed by rank-ordering the cities from the largest to the smallest and plotting these ranks on the horizontal axis against size on the vertical axis using logarithmic scales. For the most part, the long tail of these city-size distributions can be approximated by a power law—first popularized by George Kingsley Zipf in 1949—and, if this is the case, the regularity of each distribution can be approximated by a straight line. This is often referred to as Zipf's law: as we implied in chapter 1, it is one of our key principles for defining the structure of cities.[21] Cities move up and down this hierarchy quite rapidly,[22] although, in figure 2.6, the distributions are quite stable from 1950. In short, the distributions "seem" to be getting a little flatter through time, implying the larger cities are becoming slightly less significant than the smaller. In fact, there is considerable evidence from individual city systems, often organized by countries, that the rank-size—or Zipf plot—in figure 2.6 falls in its slope over time, implying that population differences between cities are slightly reducing. This

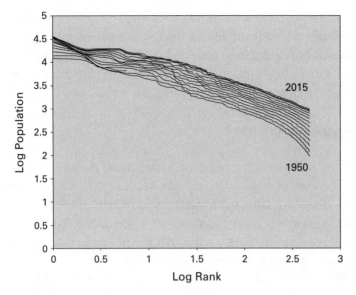

Figure 2.6
The size distribution of cities greater than 750,000 from 1950 to 2015.

is particularly the case for the United States and Canada, which are to an extent the classic exemplar because they comprise a relatively isolated continental land mass, but there is also significant literature now on estimating these functions for different systems of cities over time.

We can, of course, measure this fall in slope if we fit regression lines to the data in figure 2.6, but because the implication is that this data is lognormally distributed, we will approximate the data set by taking only the first 100 cities at each time period. This means that, in 1950, the size of cities ranges from nearly 1 million to 12 million and in 2015 from 3 million to 35 million. The regressions show good fits with $r^2=0.991$ for 1950 and $r^2=0.963$ for 2015, with the slope falling from 0.656 to 0.567 over the 65-year period. A similar gradual flattening of the size distribution can also be seen in the JRC urban agglomeration data we used earlier. We can compute the regression for the Zipf plot of the population cluster data at 1975 and at 2015, and the slope of these curves for the top 100 cities falls very slightly from 0.623 ($r^2=0.985$) to 0.615 ($r^2=0.984$). Explanations of this slow decline probably relate to the impact of new technologies on how cities increase in size with lower densities, as well as the impact of globalization and information technologies on how cities connect to one another. What this really shows is that in an entirely urbanized world, the majority of cities will still be small rather than large, notwithstanding the fact that an increasing proportion of cities will be larger rather than smaller. The implications, of course, for how we actually define cities are critical. But this is another argument we will broach in chapter 3 and elsewhere in this book.

How Many Cities Are There?

Our second question is also one of scale and distribution. If all the world is made up entirely of cities by the end of this century, we are surely entitled to ask how many such cities there will be, even though this will always be an impossible question to answer definitively. To get traction on this dilemma, we need to count the number of cities of different sizes from their frequency, and from this function extrapolate to those city sizes for which we have no data, thence working out the total number of all cities over different minimum sizes. If we then choose an absolute minimum size below which any cluster of human settlement is not a city, we will then have assembled an answer of sorts. For example, we have data from the JRC that counts all cities with greater than 50,000 population in 2015, and we can use this frequency to work out the number of cities at every threshold at or above, say, 1,000, 10,000, or any other level. We have already explored such frequencies in their rank-size form, but for the purpose of counting, we need to examine the original frequency distribution from which the rank-size plot is formed. We show this in figure 2.7 for the 13,844 settlements in 2015 with greater than 50,000 population using some 40 categories, or "bins," defined for the ranges of population size over the whole distribution.

We have plotted the absolute frequency against the logarithm of population, and, although this reduces the vertical scale, the power law is clearly evident. If we linearize the function by taking the logarithm of frequency, we can approximate the relationship that is shown in the inset by a straight line, from which we can then predict the frequencies we are not able to observe— that is, numbers of cities of less than 50,000 persons and at different levels down to a population of 10,000. (In the figure, the observed frequencies are shown by the black bars and the predicted frequencies by the white.) What this reveals is that if we examine all cities down to 10,000, we can predict the total number of these cities as 118,795—nearly 10 times the number of cities

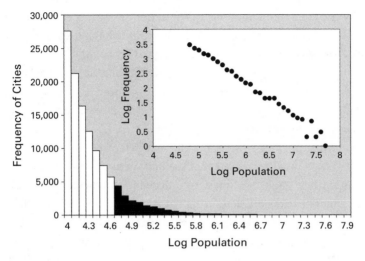

Figure 2.7
Extrapolating the total number of cities with populations greater than 10,000 in 2015.

we observe over 50,000. If we take the prediction down to all cities above 1,000 persons, we predict that there are a total of 1.644 million cities; in this context, we are assuming that the lower bound of 1,000, or 10^3, defines a continuum of cities, up to an upper bound of 10^8. This is five orders of magnitude, which essentially provide the bounds for the sizes of all the cities discussed in this book.

In fact, the distribution of cities can only be approximated with the kind of curves we have graphed as Zipf plots in figure 2.6 or as log frequencies in figure 2.7. At the very bottom of the distribution, settlements of single individuals or households are rather uncommon. Most social and economic functions require us to aggregate people into groups or communities, to agglomerate so that we can share economies of scale, and this suggests that there are pressures to reach a certain minimum size or critical mass where these functions take on city-like attributes. As we have seen, for most cities greater than 10,000, their frequency rapidly declines. but at the lowest levels, from a single individual upward, the frequency increases until it reaches a modal value that seems to vary from country to country. This suggests the frequency of city sizes is log-normal, or highly skewed to the right with a long tail. This is the current conventional wisdom based originally on work by the French scholar Robert Gibrat, but the verdict is still very much out on whether or not there is a definitive form for the distribution of city sizes.[23] Zipf's law remains a convenient approximation.

There is one more, somewhat extreme speculation we need to make before we conclude this discussion of city size. If we know (or rather guess) the total world population for the year 2100, and we assume, as we have forecast, that this entire population lives in cities, we can also guess as to the number of cities which exist above different population thresholds. To do this, we must also assume that the rank-size or frequency distribution remains entirely stable, and then, by a little bit of judicious manipulation, we can generate these predictions. In fact, we used this kind of logic to predict the number of cities at sizes below values we had observations for from the frequency distribution in figure 2.7. We will now reverse this process, noting that we can scale the log-linear frequency curve in figure 2.7 to the level where the distribution starts from a population threshold of 1,000 or 10^3, and generate a total population in the range of bins or categories that adds to our assumed world (city) population in 2100 of 10 billion.[24] The total number of cities greater than 10^3 is then 25 million; over 10^4 is 652,000; over 10^5 is 71,100; and over 10^6, or 1 million, is 1,600. We can also compute that the biggest city in this world will be on the order of 140 million, while there will be three cities with populations over 100 million, and 85 cities with populations over 10 million. These look like somewhat feasible estimates, but this future will clearly depend upon the extent to which cities might join together and fuse. To assess these issues, we need to look in much more detail at what a city is, and we will do this in the next chapter.

The Smallest and Biggest Cities

There is one last question, which we can deal with swiftly before we move back to look at the bigger picture. As we have been at pains to emphasize, cities are generated from the bottom up. They originate when individuals begin to pool their respective skills and attributes in such a way as to gain advantage from their physical juxtaposition—to gain economies of scale, while avoiding any diseconomies that come from such agglomeration. In fact, Jane Jacobs, in her second book *The Economy of Cities*, argues that the concept of the city is intrinsic to mankind itself, existing even in nomadic times as small pockets of innovation where foraging tribes quickly realized the advantages of grouping, pooling, and dividing their labor.[25] The standard classification of the smallest towns and cities starts with the idea of the hamlet and progresses to the village. Once a village reaches about 1,000 persons, it is often classed as a small town, which suggests that this population sets a lower bound on what we might consider a city. However, this etymology is historical and cultural, varying between different times and places, and there is no definitive agreement on this question. In fact, what constitutes a city in terms of historical definition is dependent on absolute size of the wider population from which cities emerge. For example, the world population during the classical era—the time of the Greeks—was on the order of about 150 million, some 2 percent of its current level. Meanwhile, the first widely accepted speculation on city size, particularly optimal city size, offered by Plato, was some 5,040 citizens. However, by the late 19th century, this number had risen to the hundreds of thousands, and became millions by the middle of the 20th century.[26]

The upper bound on the size of cities from our vantage point of the early 20th century is equally problematic. Cities could barely get beyond a million people in size prior to the beginning of the great transition—the first Industrial Revolution. It was technological innovation that enabled civilization to break through this barrier. We are still limited by the technologies we invented during the last 200 years for physical movement, and, even in an era when high-speed trains are becoming commonplace, at least in China, it is hard to think of cities where travel times are more than an hour in each direction for daily commutes. There are no hard or fast rules on how long and how far we might commute (other than the limits of the 24-hour day), but it appears that cities which spread more than 100 km (about 60 mi) from their core are unlikely to still be considered cities in traditional physical terms. In terms of their connectivity with cities that are much more remote, this changes the definition of the city quite dramatically. We will return to this issue many times during this book, for one consequence of our invention of future cities may well be that the traditional role of physical place is changed beyond all recognition.

In fact, the JRC data on city sizes we have been exploring in this chapter changes the traditional rank order of the largest cities quite substantially. For the last 50 years, the Tokyo metropolitan region has been classed as largest, currently with some 33 million persons, but in the JRC data, it is Guangzhou that leads the pack with a population of 46 million, quickly followed by Cairo and Jakarta and then Tokyo. Arguably, the biggest cities are all now in Asia, with the exception of Cairo. This pattern is likely to persist. If we look at the city-size distribution for all 13,844 cities above the threshold of 50,000, we do not find that any of these stand out as being primate. If we examine the relationship between the largest city in the set (or the top grouping of up to five cities, say), then if these cities depart radically in the sense that their populations seem much greater than what their functional form suggests, then we say these are primate cities. In many countries, such primacy is related to the domination of capital city functions, as for example in the United Kingdom and France, where London and Paris are primate cities, using an old definition from Jefferson. Pisarenko and Sornette refer to such cities as "Dragon-Kings"; just as the frequency distribution may depart from a strict power law, the existence of these Dragon-Kings implies a much more convoluted generative and competitive process leading to their emergence.[27] In fact, when we look at the JRC data, which is the most comprehensive data on city sizes to date, then there is no such primacy in the world system. If anything, the top cities have less population than the strict power law implies. If we take the top city in the JRC data set—Guangzhou—which has a population of 46 million, this is just over 1 percent of the total urbanized world population above 50,000, which is 3.82 billion. Adding the next city, Cairo, adds another percent, and when we take the top five together, these comprise 4.75 percent of this total urbanized population. There is no sense of primacy here, and even when we examine our Chandler and Modelski data over a period of 2,500 years, it is not possible to detect primacy. Our speculation is that there will never be any city worldwide, in this or the next century, that will dominate any of those that lie at the top. The same might be said for any level in the city-size hierarchy. If cities do stand out as anomalies and outliers, then the urban economy seems dynamic enough to resolve such differences quite rapidly in the quest for cities to continue to outperform and outbid competitors.

Related Transitions

The great transition that we have painted here as one of demography and urbanization is related to a whole series of transitions that will dominate our world for the next 100 years and beyond. These are primarily digital, intrinsic to the Industrial Revolution in all its guises from the first (the mechanical) to the second (the electrical) and third (the digital), and thence to the fourth, which is about to begin as a widespread deepening of technologies involving artificial intelligence, biomedicine, nanotechnology, and communications. Most of these technologies depend on the convergence of computers and communications and their embedding into the social and built environment, with the role of connectivity playing an essential part in this evolution. Although we have focused in this first chapter mainly on individual cities, their sizes, and their overall size distributions as a prelude to thinking about how these issues will play out during the rest of this century, the notion that cities are composed of interacting elements has never been far away from our concern. As cities get larger, the number of "potential" interactions scales as the square of the number of elements which connect with one another, and it is immediately obvious that this must bring qualitative change. For as cities grow, individuals face a more than proportionately expanding pool of social and economic connections. These networks, as we will see in later chapters, define different kinds and sizes of cities. In a hamlet of up to 100 people, it possible to know everyone fairly well, whereas when the settlement reaches 1,000, as in a village or small town, this is no longer possible, and as cities get ever bigger, the nature of what constitutes social and economic actions and interactions changes both quantitatively and qualitatively.

In concluding this chapter, we will not dwell in any depth on the related digital transitions that will define the future, except that it is important to impress on the reader that the kind of tipping point associated with demographic change is very different from many other transformations that are in the vanguard of the transition to a digital society. The massive miniaturization of computer power in terms of expanding memory, falling costs, and increasing speed with doubling times of something like 18 months is continuing apace, as it has for the last 50 years. Moore's law has sought to quantify this process of superexponential growth, and it shows little sign of stopping, due to the evident transitions happening in materials and their manufacture intrinsic to the development of computer hardware, as well as developments in quantum computing. The expansion of computing power due to networking enshrined in Metcalfe's law suggests that the power of linked computers, like interactions in cities, grows more than proportionately with the number of computers connected to a network. The same kinds of laws exist for the growth of software and data, and the entire edifice of automation and artificial intelligence fast being assembled in many domains at the present time depends on this kind of inexorable progress.

As population growth gives way to some sort of steady state, and as connectivity, migration, and digital communications come to dominate the global network of cities, we are likely to see much deeper and less visible physical changes in cities. These are likely to be far from the much more obvious physical forms we have been accustomed to thinking about ever since man first began to think about how quality of life might be improved by living in cities. The intensity of change defining the current wave of digital transformations shows no sign of ending, and, if anything, it is deepening in ways that both threaten as well as enhance the way we might function in cities in both immediate and longer-term futures. This is being heralded through what Brynjolfsson and McAfee have called the "second machine age"—in essence, the fourth Industrial Revolution.[28] This will transform our cities in ways that would have seemed unimaginable 60 or 70 years ago, when the digital computer was first invented. This future will be one where various kinds of singularities in information technologies, medicine, and the changing nature of work continue to dominate our thinking until solutions are found that lessen their impact and change their direction. How we map all this onto the future form of cities is the challenge we will continue to explore in the rest of this book.

3 Defining Cities

> The city in its complete sense, then, is a geographic plexus, an economic organization, an institutional process, a theater of social action, and an aesthetic symbol of collective unity. The city fosters art and is art; the city creates the theater and is the theater.
>
> —Lewis Mumford, "What Is a City?," 58–62

Ever since cities first emerged in ancient Mesopotamia some 5,000 years ago, they have had geographical integrity, meaning that the elements that enable them to function as integrated systems are always in close proximity. In this sense, the earliest cities, until classical times and perhaps even until the first Industrial Revolution, remained compact—limited to interactions based on reasonable walking distances where, for the most part, their populations needed to remain in close touch to function at all. Lewis Mumford, the great 20th-century historian of cities, makes this point in the essay from which we quote here, using the idea of a geographic plexus as his starting point. But he also portrays the city as much more than this. It is a social artifact as much as a geographical one, a theater of ideas where the critical mass of its population feeds upon itself to generate ever-greater diversity and potential for social and economic interaction. Cities, therefore, are not simply spatial systems, but are aspatial or even nonspatial, in that many of their attributes do not explicitly vary across space. Indeed, in the vast majority of writing about the city in documentaries and novels, the geographical dimension is often simply implicit.[1] In works of fact and fiction from Plato to Charles Dickens, from Herodotus to George Orwell, their writings about the city are more about their history and culture than their geography and economy.

Cities are places where people come together to pool their labor in the quest for greater prosperity and engage in many social pursuits that enrich their lives. They are places where the critical mass engendered by the density of living, as well as the social interactions that increase more than proportionately as more and more people come in contact with one another, generate innovations that drive civilization forward. Cities lie at the root of how new technologies are popularized and disseminated—not invented, necessarily, but developed and spread. In his book *Triumph of the City*, Ed Glaeser celebrates the kind of diversity large cities provide:[2]

> Cities, the dense agglomerations that dot the globe, have been the engines of innovation since Plato and Socrates bickered in the Athenian marketplace. The streets of Florence gave us the Renaissance and the streets of Birmingham gave us the Industrial Revolution. The great prosperity of contemporary London and Bangalore and Tokyo comes from their ability to produce new thinking.

In this book, we need to begin by defining what a city is so that we can map out how cities of different sizes are associated with different functions. As we have seen in the last chapter, there are many more smaller cities than big cities, and thus the notion that "we will all get richer if we live in big cities" requires some unpacking. There is little doubt that although living in big cities does bring social and economic benefits, it also brings many costs and limitations on how we might behave and function. Economies of scale, sometimes called by economists increasing returns to scale, must be set against diseconomies or decreasing returns to scale. In the late 19th century, Alfred Marshall first brought our attention to such agglomeration economies and diseconomies,[3] and as our love affair with ever-bigger cities has gathered pace from the late 20th century onwards, the notion that such economies outweigh the diseconomies has gained considerable currency. However, it is by no means clear that big cities are more preferable places to live and transact business than little cities, and thus it is absolutely essential that we learn how to define a city in appropriate ways so that we can measure these kinds of attributes. Moreover, the attributes in question are far beyond the simple geography or geometry of the city in terms of its physical extent, for they depend on the myriad ways in which we connect with one another. To this end, we need to explore the different ways in which we build connections with one another as we engage in the many aspects of daily life that define how we function in different sizes of city.

Connectivity and Hierarchy: Entangled Relations

How the elements comprising a city are connected is the all-important anchor to understanding how a city functions. These connections are not just geographical or physical but, as Mumford implies in his definition above, are also social, aesthetic, and cultural. Although the geographical definition of a city is often a good starting point, it has many characteristics that cannot be rooted primarily in geography. In fact, it is very likely that although geography has been one of the most dominant constraining factors on what constitutes a city in the past, the great transition through which we are living may well lead to cities that are not geographically connected at all. To an extent this is already the case. When people like myself spend more of their time away from their adopted city through traveling to meet like-minded colleagues, or when we engage in various transactions through email and other electronic forms of instant access that connect us to more people who are not physically near us, then the city that we inhabit has a very different extent and definition than the physical city to which we are rooted. You can see this kind of global city phenomenon with respect to the way our best universities are setting up branch campuses in world cities where there are the biggest markets for students and the largest thirst for knowledge.

In the past, we have studied cities in terms of their locations, paying much less attention to the interactions between their parts as well as to other cities of varying sizes. Even though we have recognized that traffic and land use in cities are different sides of the same coin, our focus has been much more on locations than interactions. This is changing, and the new science of cities is moving the frontier of how and what we understand cities to be into the domain of interacting systems.[4] Throughout this book, starting here, we will emphasize how important networks are—first, in terms of defining cities, and in later chapters in terms of showing how cities will function in the future as contemporary society becomes ever more digital, virtual, and physically distant but electronically connected.

At the finest scale, it is now well known that there are upper limits to the numbers of people and things to which we might be connected. Robin Dunbar's number is one such limit,[5] based on the notion that there are cognitive constraints on the number of persons one might have a stable relationship with; this number appears to be about 150. Above this figure, it is possible to form meaningful relationships, but it is likely that more and more constraints need to be imposed on the nature of the relationships for such levels to persist, and there is now evidence that such limits are affected by many different kinds of communication, particularly electronic. What Dunbar's number also shows is that in the smallest settlements, of up to 100 or so persons, it is very likely that most people all know one another, but as this increases to small towns over 1,000 persons, our ability to link is strongly determined by other factors.

In terms of social networks, it is well known that on average there are about six links from any person anywhere to any other. This is the so-called six degrees of separation. This "small-world" phenomenon was first demonstrated by Stanley Milgram in 1967 for the continental United States, when he posed an experiment essentially asking persons drawn at random to target someone whom they did not know in another part of the country.[6] They were then asked to try and establish contact with that unknown person by communicating with someone they thought might be nearer to the person in question, thus asking that person to pass on the message. This resulted in the conclusion that everyone seemed to be connected to everyone else by an average of six links in their network. It then followed that this number would likely remain invariant for different sizes of network, or at different levels of the geographical hierarchy, hence applying equally well to small and to large cities. There is, of course, some dispute about the generality of these relationships, with some arguing that the small-world phenomenon is a convenient "urban" myth, but it is, at least, a good basis on which to get going with respect to thinking of cities as connected systems.

As cities get larger, the number of potential connections increases as the square of the number of persons living in the city. This number is, of course, an upper limit. As we add more and more networks, and assuming that the networks are largely independent of one another (in that most use one network or another but not more than one at the same time), the number of connections still rises as the square of those who are connected. This is in effect Metcalfe's law,[7] noted in the previous chapter, but in reality, the total number of connections is limited by Dunbar's number, and the structure of those connections is dramatically simplified by the fact that the average degrees of connection or separation are something like six network links.

What all this implies is that as cities get bigger, there is an inexorable pressure to increase connections to others. This probably manifests itself in the kind of tensions associated with urban density, both in terms of the increasing numbers occupying the same space and increasing numbers of relationships. It is the basic argument for increasing returns to scale, and, as we will see a little later, it lies at the heart of the current fascination with scaling and qualitative change as cities get larger. Moreover, in certain cultures and economies, this is a primary thesis: that bigger cities are better in terms of the way they act as incubators and accelerators of technological progress, higher economic rewards, and more sustainable, greener, and healthier living.

Thinking of a city as a constellation of networks, which are in themselves connected by different networks, is the formal model we have in mind when we seek to define the extent of a city. One might consider the relationships formed by an individual citizen in this morass of networks as a hierarchy of sorts, if the links to those to whom that person is connected can be ordered in terms of who knows who. Constructing this morass, however, is more akin to an entangled set of hierarchies that somehow need to be simplified if we are to have any understanding of the structure of cities and who relates to whom. The simplest hierarchy was introduced in the previous chapters as a ranking of cities by their size. However, in this context, such hierarchies were simply different levels, from the largest city at the top down to many smallest cities at the bottom. The levels were not nested within one another, and our discussion of city sizes might thus be seen as a line defining the rank order. Our best definition of hierarchy within the city is easiest to visualize as smaller and smaller geographical units or communities, grouped within each higher and larger geographical level, almost like a set of Russian dolls, but with more than one doll of the same size within a doll of a bigger size. Such hierarchies are strictly ordered groups of objects nested within one another as their size decreases from the entire system down to its smallest elements. This is the familiar tree-like structure that defines our traditional and simplest conception of a hierarchy as a river-like or dendritic network. Whether or not we can simplify the city or system of cities into such ordered structures is very much an open question, because this requires the boundaries between the elements that are nested to be quite distinct—which is far from what we see in actual cities.

To best demonstrate entangled hierarchies, we can grow a city starting with its most basic elements. This is completely consistent with our view, which we emphasized in the first two chapters, that cities evolve from the bottom up. Imagine a hamlet—a couple of households who live as neighbors in a place where they pool their labor to create bigger farms, which in turn attract other farmsteads, which grow to form a village. The structure of these local communities develop stronger links when they are adjacent than when they are dispersed, and these structures form the rudiments of the emerging city. To serve the entire settlement, adjacent households group in communities, which offer services particular to their neighborhoods, and as the city grows, ever bigger districts and specialized centers emerge to service the entire system. If we assume the neighborhoods remain strictly separate, then a perfect hierarchy emerges that can be represented as a tree-like graph. In essence, the elements that comprise the hierarchy are all self-contained with respect to their sustainability, and if the tasks that take place to sustain this structure generate an economic surplus, one might imagine the urban structure would operate like a well-oiled machine. This is the model of a resilient system, first articulated in general terms by Herbert Simon in his wonderful paper entitled "The Architecture of Complexity," in which he argued that one needs to build small to create large, in much the same way that small cities begat large. If the small parts have a dense internal structure of connections, but a weaker lower density of interactions between them, the hierarchy that emerges is resilient to breaking down at the level of its most basic parts.[8]

This construction might sound like a machine, but it is not. In fact, what begins to happen to the originally distinct households and communities is that they establish ties in the normal ways, but then change their locations, or they redevelop their land, or they regenerate parts of their neighborhood while also attracting new populations into their own communities. The distinctiveness breaks down as people in one community associate with another and mix together, as much because they were once part of that community but also because social friendships and economic links evolve and change. Our perfect hierarchy is no longer nested, but consists of overlapping levels and linkages, which blur its edges. If the communities are geographically adjacent, they begin to overlap, but there is no reason why this model should be restricted to spatial neighborhoods. The relationships might be purely social, and although everyone exists in geographical space, the geographical dimension can be unimportant to the motivation for developing the network. This blurring of the hierarchy in cities was first articulated by Christopher Alexander in his paper "A City Is Not a Tree," where he argued that a strict, nested hierarchy was too simple a model for the way cities are structured and the way they have developed.[9] In fact, Alexander argued that the tree structure of the city hierarchy should be replaced by a more complicated structure, which, borrowing from mathematics, he called a semi-lattice. Alexander's thesis was that much city planning tended to simplify the world into cities composed of hierarchies, but to generate the real diversity that comprised the city—the kind of diversity Jane Jacobs and Ed Glaeser speak about in their celebrations of the richness of city life[10]— overlapping hierarchies are much better descriptors of these structures. We illustrate Alexander's varieties of hierarchy in figure 3.1.

In fact, Alexander's notion of the city as being formally represented as a semi-lattice and not a tree is a way of saying that cities are much more than hierarchies. He only assumed one kind of network, one kind of hierarchy, one kind of semi-lattice, but it is quite clear that the contemporary city is composed of multiple networks, all of which might be represented in simpler form as semi-lattices of overlapping subdivisions and subsystems. Put all these over one another and, if you can imagine them as semi-lattices, considering that there may well be links between different types of network, then entangled structures that are almost impossible to visualize emerge. Later in this chapter, we will introduce the simplest of networks to illustrate how far we have to go in defining distinct, nonoverlapping geographic communities we might take as being the right kind of elements that compose cities. How we map social networks onto economic networks, which in turn have geographic footprints, is the great challenge for a new science of cities that is theoretically consistent with what we know about how cities function economically as well as the ways in which they hold together as social artifacts.

Polis, Metropolis, Megalopolis, ...

Although we will explore the actual physical form of cities—their morphology—in the next chapter, here we need to introduce the traditional form of the city from its earliest development. Since prehistory, cities have always been small, limited by how far we can walk in a reasonable time without tiring and still be able to accomplish a day's work. This has meant that cities have rarely been more than about 6 km (3.7 mi) in radius. Where they have grown to hundreds of thousands of people, which appears to have been a tiny number from classical times—Rome in the first century CE, and later Nanjing in China in the seventh and 15th centuries CE—enormous

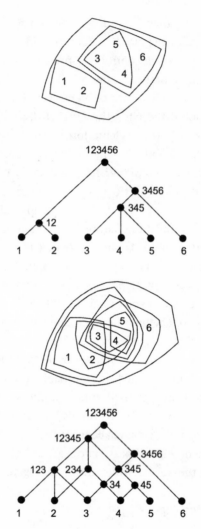

Figure 3.1
Varieties of hierarchy after Alexander (1965).

resources and political power were required to make a functioning city possible through appropriate regulation and transportation. In fact, even the largest cities remained geographically small until the beginning of the Industrial Revolution because densities for work and living were much higher than in contemporary cities, and there was very little sprawl in the absence of machine power. Rome was only about 14 km^2 (5.4 mi^2) in area, with no more than 1.1 million population; compare this with modern-day Manhattan, which is 85 km^2 (32.8 mi^2) with a population of 1.6 million.

Cities until the 18th century were generally surrounded by walls, traditionally for purposes of defense, but also to impose some political order on societies, most of which had much less developed political and administrative systems than those of today. In fact, city walls were still being built and repaired during the early to mid-19th century before developments in the technology of warfare essentially made such defensive installations obsolete. Too, urban sprawl outside the city walls did not begin until the mid- to late 19th century, first with the arrival of heavy rail and then with the arrival of the tram and omnibus, which were quickly followed by the automobile, subway, and electric rail. During this period, heavy rail also became ever more efficient, thus allowing long-distance commuting. Until the Industrial Revolution, cities tended to be pretty similar in their economic structure, acting largely as service centers for their agricultural hinterlands or as political towns, often with capital city functions of government. Various theories of human geography, such as central place theory, developed by Walter Christaller,[11] provide explanations of how strict and less-strict distinct and overlapping hierarchies of dependent services by city size relate to this pre-industrial landscape.

Insofar as scholars reflected on different kinds of town prior to the 19th century, it was the Greeks who articulated the city as a manmade artifact in describing its political and economic structure. In particular, the idea of the city, loosely called the "polis," was used as a template for establishing various philosophies and rules of law that determined how the Greek city-state was to be governed. In many respects, the polis was small in population, little more than 10,000 persons (including citizens and slaves), and its idealized structure was designed so that an army of some 1,000 soldiers could defend the city. In fact, many cities in the ancient world had much the same structure of functions—an acropolis, usually a fortified central point designed for religious and defensive retreat; an agora, or marketplace;

a coliseum; a gymnasium; a stadium, and so on. We do not know very much about cities that did not have the same well-defined structure as the Greek polis or the Roman castra (fortified camp), but it is likely that many cities in the past were essentially high-density slums with relatively little structure whose actual form and function have been lost in the mists of time. Many cities in this world were built and rebuilt over and over again using mud brick, and what we know very largely from archeological evidence is that excavation on a fairly dramatic scale would be required for a reasonably accurate picture of their form and structure to be revealed.

In the late 19th century, two scholars, Patrick Geddes and Max Weber, began to articulate a classification of cities that pertained to their forms and functions with respect to size and scale.[12] Weber made the key distinction between consumer and producer cities, with the former pertaining very largely to cities dominated by service provision as well as a political focus, while the latter pertained to the industrial city and cities before the Industrial Revolution dominated by trade. In fact, Weber's contribution was largely sociological, and his definition of the city tended to look back to the kinds of growth patterns that dominated the size and distribution of cities in the first and earliest stage of the Industrial Revolution.

Geddes's concern, however, was with the growth of cities and their evolution. He coined the term "conurbation" to identify systems of cities that had begun to fuse together: in today's parlance, these are polycentric forms of city that we will picture in the next chapter, when we unpack the way form follows function. In some respects, industrialized society—certainly in western Europe, and particularly Britain—was built on top of an earlier non-industrial agricultural base, with an original distribution of market towns serving their agricultural hinterlands. In this sense, the new industrialization led to a fusing of the ancient and modern, and new industries that drew on an earlier distribution of services provided a natural backcloth for cities to fuse together as they grew. Conurbations, therefore, were not formed by urban sprawl which came much later.

In fact, Geddes defined a conurbation as something a little more than simply a fusion of originally freestanding towns and cities. He wrote: "Some name for these city regions, these town aggregates, is wanted. Constellations we cannot call them; conglomerations is, alas, nearer the mark at present, but it might sound unappreciative; what of 'Conurbations?' That perhaps may serve as the necessary word, as an expression of this new form of population-grouping, which is already, as it were sub-consciously, developing new forms of social grouping." This was particularly perceptive of Geddes, for throughout his century and into our own, the massive and dramatic growth and fusion of settlements into one another—which are conurbations—has become the dominant pattern. In fact, Geddes went much further in his speculation of city forms. He resurrected the old word "heptarchy"—the original seven kingdoms of England—to refer to conurbations joining together, as indeed they have done in Britain during the 20th century. He thence coined the term "world city" for these city regions, a term that has massive resonance in terms of the way cities are now being connected using new information technologies.[13]

Geddes also introduced the term "megalopolis," which he implied is a fusion of fusions—cities as much connected by sprawl as by their aggregation at the metropolitan scale. His arguments about the growth of cities did much to anticipate the study of urbanization and the growth of world cities during the past century, but his was a less than completely optimistic view of urban growth, which he considered to be largely out of control. It was left to Lewis Mumford, however, his one-time disciple, to really lay out this classification of an urban future, which was even gloomier than Geddes originally anticipated. By the middle of the 20th century, Mumford was arguing that urban sprawl, which had led to megalopolitan regions such as the northeast seaboard of the United States, was running into an economic and social decline whose form and function would accelerate apocalyptic collapse. Much of this is elaborated in his book *The Culture of Cities*, which contains his own views about the future of technics and civilization. Jacobs violently disagreed with his somewhat dark view, saying this particular book "was largely a morbid and biased catalogue of ills."[14] But the term megalopolis has been used by several others, such as Jean Gottmann, whose study of the northeast seaboard is a considerably more optimistic vision of this urban future.[15] This is also the case with Constantinos Doxiadis's view of the urban future: he speculated that the world's population will reach 50 billion by the end of this century and that the future will be composed of a worldwide city, which he called an "ecumenopolis."[16]

Doxiadis is one of the few scholars to define a complete progression of city types by size, which is worth listing, for it serves to give some substance to our verbal vision of how cities change as they grow. His continuum of populations is: *anthropos*, 1 person; *room*, 2; *house*, 5; *hamlet*, 40; *village*,

250; *neighborhood*, 1,500; *small polis* (town), 10,000; *polis* (large town/city), 75,000; *small metropolis*, 500,000; *metropolis*, 4 million; *small megalopolis*, 25 million; *megalopolis*, 150 million; *small eperopolis*, 750 million; *eperopolis*, 7,500 million; and, lastly, *ecumenopolis*, 50,000 million—the entire population of the earth, as predicted back in 1976. It is instructive to note that when Doxiadis speculated about the future of cities nearly 50 years ago, the general view was one of dramatic population growth, which many then considered to be unsustainable, echoing the Malthusian predictions for the mid-20th century described in the previous chapter.

Urban Clusters as Cities

The message in the last chapter, however, was that by the end of this century we will all be living in cities of one form or another. Doxiadis's notion that this would be an *ecumenopolis*, one physical entity or superorganism that connects everyone physically, is one vision of this future. Burdett and Sudjic,[17] following in Doxiadis's tradition, call this *The Endless City* in their book of the same name. Brenner and Schmid[18] broaden this image to one of *planetary urbanization*, embracing a much more differentiated "cityness" in which urbanization is largely defined by global connectivity. Although such a connected entity is unlikely (for obvious physical reasons pertaining to the impossibility of building everywhere), the idea that cities are merging into one another, creating forms that are bigger than anything we have considered possible hitherto, increases our need for clear and unambiguous definitions of where cities begin and end in the many dimensions they embody. The largest city in the JRC database used in the last chapter reveals that this is the megalopolis that covers the Pearl River delta in southeastern China, where continuous urban development links the cities of Hong Kong and Guangzhou, embracing Macao, Zuhai, Dongguan, and many other towns within this urban constellation.

This urban cluster now contains some 46 million people. Go back 30 years, and this entity barely existed, its cities then comprising no more than 12 million. If you took the Kowloon Canton Railway from Hung Hom in Hong Kong-Kowloon, it would take about 40 minutes to reach the border with China, but from thereon, the railway ran through a different world of paddy fields and villages until, three hours later, it reached Guangzhou, which was a city of bicycles. Now you can take the metro from Hong Kong to Lo Wu on the border and transfer to one of the many high-speed "bullet" trains that crisscross the delta. These trains and all the related infrastructure that has been ploughed into this largest urban agglomeration the world has yet seen is continually increasing the accessibility of every part to every other. The fastest trains take 40 minutes to reach Guangzhou, which is now an entirely modern metropolis whose growth shows little sign of slowing down.

The emergent megalopolis plotted from the JRC data is shown in figure 3.2, where is it eminently clear how difficult it is to partition this agglomeration into distinct clusters which form a clear hierarchy. We have argued that defining cities involves more than merely using geometry and geography to determine where the city begins and ends, and this is entirely consistent with the sentiments of Jacobs, Mumford and Glaeser alluded to earlier. In fact, if you look closely at figure 3.2, it is well nigh impossible to separate individual cities from one another as quasi-independent clusters on the basis of comparing their densities with the rural hinterland. Moreover, although this massive urban entity is connected physically, it is clear from any casual knowledge of how people function in this region that its

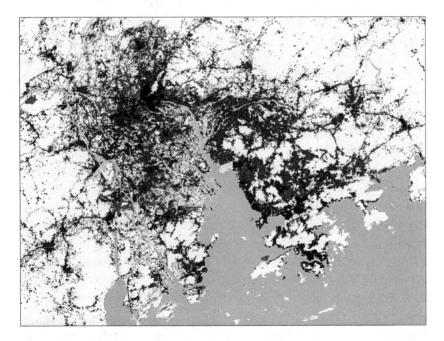

Figure 3.2
Clusters comprising the largest urban agglomeration.

component parts are individual cities that need to be considered separately for many purposes. Physical connection does not necessarily mean that all those components that connect up with one another form part of the same entity, for it necessary to disentangle function from form. Arguably, if all the pieces making up figure 3.2 were connected by substantial physical flows, illustrating the interdependence of economic activity in various locations, there might be a case for thinking of the entire entity as a single city. Or, if this were not the case, but the flows were electronic, then there is some sense in which the entire agglomeration might be treated as one mass. But the definition of individual and distinct urban clusters is more complex, and we need to be very clear about the rules for breaking up the urban mass into its component parts—cities, if you like—that make sense for purposes of measuring their various attributes.

There are three key criteria that arise time and again in defining cities. The first is density, as measured by the numbers of persons per hectare (or acre), as for example illustrated in figure 3.2. The second is some measure of interaction or dependence of any one area on another, meaning the strength of the links between aggregate populations or individuals over the whole geographical space. These interactions are usually measured in terms of material flows, such as people making the journey to work; commodity flows between different industrial areas; and even migration movements within the residential sector. As we will elaborate in the chapters that follow, electronic linkages and flows are of utmost importance in broadening our definition of cities away from the purely geographical. In fact, in this chapter, although our definition will seek to use interactions based on material and people flows, these will, in essence, be geographically grounded. The third criterion relates to geographical proximity or contiguity. The units that make up the city—whether they be individuals, households, neighborhoods, or districts—must in some sense be close to one another, notwithstanding all the potential generalizations of these definitions to nonspatial linkages and flows we will broach in later chapters.

There is quite widespread agreement about this threefold focus on defining cities with respect to densities, interactions, and contiguity or proximity (though size and political organization are also important features). Several analysts argue that, for an area to belong to a city, it must have a population density of at least 14 persons per hectare, which is 1,400 persons per square kilometer (or 540 persons per square mile). In fact, Cottineau and her colleagues[19] argue that this is a little on the low side, suggesting nearer

2,000 persons per square kilometer (or 772 persons per square mile) is a better threshold. But much depends on culture, tradition, and the level of modernity of a place. In terms of interaction, it is commuting fields that are usually used to define a city, in that any place that has more than 20 percent of its working population traveling to work outside its residential area should be considered for inclusion in a city's area. Regarding the third criterion, contiguity, places that are within a distance threshold of some 2 km (1.25 mi) are often considered to be part of a city if—and this is a very strict rule—the place in question meets the other two criteria simultaneously. Cottineau and her colleagues then propose a simple algorithm for generating cities that meet these criteria, beginning by identifying areas or cores with the highest densities, then relaxing this to consider places that have slightly less density, are adjacent, and meet a minimum commuting threshold. If there are places that are not contiguous geographically, then the distance threshold is invoked, serving to fill in "holes" that have appeared in the fabric being generated so far. The density threshold is then further relaxed and the algorithm begins again, gradually growing the cities that have emerged until they reach the minimum density threshold of 2,000 persons per square kilometer (or 772 persons per square mile), the 20 percent commuting threshold, and all the requirements for contiguity.

There are many variants on this kind of procedure, but most follow this general form. Two related criteria—a minimum size of unit for a city and whether the derived place has any administrative integrity—are often used to structure the process, either at its start or at any point in the construction of the city area. In the United States, the Census Bureau assumes a minimum size of 10,000 persons for a micropolitan area and 50,000 for a metropolitan statistical area, while the State Council in China uses a similar definition in their designation of cities in the Peoples' Republic. The JRC data, however, is not based on a functional threshold, such as commuting, since it is initially defined from remotely sensed land cover interpretations of what is urban and rural. This is much more akin to using density as the arbiter of what constitutes a city, in contrast to the Organisation for Economic Co-operation and Development (OECD) data set, which defines what have been called functional urban regions using commuting thresholds of 15 percent.[20] As we explore in the next chapter, form and function are quite closely tied together with respect to these various definitions, although there can be substantial differences when tempered by political and administrative boundary definitions.

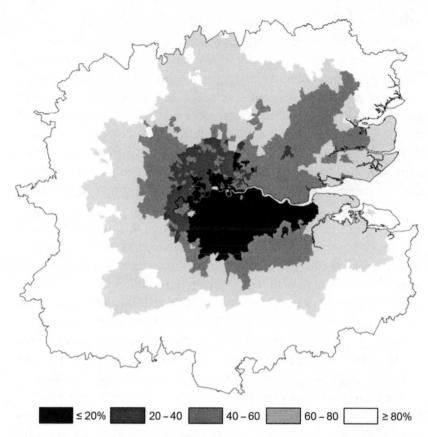

≤ 20%   20 – 40   40 – 60   60 – 80   ≥ 80%

Figure 3.3
Defining greater London at different commuting thresholds.

To give some idea of the multiple boundaries that might define a large city, we will illustrate the impact of varying these criteria for defining London. Starting with a zone at the center of its central business district—in The City at St. Paul's Cathedral—we then add an adjacent zone, one that is contiguous to the zone(s) already comprising the growing mass so that the maximum amount of interaction is contained within the mass. As we add more zones, the proportion of interaction within the city rises—we are capturing more at each stage of the aggregation, and this implies we are covering more and more activity related to the city. To pursue this process, we need a much larger bounded region, and for this we take London and its outer metropolitan area. Once we have added all the zones into this growing aggregate, we cover the entire activity of the system. From this point, we can draw boundaries, as in figure 3.3, for 20 percent, 40 percent, 60 percent, and 80 percent of activity captured, thus embodying our two criteria of commuting thresholds and adjacency. In figure 3.3, we do not use the density criteria, but this is easy to implement as an additional filter. In the sections that follow, we will explore how to define cities in a relatively simple manner to generate cities of different sizes, enabling us to examine qualitative change in structure relative to size.

Extracting Cities from the Urban Hierarchy

Prior to the first Industrial Revolution, the iconic symbol marking the city was the pinnacle of its religious and political power: in classical times, this was the acropolis, and by medieval times in Europe, it was the cathedral. But by the third decade of the 20th century with the invention of electricity and the steel frame, the iconic image had changed to that of the skyscraper. We will say much more about skyscrapers in chapter 6, but suffice it to say that the great transition is bringing another, more abstract image of the city in its wake—the network. No longer is the city about location: it is about interaction, about networks, about how we communicate and serve the built and natural environments in terms of the resource flows that sustain the organism. It is no accident that in the last 20 years, the theory of networks has grown dramatically within science and social science. Network science is fast becoming the underpinning representation for complex systems such as cities and, in a wider context, for the economy itself.[21]

In defining cities, we can think of them as being clusters within a much wider network of city systems. Networks are graphs that are composed of nodes and links—where the nodes represent locations that interact in some manner with each other across the links. Sometimes nodes and links are called vertices and arcs, sometimes hubs and spokes, and there are yet other diverse terminologies; but all convey the notion that networks are receptacles for transmitting and receiving flows and messages. In fact, the network is a good enough representation to implement the most basic elements of city definition that we introduced above. First, nodes define locations where activity takes place—where we live, work, entertain, study, and so on—and this, in turn, defines the density of any place. The more nodes within a fixed space, the greater the density, and any casual observation of a city reveals that as one moves toward its traditional center, the density of nodes usually increases. Second, the links mark the channels of communication between activities, or nodes—which might be physical or electronic routes fixed in space or varying in the ether, as, for example, in wireless connectivity. These links also define the volume of flows, and might be associated with a weighted graph where the actual flow, distance, travel time, cost, and so on define the way such links are measured. Third, links anchor the city in its geometry and geography, whether they be physical or ethereal; in this regard, this method of definition relates to various thresholds that serve to tie the nodes together through different degrees of clustering. This, of course, is the essence of defining the density and physical extent of the city.

We will begin with the simplest of all networks, the one we all have direct experience of, and that is the street network. Flows on this network are people walking or cycling or contained in vehicular traffic, and all these relate to a mixture of activities taking place at different speeds. Other networks complement these physical movements at greater scales, namely railway networks and airline networks (which are not constrained by the same physical limits). To illustrate cities and the hierarchy of places of different densities and sizes, we will take the simplest street network and show how cities can be extracted from this. This network is usually available for most countries from various national mapping agencies or from crowd-sourced versions, the most popular and widespread of which is Open Street Map.[22] In Great Britain, the most detailed network is from the Ordnance Survey. In its latest release, the survey defines some 3.5 million nodes, which are street intersections, and some 8.4 million links, which are street segments of rarely less than about 100 meters (about 100 yards) in length. A measure of the network over the whole country (England, Wales, and Scotland) can be defined by simply dividing the number of links by the number of nodes. This gives an average of 2.4 links per node, showing that this is quite a low-density network overall, notwithstanding that within it strong clusters of cities stand out.

We can define these clusters by proceeding analytically from the entire network down, splitting off the biggest clusters first and eventually ending up with cities of different sizes based on the relevant clusters. Or we can proceed the other way around, building the densest clusters first and moving up the hierarchy synthetically until we have exhausted the entire network. The precise details do not need to bother us, and there are many variants of this kind of percolation analysis that lead to slightly different realizations.

What we first do, no matter whether we start top-down or bottom-up, is to rank the links between the nodes with respect to their weight (flow), which in the example we show here is their physical distance. We then start with the smallest distance or the largest, adding nodes to form clusters from the bottom or taking them away to reveal clusters from the top. From the bottom up, we first identify the two nodes connected by the smallest distance and group these. At this first stage, we may find that we assemble chains of distances if all we do is join nodes that meet this threshold. If we find at any stage that three nodes get linked for a certain distance threshold, we then have to decide if all three have to be linked within the threshold to form the elements of a tripartite cluster (as long as we consider this to be an important requirement). In fact, given the nature of the spaces that we are working with, then sooner or later simply due to the structure of Euclidean distances, nodes that form cities will all get joined. All such methods are percolation-based, and the analogy with how we make our coffee is not lost on us in this context. A graphic of this procedure is illustrated in figure 3.4, which shows the various steps necessary to produce clusters, and this implies a method of reiterating these steps to gradually develop the entire hierarchy.

It is much easier to illustrate this method pictorially by starting with the entire graph and then decomposing it, taking the biggest distance threshold first and then relaxing the threshold, thus capturing the hierarchy of clusters that remain after each stage of thresholding. In figure 3.4, we show how we can extract a very simple hierarchy and a cluster of cities by starting at the top and gradually relaxing the distance threshold until we can go no further. What is important about this example is the fact that we can generate a very large number of clusters as we proceed. Often in a large network, there are simply too many to identify, and of course they are decomposing into ever-smaller clusters as we proceed down the hierarchy. As we are searching here for distinct cities, we do not want overlapping clusters, although the method could easily be modified to produce lattice-like hierarchies, such as that suggested by Christopher Alexander and illustrated in figure 3.1. In a world of cities where they are fusing with the urban landscape, thus becoming polycentric, it may well be necessary to consider overlapping clusters if there is ambiguity as to which node belongs to which cluster. But once again, it depends on the criteria that are used in a city's definition. So much in this world of cities is based on what we perceive as being the most intuitive way of proceeding to definitions that suit our particular purposes, and

Step 1: Rank the distances on each link in order from largest to smallest.

Step 2: Identify the largest distances and snip the links associated with these distances in order from largest to smallest. Here we take the top 5 distances.

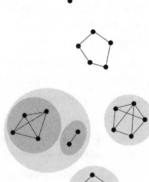

Step 3: The remaining links define the network as a more dense set of clusters.

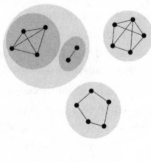

Step 4: These clusters can then be subdivided further in steps 2–3, where the next largest distances are chosen and the procedure reiterated.

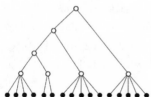

Final Step: The hierarchy is thus complete and can be visualized as a dendrite.

Figure 3.4
Defining urban clusters using percolation theory.

this in turn will vary greatly dependent on context. There are many different ways of constructing hierarchies, which we report elsewhere.[23]

We can best illustrate the method using the street network data set for Great Britain. When we start with the complete graph and proceed with our percolation from the top down, we first identify all those clusters that are more than 5 kilometers (about 3 miles) distant from one another, and at these large distance thresholds all the islands (mainly off the coast of Scotland) are separated from the mainland. As we continue to relax this threshold, first the major national divisions stand out as connected clusters—the giant cluster that is urban Scotland separates first, then the hilly areas separate from one another, and eventually the country divides into the southeast of England and the now-de-industrialized heartland of the north and west. Scotland becomes separate because it was a separate national entity until some 500 years ago, but it is clear that in passing, the different regional subdivisions reveal many political and economic characteristics that pertain to the history of industrial Britain over the last 200 years. The deindustrialized areas around the major cities starkly contrast with pockets of rural wealth and poverty, the richer southeast of the country, and London. Eventually the threshold falls to 100 meters (about 100 yards), and this is almost too low to define the cities. But cities do stand out quite nicely around the 250 meter (about 275 yard) threshold. A clear picture of the hierarchy and three pictures of the key subdivisions showing the 12 largest clusters at these three threshold levels is provided in figure 3.5 (a) and (b), respectively.

The hierarchy is not as easy to interpret as one might think. As separate clusters at any level of threshold are defined, these clusters can split off from clusters already formed, and such clusters may well decompose successively—not to reveal cities, but to reveal smaller and smaller clusters that eventually fragment into hamlets and villages, missing the city stage entirely. At some point we have to decide where to end the thresholding, but if we continue it until we get the smallest segments, we then need to perform one further stage in using this model of percolation to define cities: define the thresholds that are relevant to particular cities of different sizes, noting that if one picks a threshold with a city of one size, this city might further break into quasi-separate neighborhoods as we continue the decomposition. In essence, we need to use independent criteria to decide when a city is a city. If we look again at the hierarchy in figure 3.5, we see that the nodes at each level are in fact clusters of nodes, their size

a)

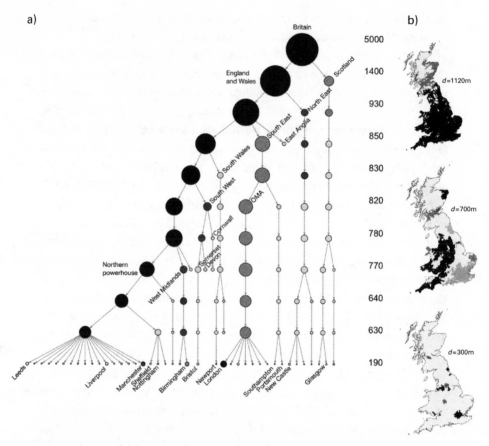

b)

Figure 3.5
The clusters defining Great Britain from its street network: (a) the national-regional and city hierarchy; (b) sample clusters at selected levels of the hierarchy.

being proportional to the number of street intersections contained in the remaining set of connected clusters. These get progressively smaller as the threshold reduces to the succession of distances needed to support clusters at that level of threshold. Arcaute and her colleagues have presented a detailed picture of how the method can be developed and generalized.[24]

There is one last point we need to make before inquiring into what this method of definition might say about clusters within cities. This relates to political and cultural, and to some extent historical, factors. In the last couple of years, the momentum for independence in Scotland has reached an all-time high, and although the vote in 2014 for Scottish Independence went against the Scottish nationalists, the vote a year later in 2015 changed the political map of Scotland beyond recognition in favor of the nationalists.[25] The vote in 2016 for leaving the European Community (Brexit, so-called) again pit Scotland against the northern heartlands of England as well as peripheral areas of the country, who all voted to leave the European Union. Scotland and the cities voted to stay. The key issue in this debate is that the kind of clusters we generate as we decompose the hierarchy are persuasively suggestive of this changing political and economic landscape, with the cities standing out as distinct enclaves of cosmopolitanism and internationalism in a sea of anti-EU sentiment. The core cities appear to be enlightened in terms of the global economy, while the de-industrialized urban swathe around the core cities—who incidentally have clearly missed out on all the benefits that have accrued to ever-bigger cities this last 30 or more years— are manifestly anti-global. This is an important signpost to the future, and we will return to it implicitly in later chapters, particularly chapter 8 where we come to grips with what these city definitions tell us about the future urban world and the ways it might be segregated.

Of course, our clusters do not stop being formed or being dissolved when we reach what we consider the correct city size. If we are building clusters from the bottom up, it is the smallest components of the city that are detected first. To be recognizable and meaningful, these smallest clusters are likely to be neighborhoods, and there is a long tradition of thinking about cities as having neighborhoods—which are cohesive and impart a sense of community, while also reflecting ethnic as well as income and social class differences. Indeed, it was Jane Jacobs[26] who argued that well-functioning cities are composed of diverse neighborhoods that are not segregated by artificial barriers like streets, while at the same time are characterized by multiple land uses. The notion of partitioning cities into discrete neighborhoods was also demolished by Christopher Alexander,[27] who argued that such distinct hierarchies are entirely artificial and, even if imposed by planners, would eventually morph into much more diverse and messy kinds of structures—that is, overlapping neighborhoods, illustrated quite effectively by figure 3.1.

Again, we will comment at greater length on this in later chapters, for much segregation is generated from forces that are undesirable, such as ghettoization. Indeed, one of the classic demonstrations of how such divisions can emerge was the subject of some highly insightful work by Thomas Schelling,[28] who showed that from simple and somewhat mild preferences

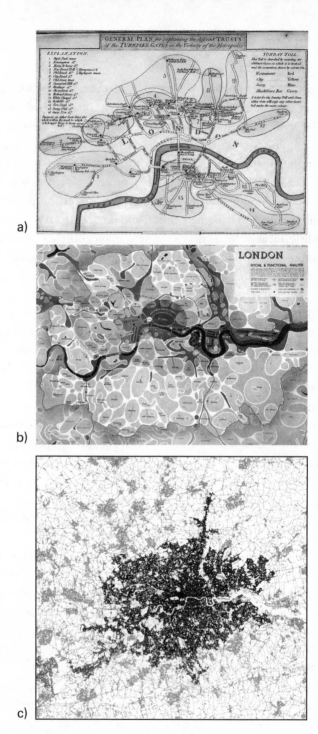

Figure 3.6
Defining neighborhoods from the bottom up: (a) Cary's map of turnpike districts in London (1790); (b) neighborhoods in Abercrombie's Greater London Plan (1945); (c) the top 12 clusters in London from bottom-up percolation.

for being a part of a neighborhood that was more similar to one's own preferences, such diversity could soon unravel once even one person began to move. Here we will conclude by illustrating that cities can be defined as distinct and separate neighborhoods using percolation, which compare to many idealizations often used for master planning. In figure 3.6, we show Cary's (1790) map of turnpike districts in London, which are a type of geographical neighborhood,[29] alongside Abercrombie's famous map of neighborhoods in London from his *Plan for Greater London*.[30] These neighborhoods do not overlap. Next to this we show clusters built using bottom-up percolation to a particular threshold level. In each case, these neighborhoods are quite distinct. More realistic pictures, of course, which reflect the messiness of the world in terms of overlapping neighborhoods are harder to interpret, despite being more realistic regarding the blurred nature of city definitions. But, for the moment, all we have done here is show that density, distance, and contiguity represent the key forces defining cities as geographical objects.

The Central Paradox of the Modern Metropolis

Several scholars and commentators on the urban condition have drawn attention to a seeming paradox: as information technologies have enabled us to spread ourselves out and communicate globally, big cities have become more polarized. In some senses, their cores are denser, but their suburbs are more spread out. Ed Glaeser[31] refers to this as the "paradox of the modern metropolis," saying, "proximity has become ever more valuable as the cost of connecting across long distances has fallen." This "death of distance" is much more than it appears, for it is a massive stretching, a transformation that enables us to live and work anywhere, but to interact with like-minded people in pursuit of the same goals at central cores in the global urban landscape that is quickly being created, as we described earlier in this chapter.[32] In the previous chapter, we also noted that the very biggest cities were increasing in size as a proportion of the top 500, 1,000, or even 10,000 biggest cities, while the distribution of cities of all sizes was tending to flatten. It is as if all cities are becoming more competitive, whatever their size, while the biggest cities are capturing an increasing share of the world's population. The paradox between needing ever more face-to-face contact in the biggest cities and the fact that we can now communicate so easily globally is something that will dominate the urban future, as form becomes more detached from function and as the complexity of how we define a city as a distinct geographic object becomes ever more problematic. We will thus use Glaeser's paradox as our second generic principle to distinguish cities of the pre-industrial age from those that are fast emerging in the post-industrial, in which the roles of geometry and time are likely to be considerably more convoluted than anything we can observe in the urban past.

At this stage, before launching into a description of how form is becoming detached from function, which will occupy our concerns in the next chapter, we should say a little about how cities are exploding physically while at the same time becoming global in terms of function. There is a tendency to think that because of information technology, all the glue and cement that ties people together to accomplish joint actions in the same places is melting—that the world of the electronic cottage where we no longer interact very much physically with one another is upon us. But a little reflection on how much time we spend in our lives with our physical neighbors provides some sobering reflections. As children, our world is very small in scale, and for most of us, we really have to reach adulthood to begin to appreciate just how large the world actually is. The number of people we interact with grows from the family unit to the classroom to the club and neighborhood for the first 20 years of our lives, and the intense interactions that take place in these small physical worlds have a dominant effect on our sense of place. After we reach adulthood, these early experiences weigh less heavily as we travel more and interact within a wider world. But as a proportion of our life experiences, the importance of place continues throughout our lives. It may become less significant, but it is a powerful lever in ensuring that we retain our sense of place, making it probable that location will continue to figure in a world which is largely composed of interactions, many of them nonphysical: a speculation, of course, but one that needs to be borne in mind as we discuss our future cities.

In this chapter, we have sketched just how hard it is to define the city as a distinct physical artifact. Although we have only noted casually, in passing, that cities are multidimensional—making it virtually impossible to collapse all their variety into a single definition—we still need to do this, for it is the only way to make comparisons about cities of different sizes with different densities and growth rates. This is a book about the future, and as our ideology about how cities grow and evolve is from the bottom up (with top-down design being relatively modest in cities' overall evolution), a generic prediction would be that such design will itself evolve during this century. Good design should be able to begin to construct modest plans that no longer have the rigid definitions of neighborhoods, districts, and entire cities—all separate from one another—that our building in the past has assumed. The plans for ideal cities produced from classical times onward, which strictly separate functions in areal terms—just as the Abercrombie[33] (1945) plan for London did, just as Le Corbusier[34] (1929) did for his City of Tomorrow and Frank Lloyd Wright[35] (1945) did for his Broadacre City—should be a thing of the past. If we have learned anything this last century about city design and construction, it is that uniformity imposed on the future city is futile and misguided: cities evolve spontaneously through the actions of individuals adapting to the wider context and to each other. Whether this is what indeed will occur is hard to say, but to broach this question more directly, we need to explore in much more detail the form and function of existing and future cities. To this, we will turn in the next chapter.

4 Form Follows Function—Or Does It?

It is the pervading law of all things organic and inorganic, of all things physical and metaphysical, of all things human and all things superhuman, of all true manifestations of the head, of the heart, of the soul, that the life is recognizable in its expression, that form ever follows function. *This is the law.*
—Louis H. Sullivan, "The Tall Office Building Artistically Considered," 408

Well, laws are meant to broken. Louis Sullivan's mantra for the modern movement—form follows function—was broken by architecture itself well before the end of the last century. With the emergence of a digital world, there are many features of cities that now underpin functioning yet no longer have physical form. In fact, in the transformation from a world based on atoms to one of bits, the nature of form is manifestly different from the kind of physicalism that has dominated our understanding of cities hitherto. Sullivan's mantra was highly appropriate for the time when he coined it, for buildings were just on the cusp of becoming truly tall. The steel frame, the elevator, and the telephone all suggested functions that enabled people to move and communicate much more effectively in space and time than they ever had before, thus generating new forms that were the immediate consequence of such inventions. A new minimalism was easy to establish in which the form of the tall building reflected the simple lines of manufactured technologies and any ornament was stripped away. Although immensely convincing at the time, such minimalism did not last long, and by the end of the 20th century, Sullivan's "law" no longer seemed very relevant. Even though there has always been an element of hyperbole in the cliché "form follows function," its gradual demise is yet another illustration of the logic of continually testing (or inventing) an idea until instances emerge where it is clearly falsified.[1] A subtler, but probably more important, consequence of the "form follows function" debate is the fact that the digital world is based on the successive invention of technologies with a very different physical presence from those that have dominated the pre-digital. These new technologies, as noted in earlier chapters, are all but invisible at first sight, and although communication through the ether does leave some physical trace, it is hard to reconcile these electronic signals with the form of cities.

Form and function as ideas go back to Aristotle, but in the modern world and particularly in biology, it was Goethe who, in the guise of morphology, provided one of the first all-encapsulating notions of form. He wrote:[2] "Form is a thing in motion, in the process of becoming, of passing away. The study of form is the study of transformation. The study of metamorphosis is the key to all the signs of nature." This conceptual definition is extremely important to our understanding of form and function in cities, for it raises the notions of growth, change, and transformation—in short, of evolution: something that is key not only to how we should understand cities in the past, but also to thinking about what form cities might take in the future. Cities are usually highly structured, reflecting their growth and qualitative transformation—features and processes we will introduce later in this chapter. But the variegation in densities associated with places where different social and economic activities take place, and the way these activities are woven together through transportation, are key elements of form. In this sense, again, we see that networks and flows are all-important in defining the functions of the city. In the past, there has been a schism between land use and transportation, one often being derived, studied, and even designed without the other.[3] But what has also been missing in the study of form is its transformation in terms of change as society develops, and in particular how new technologies, particularly those associated with communications, emerge and converge.

Thus, it is essential to see the whole panoply of transportation and communication as being key to the future city. Our quest is to broach how we might begin to articulate communications technologies that have a very different physicality and visibility than those that have dominated the city ever since it emerged in ancient Mesopotamia some 5,000 years ago. There have been attempts in the past at explaining the impact of wireless and wired communications, such as the telephone and, to a lesser extent, radio. But as these technologies have been largely passive, never interactive, in the sense of their users being able to manipulate information in a computable manner, there are hardly any studies of the impact of such communications on urban form. Claude Fischer's work on the telephone is an exception, and some of the work on the location of high-tech industries that depend on early versions of networking has been in the vanguard as well. But, by and large, there have been no serious studies of how the form and function of cities have altered or are being altered by email, online mapping, extracting information globally from the web, and the massive proliferation of apps and all sorts of social media that must be changing the city rather dramatically.[5] That we do not know any of this reflects the immense nature of the challenge.

Before reviewing what we *do* know about the shape and pattern of urban forms, it is worth noting that much, but not all, of the city is constructed from new growth that eventually ages and is then transformed through regeneration. New functions thus get layered on top of old. This complicates the picture rather dramatically, since the physical form of the city appears considerably less reactive to social and economic change than it actually is. New functions emerge and are adapted to extant forms, which in and of themselves only change on much longer time cycles than human activities. For example, the street pattern of The City of London (the financial quarter) still has strong elements of the medieval street system—even the Great Fire of 1666 made little impression on it[6]—yet what goes on in The City has changed many times in the last 500 years. This is the kind of complexity that we have to grapple with in understanding the future of the contemporary city.

We will first develop ideas about physical form in terms of its main components and how these have been changing from historical times. Our perspective is one that treats cities as developing largely from the bottom up, evolving, and thus we will introduce the notion of the growing city as the template for examining how cities add and delete functions as they change. This will take us to examining ways in which form changes—in the transformation of cities—as new technologies are invented and come to disrupt and alter older ones. In this, we will focus on qualitative change: that is, various socioeconomic indicators and how these change as a city grows. Finally, we will look at what we know about what has been called the "optimal city." This will enable us to revisit the question of the ideal city, which has been the predominant mode of dreaming about future cities. We say "dreaming," because our thesis here is that such dreaming in the past has been largely fictitious—interesting though it is—and that serious studies of the future city must come to grips with inventing it in considerably more realistic terms.

Physical Form: The Shape and Pattern of Cities

From prehistory, there have been various tensions between those who wish to impose their will on the form of the city from the top down—invariably those who hold power over the city populations they seek to control and manage—and those who exercise their decision-making capabilities as individuals by actions from the bottom up that exist within somewhat narrower domains. This mixture of styles and modes of decision-making leads to systems that are highly diverse and cannot be simply viewed as top down or bottom up, but include both, with decision-makers across many levels. In this sense, cities evolve both organically and in planned form. To some extent, cities are thus the product of a series of historical accidents, and their trajectories of development are sometimes said to be "path-dependent." In this sense, history matters, and no city can be understood without recourse to information about the dynamics and the multitude of processes that concatenate together to generate the kind of diversity that Jane Jacobs so lucidly described[7] with respect to that part of Manhattan in which she lived during the 1950s and 60s.

To an extent, ancient cities appear to contain more top-down planning than modern cities, although it could well be that the archeological record is strongly biased toward planned structures that are likely to be longer lasting, and thus built with more durable materials. This is especially so for cities that were built of mud-dried bricks, many of which have been rebuilt time and time again, as the fossil record reveals. The first cities were in fact of this form. In figure 4.1, we show a series of snapshots up until classical times. The earliest maps can be intuitively guessed from Stone Age cave paintings, but by 1500 BCE, maps were appearing on clay tablets in ancient Mesopotamia. We show these for the city of Nippur and for Babylon in figures 4.1(a) and (b), while the Sumerian city of Ga Sur, near Catal Hyuk, is abstracted in figure 4.1(c). Figures 4.1(d) and (e) show a reconstructed model and map of the ancient city of Ur at earlier times, around 4000 BCE, where the importance of the center as an inner fortified palace is shown. Three maps from cities in classical times complete our collage. Miletus, the planned Greek settlement in Asia Minor—present-day Western Turkey—indicates the power of the state dictating the grid iron plan and the disposition of uses in figure 4.2(a). Rome itself is shown in figure 4.2(b), where a much more diverse and organically organized pattern is revealed, akin to modern-day world cities. Figure 4.2(c) shows the

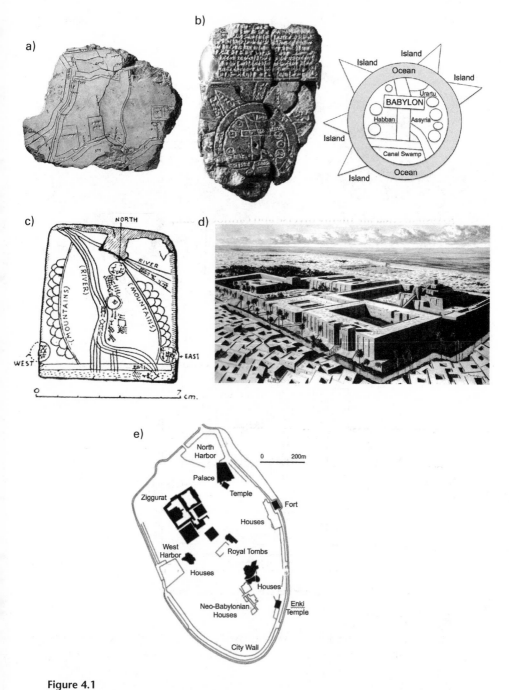

Figure 4.1

Ancient city forms: (a) a map of the city of Nippur on a clay tablet, circa 1200 BCE; (b) Babylon on a clay tablet, circa 600 BCE; (c) Ga Sur abstracted, near Catal Hyuk, 2500 BCE; (d) a reconstruction of the ancient city of Ur, circa 4000 BCE; (e) Ur abstracted, with its center clearly marked.

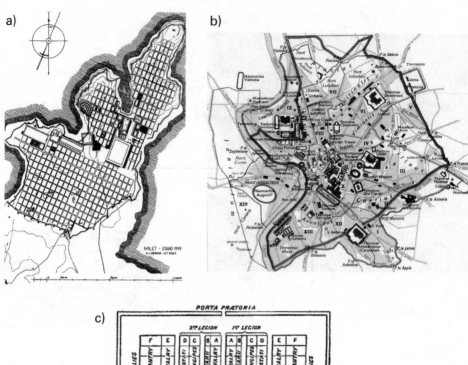

Figure 4.2
Classical unplanned and planned town-city layouts: (a) Miletus, a planned Greek settlement, 450 BCE; (b) Rome circa 200 CE; (c) an idealized model of a Roman *castrum*.

typical Roman army camp, constructed quickly over a matter of days to station legions; these camps often eventually transformed into major cities, such as London, where some of their original grid-like structure still remains.[8]

Even as far back as classical times, although cities remained compact, villages in their hinterland came to depend on their functions, and to an extent acted as suburbs. The term (*sub* meaning *near* and *urbs* meaning *city*) was used by Cicero in relation to the large villas associated with the political elite surrounding Rome, but "true" suburbs—lower-density enclaves surrounding the core—did not really become established until the mid- to late 19th century with the advent of fast transportation. Until the Industrial Revolution, towns remained relatively compact, with much higher densities than most cities in the West today; these constraints on size were largely a function of limited wealth, as well as lack of transport to move people longer distances away from the core to enjoy more space. The structure of towns or cities, from prehistory onwards, has been organized around a central core—invariably only one core rather than many, which in the last century came to be called the central business district (CBD). In the Greek polis, the agora, or marketplace, and the acropolis, the fortified seat of religious and related political power, dominated the city. Although the picture painted of ancient Greece was one of democracy, intellectual argument, and balanced reasoning, it is now clear that much of the polis was composed of fairly high-density housing, which in some contexts could be regarded as "slum conditions."

This model was revived when the art and science of classical Greece and Rome were rediscovered during the Renaissance. As Europe moved out of its Dark Ages, through the Middle Ages, and toward the Enlightenment that began in the 16th and 17th centuries, wealth slowly increased and cities came to be thought of artistically, as places of beauty. This extended to their physical layout as well as their architecture. The standard plan was a core where all intelligent debate and monetary exchange took place, but to facilitate this interaction, the ideal town was laid out in radial style, often symmetrically, while still remaining fortified. Practical tools for building, cataloged and developed by Vitruvius around 80 BCE in his *Ten Books of Architecture*, were resurrected and popularized by key thinkers such as Leonardo da Vinci, while principles of order in buildings, particularly symmetry, were implemented in the classical style by architects such as Brunelleschi, Alberti, and Palladio. Examples of Renaissance city plans[9] are presented in figures 4.3(a) to (d).

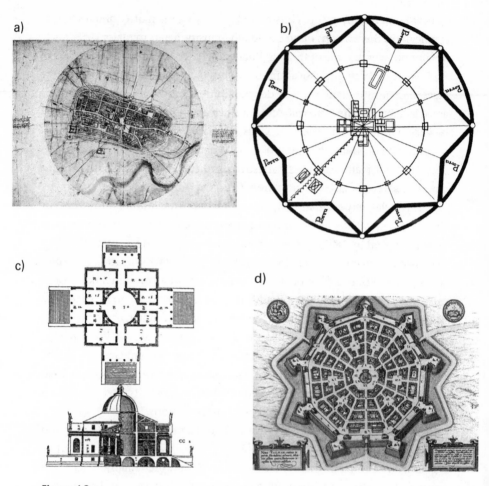

Figure 4.3
Renaissance town plans: (a) Leonardo da Vinci's 1502 Map of the Italian City of Imola;
(b) Urbino by Filareti; (c) Villa by Palladio; (d) Palmanova.

There were some big cities prior to the industrial era, in which the seeds
of extended central areas with polycentric form were sown. For example,
the area now called The City of London, the original center, emerged out of
the Roman camp and fortress established there at the beginning of the com-
mon era. In the late Middle Ages, the palace moved to Westminster, which
became an entirely separate town for royalty and the court, some miles
from The City. By the late 19th century, retailing began to occupy the land
between The City and Westminster in the so-called West End, with The

City retaining and expanding its financial services. There is now another CBD, at Canary Wharf some three miles east of The City, suggesting that London now has almost a polycentric ecology of central functions. Prior to the Industrial Revolution, most cities had small but very distinctive cores around which land use and related activities were structured into rather tight bands of similar usage. We can recognize such banding and the radial corridors that tie these bands to the central core in many cities of past eras, even as far back as the founding of the city of Ur around 4000 BCE, illustrated in figures 4.1(d) and (e). These bands were always contained within a hard periphery—usually a city wall—built for defensive purposes. However, it is not possible to determine whether qualitative change occurred in the properties of variously sized cities from the manner in which cities grew before the Industrial Revolution. This is an open question, for we do not have good data on how city functions have changed historically with size. We will return to this later in this chapter, because, as cities grow, it is clear there are significant qualitative changes we need to understand.

The Standard Model

Since the start of the first Industrial Revolution, and even before, the role of distance in structuring what goes on and where it happens in cities has been recognized. The bands of different land use and activity with respect to their distance from the center are organized according to their economic need to be near the center, while the radial routes that link these bands to the center are limited in number due to the resources required to construct them. Hence, they fill the overall space in which the city exists in the most parsimonious and efficient way. There is a standard model to account for such differentiation, developed at the beginning of the Industrial Revolution, but it was initially developed for explaining how agricultural land uses cluster around a market center. Since the mid-20th century, the model has been adapted and widely applied to explain the structuring of contemporary city systems.

Over 200 years ago, however, a German count by the name of Johann Heinrich von Thünen surveyed his estate in Mecklenburg, Lower Saxony, and came to the conclusion that the way he and his tenants had organized the planting of crops seemed to follow an arrangement of roughly circular but concentric bands of similar cultivation around a central location, which he had established to market his produce.[10] If you could have flown up 1,000 meters (about 3,300 feet), you would have seen concentric rings of different crops. Closest to the market were those that were most perishable and took the fastest time to grow, such as vegetables, while furthest away were the least perishable and took an extremely long time to grow, such as wood from forests. Between these extremes, his estate was organized into different types of crops cultivated on a seasonal basis, as well as land devoted to cattle rearing and dairying, which came in intermediate positions. Of course, von Thünen was not merely intent on simply describing this pattern, he wanted to explain it, and so he figured out what ultimately has become the basis for how a spatial economy works: products that needed to get to market fastest would attempt to locate as close to the market as possible but would pay higher rents for this privilege while incurring lower transport costs. Those that took longer to grow and were less intensively produced would incur lower rents for their land further away from the market but would generate higher transport costs. In a perfect world, von Thünen theorized, the rent payable at the place of production plus the transport cost to market would always be constant.

Von Thünen did not design this regular arrangement. It was not planned as a collective effort from the top down, but evolved over time from individual actions, and thus, its spatial organization essentially emerged from many decisions made from the bottom up. The reason why the production of different agricultural products occupied space at different distances from the market was entirely due to the economics of that production, which reflected a trade-off between the cost of transporting produce to market and the extent to which each product competed with others to determine how near the market it could be produced. Of course, the various agricultural goods produced would have to have a market—the population would have to be of a minimum size to support such production—and, in this sense, production would have to meet its costs and generate normal profits once transport costs and rent were taken into account. In good times, this would imply the boundary for production would expand, whereas in bad times it would contract. A consequence of all this was that the density of production was higher the closer it was produced to the market, the yield was thus higher, and if the producer was required to pay rent, this too would be higher the nearer production was located to the market. If the transportation routes to the market or the physical landscape for production were in some way distorted, then the circular patterns around the market would adjust to reflect such irregularities. For example, if there was a much higher-speed transport route in one direction than any other, this would lower transport costs from places adjacent to this route, and the surface would adjust accordingly. The land uses would thus be organized according to how much they could afford for occupying land at different distances from the market center, with a river or canal providing relatively lower transport costs to market, as shown in figure 4.4(a).

Von Thünen did not consider how many market centers defining a system of central places would modify this pattern, nor did he speculate on how a real system might develop with all the noise and heterogeneity of the real world. But his ideas have remained intact, and they have become the basis for how we think the spatial forms of entire cities are structured in the modern age. If we fast-forward to modern times and ask how are our town and cities are organized spatially, they still approximate von Thünen's rings. If you look at a large city, certainly among those that have developed over the last 100 to 200 years anywhere in the world, their structure can also be seen as reflecting a strong market core—the CBD—followed by circular rings of different land uses, which reflect increasingly high rents as one approaches the center. Although the classic example is Chicago, many cities show similar patterns. For a very long time during the last century, we thought that this concentricity, punctuated by radial networks which enabled people to travel more quickly to the center for work and shopping, represented an almost ideal type when it came to cities. It seemed to be the "natural" way of things. It portrayed an equilibrium that went back well before the Industrial Revolution—to the medieval city and even to classical times, while the industrial era itself did not really upset the balance. It simply reinforced it, with the central city getting bigger and more specialized and the suburbs growing less densely at ever-greater distances from the core.

In the standard model, portrayed in figure 4.4(a), different agricultural land uses are arranged concentrically around the market center, and their usage is determined by the trade-off between yield (rent) and transport cost. In adapting this to the industrial city, Robert Park and Ernest Burgess in their book *The City* used Chicago to demonstrate how poorer groups were forced to live at higher densities near the center, while richer groups could afford more space at lower densities toward the edge.[11] Commuting is all-important to this picture. In this illustration, concentric zones end at the lake (the solid gray line), demonstrating the effect of geometry on the form of cities, which we show in figure 4.4(b).

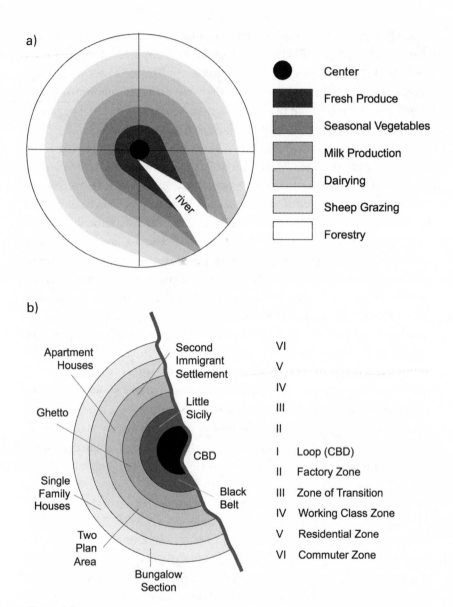

Figure 4.4
The organization of cities into concentric rings and radial routes: (a) Von Thünen's rings around an agricultural market center; (b) Park and Burgess's model of Chicago, 1925.

This model of city development is assumed to represent a structure that is balanced in terms of the ability of urban activities to compete for space and pay an economic rent that reflects transport cost to the CBD, but it is by no means a perfect market. To an extent, von Thünen's basic model, which now lies at the core of urban economics,[12] was predicated on notions of perfect competition, but there are many missing pieces when it comes to modern day cities, where income differentials and inequalities are rife. For example, although rents are higher near the center of the city, and one might assume that rich people are more likely to live there, outbidding the poor for such premium space, it turns out that—in most Western cities, at least—richer people live on the edge, although there is some speculation that this pattern is beginning to break down.[13] On the periphery of the city, the rich can get more space and afford the transport costs, while poorer people are crammed into more congested space nearer the center. Poor people thus end up paying more for their housing per unit of space consumed than rich people, and this is hardly perfect competition. To an extent, it makes the central and inner zones of modern cities poverty traps, zones where disadvantaged populations are forced to live, where crime is often rife, average lifetimes shorter, and access to good education is much less available.

Chicago again is our classic exemplar. In the 1920s, a group of self-styled "social ecologists," led by Park and Burgess, produced diagrams of the evident circularity of the city in the form of concentric zones. These reflected, not different products, but different types of residential neighborhood, demonstrating that the poor and underprivileged were concentrated in high-rent, low-quality housing in the inner part of the city.[14] Waves of newcomers coming to the city tended to occupy the inner areas first—with the richest, who in the 1920s were first called "commuters," the furthest out. This "invasion, then succession," as the social ecologists described it, marked the way the city exploded from the mid-19th century on as it grew seemingly without bound. These waves, or rings of growth, imply a city continually in transition. As the city grows and gets wealthier, the richer move further out and the poorer move in, thus determining the classic social ecology, as illustrated for Chicago in figure 4.4(b).

This world of concentric zones and radial networks is fast disappearing as cities continue to both spread out and polarize, reflecting Glaeser's paradox.[15] Increasing wealth and faster transportation from the mid-19th to the mid-20th century accelerated the growth of suburbs and reinforced the automobile as the dominant form of transportation. In American cities, in particular, the downtown core—not perhaps in the biggest cities, but certainly in most—lost its attraction, while cities began to fuse in polycentric fashion, creating the kinds of megalopolis explored in chapter 3. The dominant urban pattern that had emerged by the late 20th century was a landscape of multiple centers. Think of scattering many von Thünen ring models across a landscape of routes that connect the cores, and then modifying land uses to reflect composite patterns of accessibility, and you have some image of what the urban world now looks like. Paul Krugman sums it up extremely well when he writes:[16]

> The monocentric model pictures a metropolitan area as something like a slice from an onion, with rings arrayed around a single center. The reality of all metropolitan areas in the United States today, even those of New York or Chicago that have huge, vital downtown office districts, is that they are less like an onion slice and more like Jack Horner's plum pudding, in which edge cities correspond to the plums.

Add to this the kind of polarization and segregation that is evident within the city itself, and the picture becomes more complete and recognizable in terms of the world we now live in. A far cry from the standard model.

The 20th-century version of the contemporary city is a mixture of New York and Phoenix, Paris and Guangzhou, Melbourne and Manchester. The kinds of polycentric structures that have emerged are now peppered with specialized, so-called edge cities, a term popularized by Joel Garreau in his book of the same name.[17] There are many images of these kinds of agglomeration; the pattern of development for Guangzhou in the Pearl River delta is illustrated in figure 3.2 in chapter 3. Cities are now highly heterogeneous in terms of their relation to one another as well as their intraurban configurations and dispositions of land uses, social groups, and economic activities. The standard model now only bears a slight resemblance to what we see in the modern city, but so far there has been nothing to replace it. At the same time, as the mechanical and electrical revolutions have given rise to the digital, new modes of electronic communication via wireless networks have barely been charted.[18] Arguably these forces are just beginning to work themselves through the urban fabric, but we have had far too little time to make much sense of these changes.

The rates at which these new technologies are being developed, layered on top of, and woven within the processes that determine how the contemporary city functions are likely to change the city radically and quickly, even in the short term. The disconnect between form and function that this implies is likely to be dramatic, and the great transition from a world of super-exponential growth to one where growth is largely between existing cities through migration will dominate our thinking about cities during the rest of this century. The image of a city based on ordered, homogenous zones connected by well-defined transportation routes is fast merging into one where heterogeneity of use is the order of the day. The idea of physical networks is being thrown up in the air through communications that are essentially location-free and global. The challenge is to understand what the form of the future city is likely to be and whether we can continue to think about form and function in the same ways we always have in the past.

Growing Cities: Networks and Flows

As we have been at pains to point out, the form of a city must be successively unpacked into its separate layers. A key feature of this process is that its locations are essentially products of interactions: what happens in any location is a summation or synthesis of interactions. Locations cannot be understood without recourse to interactions, and this is particularly relevant to an urban future that merges digital and physical domains. In this, networks and flows are critical. Although networks underpin this rationale for cities, the dominant focus for the last century or longer has been on searching for patterns in the location of different activities, with populations defined largely by radial routes and concentric rings, as in the standard model. This still dominates the morphology of the contemporary city. Location has taken pride of place over interactions or networks, largely because it is easier to see pattern in location and because cities, certainly until the Industrial Revolution, manifested very close associations between the networks of distribution that defined their roles in exchange and the patterns of location that emerged to support these networks. This, as I argue, is changing beyond all recognition as the city evolves into the digital era. Thus, if we focus on location, this now gives us an entirely false sense of what cities are all about. Although most cities still have well-defined central cores that function to tie economic and social activities together, the networks that sustain these cores are becoming ever more complex, diversified, and diffuse. In a global world, it is no longer possible to trace the ramifications of the networks that support our cities in the simpler, local manner that defined an earlier world. For example, even though world cities still have very strong CBDs, the amount of activity in such cores is often considerably less than in the rest of their urban area. Even in a strongly monocentric city like London, which has about 4 million jobs in its metropolitan administrative area, only half of these jobs are located in its extended CBD, with the other half scattered around the rest of the metropolis. If we then add to this the amount of physical traffic that crisscrosses the metropolis—and then consider the vast amounts of electronic information that are transmitted daily through the city from all over the globe—it becomes clear that trying to understand the functioning of the city purely on the basis of its patterns of location poses enormous limits on our understanding. It is imperative that we move well beyond an understanding that is primarily locational. As we keep continually reminding the reader, this is the message we are intent on advancing here and the challenges that spin off from this.

Location in cities, then, is no longer and probably never has been the essential focus: it is interactions between locations—that is, actions that involve two or more locations. Locations can be seen as aggregations or agglomerations of interactions: clusters of people, for example, who work in one location but live elsewhere; retail customers who shop in a center but live elsewhere; clusters of commodities that are delivered to centers of production from a more remote and wider hinterland; and so on. Add to this the myriad of flows that involve the transfer of electronic information, and it is easy to see how complex such a constellation of urban functions might be, with little chance that location by itself even approaches providing the understanding necessary for us to grasp how such systems work.[19] Flows of people and commodities represent material interactions and tend to be more visible than electronic flows occupying the ether, which makes them much less visible. As these varieties of flow proliferate in a global world, the complexity of cities becomes ever greater, and the challenge to our understanding more daunting.

The city forms illustrated in figures 4.1 to 4.3 involve street networks that are very tightly coupled with their land use at densities and city sizes limited by technologies of movement, which before the Industrial Revolution were based on walking or various forms of horse-drawn vehicle. Villages tended to be no farther than 10 kilometers (about 6 miles) apart, and the biggest cities—much more compact in structure than today—never reached more than a few hundred thousand persons. The invention of the internal combustion engine changed all this, and very well-defined physical networks for trains and automobiles came to dominate the city by the early 20th century. This enabled a disconnect between location and transportation, with populations able to exercise much more choice over their location and the ways in which they interacted and engaged with activities and social groups. The earliest city plans represented rudimentary networks, although it was not until the Renaissance in Italy that speculations about networks in cities were made by scholars such as da Vinci, who was among the first to conceive of cities as analogous to the human body and its networks. Leonardo's maps, however, embedded networks into street blocks and vice versa; his 1502 map of the city of Imola, shown in figure 4.3(a), is as good an example as one might find of urban form in the medieval and Renaissance city. Indeed, many idealized town plans at the time reflected the close association between networks for movement and locational activities. These implied relatively modest interactions, all contained with clearly articulated urban spaces that were often defined by city walls and related fortifications. Some of these embedded networks were also evident in figure 4.3 above.

The idea of energy flowing through the city and binding its parts together gained massive momentum with the advent of the Industrial Revolution. Once machines for moving goods and people became widespread, a hierarchy of networks emerged for rail and then for road, while in the 20th century, the airline network reinforced the emergent global hierarchy of communications. In fact, the idea of abstracting street networks began over 200 years ago. In empirical terms, Cary's map of the "high roads" in London, produced in 1790 and shown in figure 4.5(a), is reminiscent of the way we abstract road networks today. If you compare this to his clustering of toll road areas, illustrated in the last chapter when we examined the clustering of neighborhoods in London, there is a sense in which the notion of form following function has been writ large on our imagining how cities work since long before the Industrial Revolution. Kohl's idealization of the network structure of a town, produced in 1840 and shown in figure 4.5(b), clearly defines the role of hierarchy in the dendritic—or fractal—street network. Minard's maps, produced in the 1850s, assigned the flows associated with these interactions to actual networks, as in figure 4.5(c) for Paris, while Unwin in 1909 pointed to a typical flow diagram for railway traffic, shown in figure 4.5(d). These visual tools had, by mid-century, been picked up

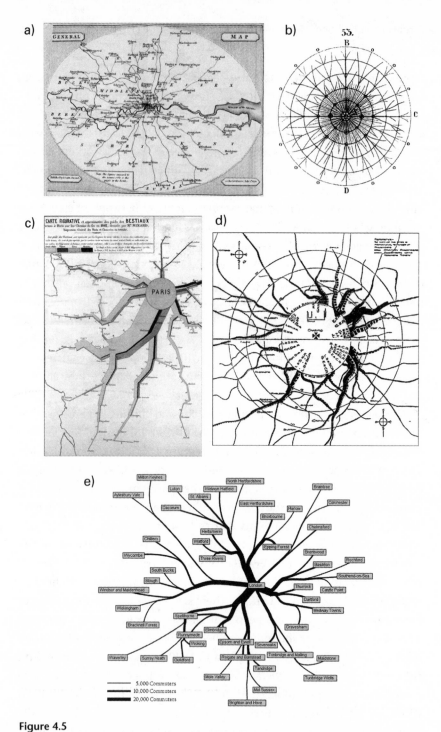

Figure 4.5

The earliest abstracted city networks: (a) Cary's London high roads (toll roads) in 1790; (b) Kohn's theoretical dendrites, 1841; (c) Minard's traffic flows, 1850; (d) Unwin's traffic flows, 1909; (e) Rae's commuter flows in the London region, 2017.

and exploited extensively for visualizing movement in cities. A more recent abstraction produced by Rae, illustrated in figure 4.5 (e), shows how such flows might be simplified even further for the wider London region.[20]

Throughout the 19th and 20th centuries, networks delivering energy of various kinds dominated the form of the city, and physical channels became prominent features in the urban landscape. Generally, these systems radiated from the traditional central core of cities at different scales as cities grew bigger. Meanwhile, peripheral routes—ring roads and beltways—began to appear, with new urban cores growing in peripheral locations, massively improving accessibility through the confluence of various transport hubs. Thus, the form of the city was transformed during the 20th century from strongly monocentric to polycentric based on combinations of single towns growing into one another to form metropolitan agglomerations. Edge cities then appeared at points where hinterlands of population demand could easily sustain intense developments of retail and commercial activity. It is in this context that electronic networks that are dramatically changing our conceptions of location and interaction have emerged.

The last century was largely dominated by the idea that the city could be treated as a machine. But as far back as Leonardo, there were glimmerings of metaphors and analogies between the city and the body in terms of the flow of blood, the nervous system, and other organisms. Victor Gruen's book *The Heart of Our Cities* emphasized the idea that the city could be seen as a network of flows delivering energy to its parts.[21] He went further in articulating this in terms of location, writing: "I can visualize a metropolitan organism in which cells, each one consisting of a nucleus and a protoplasm, are combined into clusterizations to form specialized organs like towns." His analogy with the flow of blood echoes animations of the flow of traffic over the diurnal cycle, reminiscent of the pulsing of the heart but focused on the distinct peaks and troughs in such activity that reflect the morning and evening rush hours. In the next chapter, when we explore "the pulse of the city," we will visualize some of these flow systems, which can enable us to better understand how the form and function of the city change over the very short term.

Flows are thus complementary to networks. Although traditionally such flows have been hard to measure, as the world becomes ever more digital, they can now be measured routinely, often in real time, such as in these "blood flow" maps of traffic noted above. To an extent, networks as physical infrastructures are easier to measure, and only now is it possible to measure physical traffic that uses such networks in any complete way. Really complex systems, built on networks with many nodes, encapsulate flows that require visualizations involving assignments of the kind first pictured by Minard and Unwin shown above. However, better pictures of the functional structure of locations require vector flows of the kind first visualized for cities and regions by Ravenstein in the late 19th century.[22] In figure 4.6, we show such flows based on the journey to work between small census units at two scales—for England and Wales, where the hierarchy of towns is quite clear, and for metropolitan London and to its southeast, where the monocentric bias of the city is very clearly evident. The vectors here are based on movements from home to work and are scaled proportionally to the average flow from each node in the network to all others. The direction for each vector is an average of all the directions from the place in question.

The idea that form is composed of flows is as old as science itself. Plato is credited with saying "all is flux, nothing stays still." And, as noted above, da Vinci speculated that landscapes mirrored the fluid flows in the structure of the human body, his paintings often reflecting the pattern of water and its turbulence in the landscape.[23] Contemporary landscapes in populated places reflect not only physical flows but also human, and a particularly intriguing perspective is the one that seeks to integrate patterns in form that are woven together by human and physical movements.

These ideas are not new. Nearly a century ago, Benton MacKaye defined regional landscapes as being a synthesis of flows originating from geological and climatic changes through which agricultural patterns had evolved, thence being influenced by manmade structures. In *The New Exploration*, published in the 1920s, he defined how the old evolved into a new urban landscape using a model of flow that we will extend and apply in our discussion here.[24] This is strangely prescient in relation to our current concerns for capturing and simulating what is happening in cities using new digital tools, which now allow us to articulate and visualize complexity in ways that could only be imagined in that bygone age.

MacKaye's model of a developed urban landscape assumes a bounded hinterland or basin, which is drained in what he called its indigenous structure. The flows that characterized this landscape included everything from water to people, all usually focused on some sink point, often the center of a market—the CBD—where physical flows discharge. This he

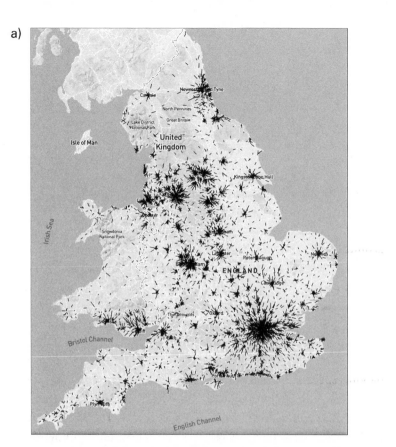

Figure 4.6
Predominant vector flows from home to work: (a) England and Wales;
(b) metropolitan London.

called the "inflow." In almost symmetrical but opposite fashion, he defined "outflow" as the movement of peoples and materials out from the market to the hinterland, arguing that these two reversible sets of flows, when balanced, defined a sustainable landscape: a pattern of circular flows mirroring production and consumption. He then argued that this sustainability was in fact being destroyed in contemporary urban systems by a "backflow." which results when too much activity is attracted to the sink—when cities, for example, become so large that their economies of agglomeration disappear and diseconomies of scale set in. (In fact, in the evolution of such a landscape, he talks of a "reflow," a second wave of inflow.)

In essence, his model is one that treats any landscape as a complex co-evolution and convolution of these flow patterns. As our concern with location per se has lessened and as networks have become the key organizing concept on which urban form is built, such outflows and inflows, backflows and reflows are rapidly becoming a new vocabulary around which to discuss contemporary spatial organization. We show MacKaye's flows for Boston in figure 4.7, which were based on the emergent sprawl of the expanding metropolis. There are many such pictures that mirror the centralizing and decentralizing forces and fluxes in the city, but nowhere are they as clear as in the detailed digital traces that can now be routinely archived and measured from a variety of passive and active digital devices. We will show several of these in the next chapter.

Although telecommunication networks have been significant in cities for nearly a century, there are a surprisingly limited number of examples of such networks that have been measured and visualized. With the advent of email in the late 1980s and the web from the mid-1990s on, there is now a plethora of digital networks underpinning cities and regions. Flickr feeds, maps of where we tweet, movements based on smart card usage on subways and related transit systems, and flows of credit card transactions are all being visualized to show the complexity of urban movements. But it is extremely hard to extract networks from social media data; interactions from social networks must be inferred, while most such data is not geotagged in any case. Data from mobile phone calls does generate network flow data, although the networks tend to be invisible with transmissions through the ether, while financial flows in terms of online marketing and sales, flows of capital, and so on are exceptionally hard to observe. Thus there are few examples of such visualizations, and this reveals a major problem in

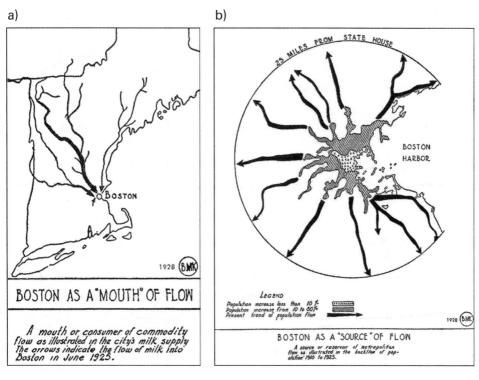

Figure 4.7
Force and flux in the modern metropolis after Benton MacKaye, 1928: (a) inflows;
(b) outflows.

understanding how the physical and informational worlds underpinning
the functioning of cities actually work. This problem is getting ever more
severe as more and more information technologies are coming to dominate
the way we live in cities, and this is part of the growing complexity of urban
form and function. The visualizations of such electronic traces that do exist
do not reveal much that is different from our view of cities as physical networks and flows.[25] But as yet, so little has been observed and so much of
the physical stock of cities is long-lived and inert compared to the volatility
of electronic and informational flows, that we do not yet have any sense of
whether cities will dramatically expand spatially as this century progresses
or become denser, more clustered, and more compact due to the impact of
new information technologies.

Urban Transformations and Qualitative Change

We all agree that as cities grow, they change qualitatively. Their shape transforms in ways that influence various aspects of how we move and interact with others with whom we come into contact. For example, we tend to walk faster in bigger cities, we tend to use different modes of transport because congestion increases, and we have access to very different ranges of facilities that are determined by different patterns of demand generated by different sizes of city. There are many ways of charting how objects change in shape as they grow: in biology, formal methods for explaining such change are subsumed under the heading of allometry. Allometric growth is relative growth that defines differentials of transformation with respect to the various dimensions along which an object changes shape. Objects whose dimensions remain the same are usually called isometric, while those that deviate from this baseline are positively or negatively allometric depending on whether the object grows more than or less than proportionately.

It was the biologist D'Arcy Wentworth Thompson who was the first to reintroduce these ideas to the scientific world in the early years of the 20th century. But, in fact, these notions of similitude go back to Galileo, da Vinci, and several other Renaissance scholars and were also exploited by a new generation of evolutionists such as Haldane and Huxley in the interwar years.[26] Thompson's approach, however, is highly resonant with respect to the form of cities, because his treatment focuses on ways in which animal and plant populations change their Euclidean shape as they grow. He introduces the notion that form might be determined as a "diagram of forces" that dictate transformations in different directions, leading to a series of trajectories that change the shape of the object as it gets larger (or occasionally smaller). Thompson's seminal book *On Growth and Form* is full of examples of how fish, plants, mammals, and so on change shape from one population to another.[27] Despite the fact that many scholars who have studied cities in the last 50 years are well aware of his work, somewhat remarkably there do not seem to be any examples in which such physical transformations have been used to describe how cities change as they get bigger. One might imagine how a village transforms to a market town to a medium-sized city, and thence into a metropolis, but no such descriptive examples seem to exist. This might be because we do not have good records on the historical development of towns anywhere, and what data we can get is often of too short a time series to infer such geometric changes. Or it might be because we have only recently acquired the computational resources that enable us to visualize such changes in the growth of cities.

Nevertheless, Thompson's work is important. He characterizes morphology as "not only a study of material things," but work that "has its dynamical aspect, in which we deal with the interpretation, in terms of force, of the operations of energy."[28] This introduces the notion of networks, and although he does not really deal with such patterns, they are implicit in his treatment of growth and form. They are, of course, essential when we come to physical transformations of cities. It is worth noting that Patrick Geddes, who articulated various physical ideas about the size and shape of cities in his book *Cities in Evolution*, published a couple of years before Thompson's great book, was a friend and colleague in the same department at University College Dundee. Although both their books have and continue to make an enormous impact on those of us pursuing the science, philosophy, and planning of cities, and although both authors expressed a certain skepticism about pure Darwinism, they did not seem to share ideas about cities and form, despite their close proximity and slightly maverick lifestyles away from the mainstream of biology. This is despite the fact that both of them used similar biological examples to illustrate their principles of spatial growth. In 1915, Geddes said: "The octopus of London, polypus rather, is something curious exceedingly, a vast irregular growth without parallel on the world of life—perhaps likest to the spreadings of a great coral reef"; while Thompson, in talking of the emergence of crystalline structures, said: "It begins by the appearance of small isolated particles ... whose form has little relation to the form of the organism; it culminates in the massive skeleton of the corals."[29]

We do not yet have a detailed understanding about what happens to various properties and attributes of cities as they grow and change in scale, but there is some progress. This is a science in the making, and it requires us to derive quantitative and statistical changes that we can link to the qualitative. Geoffrey West has laid out the rudiments of such a science in popular terms focused around ideas of scale, linking such relations to allometry.[30] Marc Barthelemy has begun to measure such changes using ideas from physics, tying together notions about city size with their shape and movement patterns and linking these to ideas that we introduced in the first two chapters of this book.[31] One of the best-cataloged of such facts is that as cities get bigger, they get denser. Density is a measure of the intensity of land use by population residing on that land, and it is usually defined as the population count divided by the land area occupied by that population. Many sources suggest that in both historical and contemporary cities, density increases as cities get bigger in terms of area, but this increase occurs at a decreasing rate.[32] Writing this the other way around, the land area for one unit of population (land area per capita) gets smaller as population increases, and this suggests that other measures of land uses, such as the amount of space given over to transport (streets etc.) might also get smaller per capita. Indeed, this is borne out in many studies, particularly those by Luis Bettencourt and his colleagues,[33]who show that several physical measures involving roads, railways, and utility lines are used more intensively as cities increase in their population size.

What all this implies is that transport and its networks tend to change in form as cities get bigger. It is well known that just as cities in the past have been unable to grow beyond an upper bound due to limits imposed by their available technology of movement (1 million persons or so in the case of classical Rome), mass transit in the form of subways and surface commuter rail is rarely developed today for cities that have less than 2 to 3 million in population. The city needs to reach this threshold before resources become available for such transit, while the physical structure of the city itself begins to generate levels of congestion at the threshold that need to be tackled using mass rail transportation systems. There is a mild correlation between the number of subway stations and population size,[34] but, as in the case of densities, history and culture matter. Different populations seem to adapt to different levels of density and congestion in different ways, and these distort the standard allometric relationships. Changes in shape as cities grow bigger are harder to track when it comes to transport, but there is no doubt that inside the city, there are also changes with respect to densities. Over the last century, in many Western cities, density of population in the CBD has fallen as residential populations have decanted to the suburbs, but only in the last 20 years has there been any evidence that this trend is coming to an end, with some population returning to live in the cores of large cities. Even this evidence is mixed. The most we can say about what happens to density as cities grow is that, in general, overall densities increase—but this must be tempered by cultural and economic factors that pertain to car ownership, the cost of gasoline, costs for different varieties of housing, local regulations, and a whole range of factors that cannot easily be generalized with respect to city size.

Yet the most important qualitative changes relate to prosperity. In general, as cities grow, the number of potential interactions, notwithstanding Dunbar's number,[35] increases more than proportionately. Although there may be upper limits on the number of people who we are linked to, the number of friends we might be able to manage, the number of work colleagues we relate to, the potential number we can select from increases as the square of the population of the city itself. This gives population in bigger cities ever more opportunities to find their niche and, in turn, this seems to generate greater prosperity. In short, these are economies of scale or agglomeration that define the very rationale for our coming together to concentrate activities in cities by "pooling our labor," as Marshall first drew our attention to in the late 19th century. Bettencourt and his colleagues have demonstrated fairly conclusively that, as cities get bigger in the United States, incomes per capita rise more than proportionately with population.[36] They have extended these results to other parts of the world, and suggest that incomes generally rise by up to 10 percent for every doubling of a city's population. At face value, this provides a strong argument for living in ever-bigger cities, but it is subject to numerous qualifications—not least of which is the fact that many surveys about quality of life in cities invariably suggest that it is in smaller cities that the highest quality of life is achieved.

We must spell out these qualifications, for they are important in that they reveal other significant, qualitative changes as cities get bigger. The basic problem with these results pertains to what constitutes a city, the issue raised in the early chapters and dealt with extensively in chapter 3. Although we are approaching cities in this book from the perspective of their physical form, at least in the first instance, our argument throughout is that physical boundaries to the city are being fast eroded as we move headlong into the digital world—where many, if not most, activities will be informed by communications that are, to an extent, placeless. Location is losing its power, while interactions are becoming ever more important. We still require bounded systems in which to root our measurements of cities, however, and thus the argument about how reliable the West-Bettencourt results are rests on how good the definition of cities is. But no matter how good, we know that the bigger the city, the more open it is to the world economy and other world cities. For example, London is a very rich city in per capita income terms. Average incomes there are 50 percent more than the UK average, with the average in The City at least double this national average. But this average is dramatically weighted by income earned from the rest of the world, not from the city itself or its local hinterland. London's GDP is some 22 percent of the United Kingdom, whereas its population is only 13 percent. The definition of the city remains ambiguous, but we know that many of the linkages between the city and the rest of the world are based on very special political relationships, some historically grounded, some based on London's role as a capital city, some based on the way the economy deals with regulation, and so on. In short, it is not possible to directly compare London in these terms to an equivalently sized city in other economies with the same level of prosperity. The same limitations with respect to boundaries of the city relate to other allometries such as density, congestion, creative industries, innovative activities, and so on.

Other issues are problematic. As cities get bigger, they get richer, but their levels of poverty also increase. Although there is not much data on this, it appears that cities get more unequal in terms of their internal distribution of income as they get bigger; in short, just as income per capita increases more than proportionately, so does poverty per capita (which is lack of income). What this implies is that even though the number of persons earning ever-greater incomes increases as a city gets bigger, the numbers of persons in poverty increases even faster, though the growth in income outweighs the increase in poverty, and thus the average per capita income still increases. The additional income masks the increase in poverty. To an extent, a similar phenomenon has been demonstrated in terms of more than proportionate increases in crime per capita as cities get bigger.

There are also counterintuitive results when it comes to such allometric scaling. Arcaute and her colleagues have clearly demonstrated that in the United Kingdom, average per capita income does not increase with city size, with London being a massive outlier.[37] We can speculate that this is due to cultural factors, but it is probably also related to regional policy: large amounts of capital have been moved from London to regions of Britain such as the North, and massive amounts of tax payments move back to the capital. This is clearly influenced by the highly centralized role of London in the national economy—and it is probably only explicable in terms of the fact that the United Kingdom might now be one large city that cannot be subdivided in the way we have traditionally assumed. The emergence of polycentric urban forms due to the growth of previously freestanding cities also distorts the allometry, since it is not possible to simply fuse relations together and hope that the original distribution of cities by size is maintained in any way. In short, what we see in the United Kingdom and London may well be the future: urban development in which it is impossible to separate cities from one another in a global urban world where everyone is connected to everyone else, and where what we produce and consume is no longer dictated by what happens in the locations where we decide to live and work.

The Optimal City: Inventing Urban Futures

Most idealized cities envisioned during the last century are based on distinct sizes, which are rather small, as in Plato's *Republic*, or rather large, such as those associated with architects whose sentiments lie with large-scale megastructures. The advocate for largest city size was Le Corbusier, who in his plan for *The City of Tomorrow* suggested that 3 million would be an ideal size population, organized via a core of 60-story tower blocks regularly spaced in wide open parkland surrounded by residential blocks some six stories high.[38] In 1929, this fictional proposal was of the same order of magnitude as the largest cities in existence (New York had 8 million persons at the time, and London 7 million). It is tempting to think that had cities been even bigger, such as today's Hong Kong–Guangzhou in the Pearl River delta, which has reached more than 46 million, Le Corbusier would have proposed an even bigger number. A more compact, but equally fictitious, proposal based on compressing activities horizontally and to some extent vertically was developed some 50 years later by Dantzig and Saaty (1973). Their *Compact City* was designed to house around 250,000 people and then grow in modular fashion up to a maximum of 2 million. They developed their argument geometrically, in much the same way Plato argued his case for an optimal town of 5,040 persons, using up-to-date technologies. In contrast, Ebenezer Howard suggested that the ideal garden city should have a population of some 30,000, which became the model for the British new towns in the mid-20th century.[39]

It is worth noting that garden cities and new towns were largely a British phenomenon, almost a shorthand for the ideal city, introduced in the late 19th century as a solution to the problems posed by very rapid industrialization and urban growth that led to slum housing. Howard was one of the first to propose a model based on building lower-density new towns in the hinterland of the industrial parent city to relieve congestion and to infuse a degree of "rurality" back into the town. We will briefly return to these ideas in later chapters, particularly in chapter 8 where we show examples of more recent ideal cities conceptualized around the same idea.

To complete these examples, the other great architect of the early 20th century, Frank Lloyd Wright, hedged his bets somewhat by proposing in 1932 a lowish-density but sprawling structure, called Broadacre City, about 4 square miles in area that would contain some 20,000 persons. Toward the end of his life, he sketched out a mile-high skyscraper, the Illinois, which could house over 25,000 persons.[40] Yet in all these cases, the proposals could only be realized if there were very strong central control exercised from the top down. In fact, most of these structures were never worked out other than in purely visual terms. There is a suspicion that most would not have been able to function due to local congestion and the inability of the structures to serve residents' living requirements, but since they were never developed, we can only speculate. These idealizations are, indeed, extreme examples of how form follows the simplest of functions and where a single idea dominates the structure proposed. In fact, these ideas largely illustrate the fact that extreme densities give rise to extreme forms, which can be very large in two as well as three dimensions, or based on simple hierarchical premises of the kind critiqued by Alexander in his article[41] "A City Is Not a Tree." We illustrate these plans in figure 4.8, where the focus on aesthetic principles is very clear (perhaps with the exception of Compact City). Our view is that such proposals simply demonstrate one kind of vision among a multitude of ideas. They are "thought experiments" about the future, notwithstanding that they do generate some interest in thinking laterally about that future—out of the box, so to speak. But they bear little resemblance to anything that is likely to be built, and although it is certain that such visions will continue to be proposed, the future will likely always be very different from that envisioned by these idealists. In the rest of this book, we will develop different alternative conceptions, many of which do not need to be explained in terms of the physical city, per se, or even to lend themselves to visualizations in terms of maps and models.

In stark contrast, another movement—largely inspired by economists—has sought to define the optimal city both theoretically and empirically in terms of the monetary gains that accrue to cities of different sizes. This approach became popular in the 1970s when William Alonso published "The Economics of Urban Size," which postulated that, as cities grew, the costs of locating in them could be compared to the benefits received, this difference

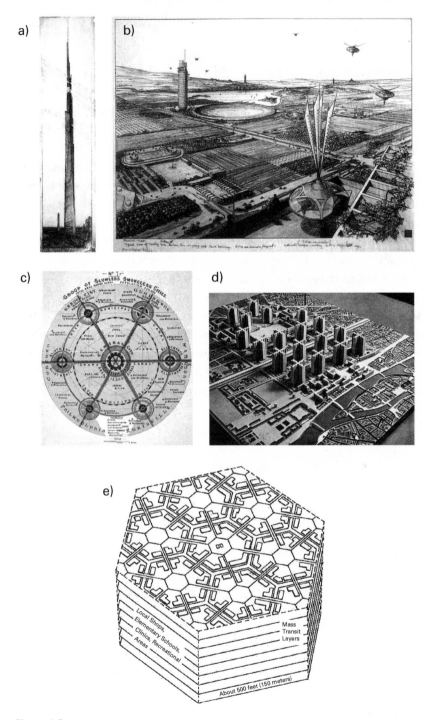

Figure 4.8
Cities of tomorrow: (a) Frank Lloyd Wright's mile-high Illinois building, 1957; (b) Frank Lloyd Wright's Broadacre City, 1932; (c) Ebenezer Howard's Garden City of Tomorrow, 1898; (d) Le Corbusier's La Ville Radieuse, 1923; (e) a neighborhood in Dantzig and Saaty's Compact City, 1973.

being taken as being an index of their optimality or performance.[42] The difference between benefits and costs could thus be used to define an optimum, on the assumption this difference was positive. The simple argument was that as cities got bigger, the functions defining their costs and benefits differed in shape—costs following a U-shaped curve, while benefits would increase linearly. Optimum points could thus be defined where total benefits exceeded total costs by the greatest amount, or where marginal costs equaled marginal benefits. In typical economic parlance, many variations on these optima could then be defined. Some economists have explored this kind of approach empirically, but the evidence is ambiguous, despite the implication that cities of some 250,000 appear to generate higher benefit-to-cost ratios or differences than those that are smaller or larger. In a similar but more theoretical tradition, in the heyday of the new "urban economics" of the 1960s and 1970s, there were several attempts at adding a welfare function to the standard monocentric model. These extensions could generate configurations that implied an optimal population size for a town but, once again, also suggested that much depended on local conditions. Conclusive results were hard to draw with respect to optimum size, despite some intriguing attempts.[43]

5 The Pulse of the City

Tell me the size of a mammal and I can tell you, to about 85 per cent level, pretty much everything about its physiology and life history, such as how long it is going to live, how many offspring it will have, the length of its aorta, how long it will take to mature, what is the pulse rate in the ninth branch of its circuitry.

—Geoffrey West, *Scale: The Universal Laws of Life and Death in Organisms, Cities and Companies*, 451

Let us see if Geoff West is right. The heart of a mouse pulses at 650 beats per minute and its average lifetime is some three years. Its life is thus just over 1 billion (1,025 million) heartbeats in length, and this number is the one that biologists have confirmed as a "law" that applies to most mammals. Applying this to an elephant whose heart pulses much more slowly, at 30 beats per second, then its average lifespan can be predicted as 1025 million divided by 30 beats, or 65 years. This is about right. Not bad, I hear you say, and West goes on to describe how this law and many other features of our physiology generalize across many species. In fact, humans mess up the "law" somewhat, since it only appears to apply to our average lifespans before the Industrial Revolution, when life expectancy was no more than 30 years.[1] The great transition has increased our lifespans dramatically, and as we implied in chapters 1 and 2, we stand at a threshold where medical advances might further accelerate this change. It would be nice to think that we could have a theory about cities with the power that West ascribes to our own physiology, and although much of that theory does resonate with how cities form and function, cities are much more complex systems than those in the animal world. As we will see in this chapter, however, there are deep and consistent regularities in the way cities function, both in the short and long term, but there are no fundamentally conservative properties such as those that we find in the biological world. The fact that in animal lifetimes, all hearts beat a similar number of times finds no equivalent when it comes to cities.

We have already demonstrated this, albeit indirectly, in the last chapter in showing that cities manifest allometry with respect to how the resources they generate or attract scale more than or less than proportionately as they grow in size. In fact, although the iron laws of animal physiology do not apply to manmade structures such as cities, allometry does provide a wonderful analogy that enables us to measure departures from such laws.[2] The economies of scale that generate increasing average incomes as cities get bigger reveal that certain processes intensify—and the one that is closest to our notion of the pulse is the speed at which we walk. That we seem to walk faster in bigger cities has been reported for many years. As far back as 1976, Marc and Helen Bornstein produced some fairly definitive evidence that we walk faster in big cities than in small, demonstrating that in places like Brooklyn people walked at speeds of 1.5 meters (nearly 5 feet) per second, twice as fast as in the small Greek villages they surveyed.[3] More recently, Walmsley and Lewis reported speeds of up to 1.68 meters (about 5.5 feet) per second for walking in London.[4] In 1970, Stanley Milgram (who we came across in chapter 3, where we introduced his work on small worlds) produced a more general summary of the pace of life in cities, characterizing how people undertook a range of activities at much faster speeds in bigger cities.[5] As a corollary, it seems vehicular traffic congestion also increases with city size. Using Google's drive speeds and routing algorithms, speeds per hour in US cities increase from an average of about 25 kmph (15.5 mph) in New York City, which has a population of around 8.5 million, to around 65 kmph (40 mph) for metro areas like Kansas City, whose population is some 480,000. If we look at speeds in the core of cities, anecdotal evidence suggests that in places like London's central business district (CBD), it is often faster to walk, since vehicular speeds hover around 10 kilometers (about 6 miles) or less per hour in the center. And in the biggest and oldest cities, these speeds seem to have remained pretty constant for several hundred years.[6]

Defining the pulse of the city is highly problematic. The word is used rather casually, and aggregating individual responses and taking averages for comparisons between different levels of activity is tricky. Much depends on cultural factors that cannot be quantified and on the historical evolution of the city with respect to its focus on activities such as entertainment and retailing. It is difficult to compare Las Vegas, for example, a city that is based on 24-hour gambling, with San Francisco, which reportedly has a population that on average sleeps less than any other in the United States. The activities during day and night are so different that comparisons are futile.[7] However, before we explore the different pulses that define our cities and speculate on how the new digital world is yielding ever more data and information about how our cities function, we need to reflect a little on the way we look at cities with respect to how they change over time. Traditionally—and this is very clear from the last chapter—the way we have approached cities in the past is largely as though they are timeless; that is, frozen eternally at a moment in time. Although city planning does deal with the city of the future, the kind of master plans that have been the modus operandi of planners for at least a century assume an unspecified temporal future that will be reached at some point, but is invariably a convenient fiction to provide a focus. We do not yet understand, however, how the city forms gathered together as illustrations in chapter 4 actually evolved to the point where we could discern their structure, nor how the key processes of development that led to those forms will play out in the future. Past speculation has been solely confined to how cities have evolved over long historical time periods—over eras and epochs—in the manner used to explore long-term futures in chapter 2. Not that this was irrelevant, far from it, but it does not provide the basis for a requisite understanding of how cities evolve over decades and generations. In short, in most studies of urban form and function, there has been very little emphasis on urban dynamics.

Our thoughts about how cities function over much shorter periods, such as the 24-hour diurnal cycle, are not new—they go back at least to Chapin and Stewart's 1953 article *Population Densities Around the Clock*. Yet little could be done in terms of understanding these cycles until quite recently.[8] Richard Meier's attempts to construct a theory for urban structure based on thinking about social life in terms of communications theory provided a brave attempt long before its time.[9] But only when the digital world emerged, with all its sensors enabling us to track what is happening second by second, has the prospect of an entirely different way of thinking about cities emerged. Most of our focus in cities to date has been on densities that pertain to space, rather than intensities that relate to time. But this is changing rapidly, and in some respects this chapter, with its rather generic title pertaining to "pulse," redresses the balance—by thinking about cities in time, which is key to understanding their dynamics. In the past, our focus has been on cities in equilibrium, and although there have been attempts to examine abrupt change, such as catastrophes, chaos, and singularities that pertain to urban discontinuities, these have been over longer rather than shorter periods of time. Although complexity theory, alluded to in chapters 1 and 2, did change the emphasis on equilibrium to thinking about cities as being perpetually in disequilibrium in the short term and always being far from equilibrium in the long term, its focus has still been on change over decades or longer.[10] There have, of course, been attempts at looking at economic cycles pertaining to cities, which range from those associated with long waves such as Kondratieff cycles to various kinds of trade cycle, and we will address some of these in later chapters. But these have never been really linked to spatial change. The move to the very short term is a recent phenomenon, one that largely dates from the data gathered second by second at a very fine spatial scale, invariably using new generations of sensors and computers that have appeared only in the last 10 years. And thus the focus of this chapter is on exploring what is possible using these new kinds of data and dynamics.

Temporal Cycles, Flows, and Flux

When we examine how individuals and groups in cities function in time, we can classify their schedules and activities into nested cycles that define their behavior at different levels of aggregation. To an extent, the previous chapters have gradually focused in on more and more detailed kinds of behavior, starting from long waves and cycles characterizing technological change in our first two chapters, to more detailed implications of how cities change their form and function in the previous chapter. Economic cycles over generations and decades determine the state of the economy and the development of new technologies, and, within these, development processes determine how land use, transport, and economic activities change their locations as cities evolve over years and decades. Focusing our microscope on the finest temporal intervals, however, is where we reveal the detailed pulses, flows, and fluxes that characterize urban behavior, where the key cycles are diurnal—based largely on how our bodily functions relate to the presence of night and day—and determine the ways in which we work and play. Mobility is central to these processes, and in relating such movements to location, once again the notion of the network takes pride of place.

We can also characterize key cycles at slightly more aggregate levels—for example, seasonal change and its influence on behaviors. This makes a difference to the times and places where specific events take place, for many activities in cities are organized on a yearly basis, in particular education. In fact, although there are diurnal and seasonal rhythms particularly relating to work, entertainment, education, and so on, peppered within these cycles there are distinct one-off as well as repeating events that stand out as critical to the way cities function and are organized, especially in sport and entertainment. Many flows that can be recorded at very detailed temporal scales, such as second by second, or at least minute by minute, can almost be visualized as fluids, with their liquid flow being punctuated by discrete events. Thus, frequency of flow is key to an understanding of such changes, and in this chapter we will characterize a series of examples that define the contemporary city. However, our quest is to go well beyond this, and to imply how we might link all these together in generating a much more profound understanding of how cities evolve. Although our focus will be on the very short term, the short term becomes the long term if enough events and flows are recorded over ever-longer time periods. Thus, from the short term, we should be able to observe secular trends that manifest themselves over much longer time horizons. This is the challenge we face in linking small-scale change to long term, and short term functions to the evolution of urban form.

The flows that define our current understanding of how elements in cities relate to one another are almost entirely material and deal with movements, such as the journey to work or to other distinct functions such as retailing, commercial activities, education, health provision, leisure pursuits, and so on. Added to this, movements between economic activities, such as the transport of goods and commodities using many different networks, together with the flow of individuals to commercial activities, define a hierarchy of markets used in exchange. In turn, it is possible to see this constellation of movements as determining the demand and supply of goods, reflecting how prices are determined, and ultimately the way in which wealth is generated in an economy. As a consequence, some have recently invoked the idea of the network as the basis of the modern urban economy.[11] Movements take place diurnally, at discrete times, and seasonally. But layered on top of these patterns, land uses, individuals and households, businesses, as well as the many activities that comprise agencies and institutions in the public sector, all move and relocate for a multitude of reasons that pertain to the economic constraints or opportunities they have to confront. While these movements generate patterns of migration when they are aggregated to longer time scales, essentially each is composed of individual actions that take place at very distinct points in time, although some of these processes work themselves out over longer time periods. Traditionally, information central to the operation of the economy has been material in some form; prior to the Industrial Revolution, most information involved face-to-face contacts or letters that were passed using the technologies of the time—horse and carriage, dispatch rider on horseback, or complex forms of manual signaling, as used during the Napoleonic wars, for example.

Once the Industrial Revolution began, new technologies were quickly invented that enabled all the elements that comprise the city, as well as new innovations generated from these technologies, to change the basis of exchange and movement. The internal combustion engine, in the first Industrial Revolution, and the electric motor, in the second, continue to dominate the way we move around cities. But it was in terms of the flow of written information—data—that the changes we are currently in the midst of began. Even in classical times, information passed by messengers on horseback was the fastest way to communicate any nontrivial conversation over distances longer than a mile, while bonfires and smoke signals have been time-honored ways of passing "bits" of information since pre-history. Logical signaling systems such as semaphore were used in the early Industrial Revolution, and in the mid-19th century, the telegraph and Morse code were invented. Hard on their heels came the telephone, and together these technologies marked the first "death of distance" as new worlds were quite literally opened up due to this communication. Together with the railway, these technologies changed the world.

As we have pointed out in earlier chapters, cities would not have grown had such technologies not come into play; and, of course, this changed the basis of global trade. One of the reasons we consider that the real divide between the old world and the new began with the first Industrial Revolution is this development of both material and communications technologies, which generate their own positive feedback. The characterization of this era as the "Victorian Internet" by Standage[12] reflects that fact that our current digital age is simply an extension, a deepening, and an integration of changes that began more than two centuries ago, when the world first began to divide between previous eras of hardly any cities at all to a time when everybody will eventually live in cities.

Television was invented in the 1920s, but it was not until the development of the digital computer during World War II that the interactive manipulation of information really came onto the agenda. We have recounted a little of this history in our second chapter, and we will say more in later ones, but it was not until the convergence of computers and telecommunications, which reached its zenith in the 1990s, that truly interactive computation began. Moreover, computing at a distance became a reality with the invention of hypertext, and with its use on the Internet via the web, the impact of computers and communications on locations and interactions has become massive. There are now many forms of electronic interaction that take place between fixed locations where no material product is being exchanged. All of these are likely to have some impact on the way in which we behave with respect to economic and social interactions, but as they are largely invisible, at least at first glance, and because they are all conducted at the individual level without very obvious sources that aggregate this activity, it is hard to extract their meaning with respect to patterns of location and physical movement in cities. In short, these new ways of communicating data and information—indeed, as we will see, generating new kinds of information—must have an impact on how and where we locate and how we use the traditional functions of the city, which are translated ultimately into physical forms.

In particular, we need to define the range of such digital information. First and foremost, there is email, which is highly liquid. It is almost impossible to guess the number of emails sent worldwide each day—large quantities are spam or junk—but a conservative estimate (from February 2015) is around 200 billion per day. The number of Google searches per day is about 3.5 billion. We can repeat such superlative numbers for many media involving the Internet.[13] In fact, since so many of these media use the Internet and web browser technology to generate their content on web pages, the number of web pages accessed each day is not very meaningful. Breaking all this down to location, or rather to city-specific terms, is highly problematic. Even though many devices that are used to access this information are geo-enabled—their location can be fixed from geo-positioning satellites—there is considerable noise associated with this, since many users do not enable their location in any way. This is not likely to change in the near future, either, although most Internet providers do capture and archive such data for their own use. Much of this electronic data is from social media that intersects with the economy to an extent but is largely individual. When it comes to business-related data and interaction, the picture is even more confused—but in any case, the sheer volume of such data now is so great that there is no synoptic vision regarding how to make sense of it all, notwithstanding the fact that much of it is inaccessible in any case.

In the past, with rather small amounts of data on location and interaction in cities, we were able to aggregate the data quickly, easily producing flow tables, patterns of locational activity, and so on. Our understanding was limited by the data available, and thus theories of how cities evolved in terms of their form and function, usually at a specific cross-section in time, were manageable, while attempts were made to make such theory consistent with what was observed. No such theoretical superstructure exists for this new digital world. In fact, it may take a while for any to emerge, for the rate of change in what is happening in cities and society appears to be much faster than the rate at which we are able to absorb the new data and make sense of it via our traditional or even new ways of looking at cities.[14]

Notions about how we might represent space and time as individual profiles have been developed for cities before. The so-called space-time cube has been popular for many years. Credited to Hägerstrand's work[15] in the 1960s, with it individual travel profiles are visualized related to activities undertaken on daily basis. These profiles are richly descriptive, but there has not been much progress in stitching individual profiles together to generate more aggregate behavioral relationships pertaining to daily time budgets and travel patterns. The same is true for more microsimulations of city form and function. Ultimately, we have to contemplate the possibility of there never being any comprehensive aggregate theory of how cities form and function, given their current level of complexity. We may be doomed to a world where only partial theories are possible, where all our understanding is contingent on what we observe over short periods of time and at particular instants. In some senses, this is already the case. Notions about cities based, for example, on the "standard model" are now being partly eclipsed by new forms of behavior and new sets of values that have a very different expression in cities from the ideas we held in the past.

In his book *Radical Technologies*, Adam Greenfield begins with a vignette based on how many very different individuals access social media and use various sensor technologies in their daily lives.[16] This contrasts with a world at the turn of the millennium where no such behaviors were possible and we did not have access to the sorts of technology that are now widespread. The rate of change in this domain has been daunting, with the iPhone introduced just over 10 years ago (at the time of writing) in mid-2007. This device is in the vanguard of such change, with the latest estimate of smartphones in use numbered at more than 2.8 billion, about one for every three persons on the planet. There are now more mobile devices than people, levels of penetration that are still increasing very rapidly, with complete saturation—that is, everyone having such a device—possible within the next decade.

The implications for how we think about cities are very dramatic. Meier,[17] in some respects, anticipated this nearly 60 years ago in talking of cities as being environments where everyone "is continually bombarded by messages from other persons." But Greenfield's summary of what an individual does through their "normal" day catalogs this richness—a person wakes and answers email, checks website news, sends tweets, taps in and out of transit system locations, reads ebooks, accesses web information for work, downloads and uploads data at work, buys lunch with a credit or debit card, and so on and so forth. This rich diet of digital access supplies a locational and temporal record that could go some way to understanding how an individual behaves, which is part and parcel of the quantified self.[18] As we have implied, scaling this up to overall space-time patterns of demand and incorporating one-off events into this picture is quite problematic and has rarely been attempted. Add to this the patterns of city facilities supply provided by government and businesses, which are also controlled by digital technologies—often via individuals accessing them to enable management—and the problem of synthesizing all these options is writ large.

In the rest of this chapter, we will broach these questions, first with respect to the data, largely focused on transit and mobility, becoming available from routine sensors, and then explore the flows and networks that can be extracted from such data for cities of different sizes. We will broach, though hardly answer, the question of what social media can tell us about the future city, and we will finish with some speculation regarding what all this might mean for the city in this century and beyond.

Sensing the City and Real-Time Streaming

For the last 200 years, if not longer, it has been generally accepted that to alleviate the many problems that plague the city and to improve the quality of life of its citizens, physical change to the city's form (and hence, its function) has been the preferred and perhaps least intrusive way. To this end, the forms reviewed in the last chapter and changes to their physical planning, usually focused on arranging land use and transportation in different ways, have been the dominant approach. Moreover, we have assumed that for changes to urban form to have any impact, plans are implemented over long time periods—years and decades, rather than weeks or months—consistent with the fact that our observations of how cities function is over similar and rather long periods of time. We might consider such observations to be a type of sensing, although what data we have had available is collected periodically, with low frequency—every 10 years, for example, in the case of population censuses—and, of course, such data is usually gleaned from direct questionnaires administered manually.

This concept depends on separating the real city from any ideas, practice, and theory we have about it. It is the paradigm adopted by those who are guardians of those ideas, practice, and theory—who exercise control, management, and planning over the real city, while all the time generating data that is then converted to information so our understanding (hence, control) can be better executed. Ever since computers were developed, digital simulations of the city have been attempted, first as models of location and interaction at coarse spatial scales, and more recently as digital visualizations of cities in terms of their geometry in two and three dimensions; and, of course, data itself has become almost entirely digital along the way. What is different is that within the past 10, and certainly 20, years, digital devices—computers and sensors—have been directly introduced into the real city for purposes of planning and control to improve efficiency as well as generate better planning and quality of life. From this embedding into the physical fabric of the city have come new streams of data, which is often generated at very fine temporal intervals—second by second, or even finer. This data is a by-product of the digital mechanisms used to control the city, and in this sense it is a kind of "exhaust." It is often highly unstructured and thus requires special techniques to make sense of it, and it is usually voluminous—hence the term "big data."

This change in the paradigm involves a switch in focus to much shorter time intervals associated with how cities work. Data gathered automatically using such sensors can be used in some cases for real-time management, as in the variety of control centers that have mushroomed in the last decade in the biggest cities, where traffic, in particular, as well as emergency services need constant monitoring and intervention so that such systems work smoothly. This new paradigm is often referred to as the "smart city," but other terms have been used: the information city, virtual city, digital city, electric city, and, earlier, even the wired city. In essence, this implies a massive change in focus from long term to short term, from large scale in spatial terms to much finer scale in individual terms, and from strategic to routine in terms of management and control (although, as noted, the short term eventually turns into the long term if enough data is collected over a long enough period of time). This represents a very different use of computers from that traditionally used to model cities and transportation to inform better planning. The fact that we can use the same devices to understand the city as those that generate data from it and control its functions is yet another demonstration of Turing's insight that the computer is "the" universal machine.

We can divide the way we sense the city into three regimes. First, we can introduce sensors to monitor the performance of built and natural environments we might condition in some way. This is physical in focus, for many of these sensors are organized to pick up the operations of natural and manmade systems and do not involve any human intervention other than periodic maintenance to capture the data generated and to ensure they are working. Such systems range from inductive-loop traffic detectors, which have existed in analog form for many years, to new forms of energy monitors that are part of the quest to automate buildings and the home. In contrast, there are also social sensors, which are devices we use ourselves. The entire panoply of social media is configured around our devices, which enable us to get access to this virtual world. In short, we decide when they are used on an event-by-event basis. Although the line between the social and the physical can be blurred, if we program our machines to perform routine tasks even at the individual level, the distinction is obvious. Somewhere in the middle are sensors we activate in a routine fashion. When individuals are scaled up to very large aggregate populations, such as those accessing a stock market, using a transit system, or even watching television, then such data is easily seen in real-time streams, despite the fact that it is made up of many individual objects and people. Another way of thinking of such data is as being passively or actively collected; the differences between these two methods can be profound with respect to our ability to use such data in making generalizations.

Passively generated data pertaining to manmade and natural objects usually generates information about different spatial locations. Movements of automated vehicles can be tracked, but it is data actively generated by ourselves that is more likely to be associated with network flows, in particular ways in which our devices are able to track our movements. In fact, we will not focus in this chapter on every possible kind of social and physical media developed over the last decade that yield information about where and when activities in cities take place and the particular individuals involved. We will examine short text messaging as an example of social media and movement data from smart card activations, which represent a blend of the social and physical. We will also look at the automated generation of data about vehicles, such as subway trains, where the vehicles themselves or their operators, not their users, activate the system in event-by-event mode.

Since so much data is now being generated routinely as real-time streams, and the variety of such data is quite wide and somewhat idiosyncratic, various portals have emerged that attempt to pull very diverse data together in the form of dashboards.[19] These are popular with city authorities who want an instant and immediate picture of what is happening with respect to more than one data stream, and they are easy to build at a crude level, for there are now many interfaces to such real-time streams or to archives of such data that are made available with short time lags. In figure 5.1(a), we show a very simple dashboard that pulls together real-time streamed data for London, and in figure 5.1(b) the web-based London Panopticon, which provides camera images of what is happening at the eight compass points around high-profile landmarks. All of these, of course, are in the public domain and can be accessed easily, but a dashboard collects and displays them in relatively comprehensible form. If one watches such a dashboard or portal for more than a few moments, trends can be observed. But the ones shown in figure 5.1 have no intelligence, although more useful analytics are being rapidly developed. What these do at present is provide some sense of how such data can be mobilized and how it is being used for short-term, often crisis-related management. As such, these dashboards and portals provide an intuitive synthesis of the "state" of a city, in comparison with those examining much more abstract data on less frequent cycles.[20]

There are now many online systems that enable us to extract data from cities in real time. Even map interfaces such as Google Maps and Google Earth allow data to be captured at various levels, which can then be used to explore

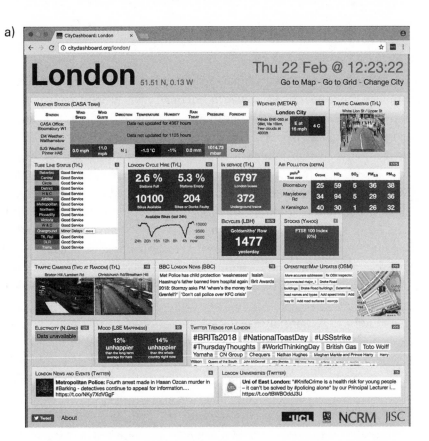

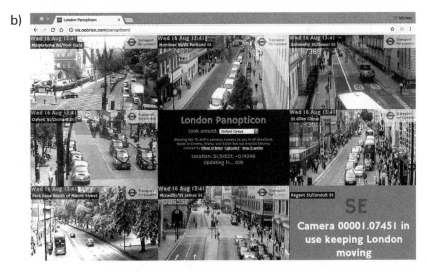

Figure 5.1
Organizing real-time streamed data: (a) in a city dashboard (http://www.citydashboard
.org); (b) in a web-camera portal (http://vis.oobrien.com/panopticon).

cities. NASA night lights data from satellite sensors has become popular, and although this is not quite available in real time, it will be soon and will then allow all kinds of real-time applications. Virtually everything that can be sensed and digitized in cities is now being processed, and the rate of change in addition to such real-time streaming is now so great that this section of our exploration of future cities is inevitably the most incomplete in this book. The data deluge is so massive that it threatens to overwhelm us. Everything about the digital age is dominated by superlatives, with that associated with data being the most dramatic. Current estimates[21] (from December 2016) suggest "90 percent of the data in the world today has been created in the last two years alone"—at some 2.5 quintillion bytes of data a day! The challenge of dealing with such big data, even at the city level, is enormous—plagued by problems of confidentiality, lack of structure in the raw data, missing data due to noise in sensors, diverse and often inconsistent attribute tracking of an individual's social media, and a host of issues pertaining to the general invisibility of important data such as email, web access, and so on. We will focus on all these issues in the next section, where we explore typical examples of the diurnal cycles that dominate the structure of city data.

Rhythms of Transportation: Demand and Supply from Online Data

The basic rhythm of the city is the regular and routine movement of people who work for a living, usually in cities in the developed world, five days a week. People mainly start work in the early morning and finish in the early evening, notwithstanding that there are deep cultural differences, reinforced by levels of prosperity and culture associated with differing social contexts, that in turn affect these patterns. For each working day (usually a weekday), there is a short, more intense peak of travel in the early morning, a slight decrease in the trough that occurs in the middle of the day, and then a more elongated peak in the late afternoon to early evening. In big cities, there is often a late-night peak, which is much smaller but nevertheless quite distinct, associated with entertainment venues. Weekend days are quite different in that there are no morning or evening peaks, but usually an increase toward the middle of the day and a long tail falling off as the evening approaches. There is sometimes a peak on Saturday nights. Seasonal changes confound this pattern somewhat, particularly with respect to education when school holidays start and end. The months in the middle of the year are mostly associated with holidays—usually July and August in the northern hemisphere—and these affect the volumes, while severe (hot or cold) climates can also alter the diurnal profile. One-off events show up in various profiles, particularly related to sport, concerts, and festivals, and these can be factored into different layers that separate routine from less regular patterns. In fact, there are many different levels of routine events. In some sense, the peaks themselves are one-off events based on individual travel decisions but are intensely clustered to become routine, while regular entertainment events are often organized on a less frequent but continual basis; and then there are simply events that are not predictable but have to be factored into the picture.

If you look at transit systems in the biggest cities, most of these have now developed smart card technologies that enable automated payment. This is largely because such systems tend to move very large numbers of passengers, and automation clearly speeds the process. Sensors enable these volumes as well as their related payments to be easily captured, sometimes for real-time control, but always in archived form so that policy analysts can gain a better understanding of the system in hindsight and develop appropriate policies for short- and medium-term control. These kinds of system are usually based on registering the start of a trip by a tap-in on a sensor and the end by a tap-out, but there are various more sophisticated systems that enable users to travel on more than one mode for the same price if within a fixed maximum time. When passenger data is captured in this way, it reveals the demand for transit as compared to the supply (which is the positioning and direction of travel of the vehicles themselves). Figure 5.2(a) shows the aggregate tap-in and tap-outs over the whole working day for the use of tube trains (subways) in London on a typical November day in 2010. The two peaks are clear, and the distinction between tap-ins (entries) and tap-outs (exits) is lagged, with the differences between the profiles showing the rise and fall of each peak. In figure 5.2(b), we show the diurnal profile for every one of 270 tube stations, which reveals that the routine features of the aggregate travel are clearly mirrored at more local levels, indicating very substantial order in how the network performs and the flows that characterize movement on it.[22]

This kind of data provides a clear picture of the demand for transit, but there is now routine data available online and in real time for the supply of transit—the positioning of the trains, how close they are to their predetermined timetable, any problems that pertain to their operation, and so

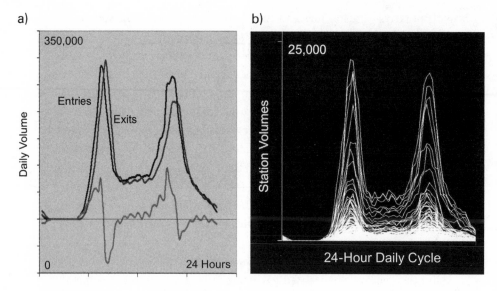

Figure 5.2
Diurnal passenger volumes on the London Tube: (a) aggregate diurnal flows; (b) diurnal flows at each underground station.

on. Much of this information is used in communicating with passengers if trains are delayed or disrupted. The supply data is entirely automatic, collected through the operation of the trains. This is what we referred to earlier as physically structured automated data, not dependent on any human input for activation or transmission, unlike the smart card passenger data, which is individually user generated. In fact, these vehicle sensors are by no means as reliable as those used for passenger demand inputs, and they have to be reset frequently to ensure continued operation. In short, there is more noise in this data. Data on the position of trains can be categorized by the tube lines, and in figure 5.3, we show a snap shot of four months' worth of weekly data colored by each tube line and accumulated for each time during the day of the week.[23] Much the same distribution of peaks and troughs during the working week that we see in the passenger demand are reflected in this data. But from these pictures, it is quite hard to distinguish any obvious seasonal change, other than the weeks when there are school holidays, where the total numbers of trains are clearly reduced, presumably according to predictable lower demand. In fact, the supply position in terms of trains has much less flexibility than that in the passenger demand data, simply due to the fact that individuals determine demand, while trains of different

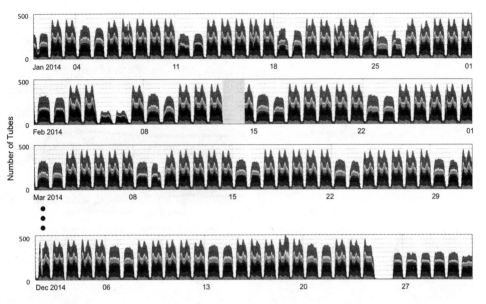

Figure 5.3
Train volumes on the London Tube over different months in a year.

sizes cannot be subdivided at will, hence there is much less flexibility in
their deployment.

These patterns pertain to every system or sector that varies its functions
in time and space. Thus all our illustrations here are applicable to other data
streamed in real time and associated with the actions of individuals, ranging
from retailing to social media. For transit data, we can examine how locations change over time—the hubs or stations where travelers connect up
with trains—and how the flows between locations vary during the day. In
figure 5.4(a), we provide a snapshot of tap-ins and tap-outs in the morning
peak in central London, while in figures 5.4(b) to 5.4(d) we show the flows
between stations at the morning peak, the midday trough, and the evening
peak. Cities, as we know, are fluid systems that are in continual motion, and
the best pictures we can use to communicate their dynamics are animations
of how locations and flows change. We cannot use the printed page to illustrate changes over 24 hours—instead, we take three time instants in figure
5.4(b) to 5.4(d)—or for longer time periods, but a movie, created by Jon
Reades from digital passenger demand data, is available online.[24]

Some rather good visualizations also exist for other cities, in particular
for Lisbon, reminding us again that cities are like organisms, with traffic

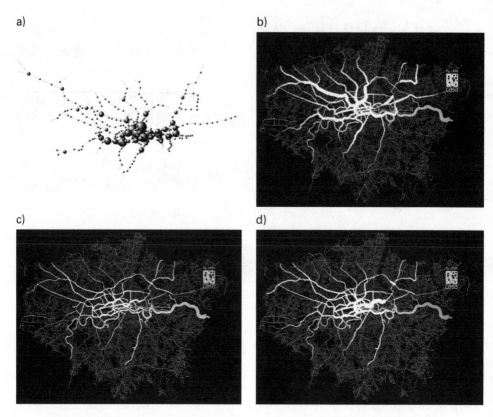

Figure 5.4
Locations and flows during the daily cycle: (a) aggregate flows at station locations; (b) flows in the morning peak, 8am; (c) flows in the noon hour; (d) flows in the evening peak, 6pm.

acting as their life force, these flows being similar to the way blood flows through the human body[25]; indeed, every flow of this kind one can imagine provides a similar demonstration of the many processes that encapsulate how we interact with one another to enable the city we live in to function in a workable, perhaps even optimal way. When the city becomes unworkable, congestion takes place, and the flows in these animations clog—the analogy to the human body is one of blood clots forming, traffic jamming. The implications for thinking about cities in these terms are fairly obvious: we need to design cities that do not clog but gain the advantages of traffic that flows fast and efficiently. This is a balance that is forever changing. It involves a complex spectrum of patterns whose variety and volatility imply

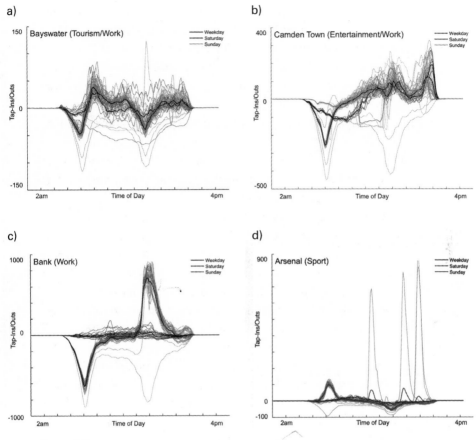

Figure 5.5
Temporal profile–based tap-outs at typical London subway stations: (a) Bayswater;
(b) Camden; (c) Bank; (d) Arsenal.

a healthy functioning system analogous to the rhythms that define bodily
functions.

When we examine these patterns in terms of locations, which in this
case are the volumes associated with the subway stations, we produce a very
detailed picture of the remarkable heterogeneity of travel behaviors associated with different places. In figures 5.5(a) to (d), we show four subway stations in London in terms of their weekly and weekend diurnal profiles, and
it is clear these are very different. These are all shown as deviations from
their baseline flow in terms of tap-outs, so they cannot be compared in absolute terms, but what is clear is that each has some semblance of morning and

evening peaks. If you know these areas, then entertainment dominates (a) and (b), work (c), and sport (d), the last accounting for the three spikes in this graph relating to football games that happen at the Arsenal.[26]

Joining these patterns together to provide a synthetic view of the city will give us a better understanding, but there are many pitfalls along the way. For example, we have good data on the demand for travel by passengers and the supply of trains that will meet this demand in the examples we have introduced. But to really make sense of the way the transit system operates, we need to examine how passengers and trains are connected. If we are interested in disruptions and failures of equipment on the system, then we need to figure out how to connect passengers to trains. Subway stations can be very convoluted in terms of their layout, and there are many ways of getting from a tap-in point to a train; passengers have different cognitive abilities to make such connections, but if we seek a detailed and accurate picture of how a passenger is disrupted on a particular train, we need to be able to observe this link. In fact, in the London tube, there are very specific restrictions on tracking people using Wi-Fi, which is not allowed at present without special safeguards because of privacy concerns. Add to this the fact that the system is by no means foolproof with respect to tracking demand, because often barriers or gates are left open, and there are several groups of passengers who are not penalized if they do not tap-in or tap-out, making the problem of getting accurate data on disruption quite serious. It is not our intention in this book to inquire into the detail of big data of this variety, for we only wish to emphasize just how much this is changing our perceptions of what we consider important in cities and, in particular, in future cities. Yet although this revolution has the potential to provide us with a new understanding of location and interaction in cities and is giving us a massive variety of individual data pertaining to behavior, it raises many new problems that need to be resolved.

Cities as Networks of Social Media

To provide a comprehensive picture of the various pulses that characterize the rhythms present in the city at different scales and over different time periods, we probably need to consider some sort of classification of the city into different activities. This would let us integrate the various signatures of these activities so that we could see how they coordinate or conflict with one another. No such discussion, however, is yet possible, and all we can do is produce fragments of the various profiles that describe how the city works in the short term as well as implying that such profiles extend to the long term. In the last section, most of the activity associated with transit pertains to working, schooling, and possibly shopping, but all the activities that define a city are tied up in these profiles, as figure 5.5 makes very clear. There is now substantial information available pertaining to retail transactions, but most of this is proprietary and its spatial and temporal distribution is hard to visualize because there are few attempts so far to integrate such data. Where it is mainly used is in marketing and determining the location of new stores that maximize the profits of operators.

However, we are able to show data pertaining to credit card transactions in the city of Barcelona for a whole year (2011). Carlo Ratti and his group have produced a fascinating visualization of credit card flows for Spain from this data, which is available as a YouTube movie.[27] The annual cycle does not have the same sort of peaks that the transit cycles in the previous section show, but what is possible are visualizations of the patterns of demand and supply for various zones into which Barcelona can be divided. We show the flows for the maps of purchases where individuals reside and expenditure and revenues where sales take place in figures 5.6(a) and (b), respectively, with the mismatch between them relating to the differentials in spatial purchasing associated with the use of these cards. However, this does not map into the actual flows. We show samples of the aggregated expenditure and revenue flows for the top 30 locations in Barcelona in the abstracted circular graph in figure 5.6(c), where we plot the top 2 percent of flows in the darker gray colors. As you might imagine, there are flows from every place to every other place, and it is a challenge to visualize them so that we can extract informative patterns in the data.[28] Thus our illustrations are highly impressionistic, but it is not our purpose to conduct a detailed analysis here; we simply give the reader some sense of the kinds of exploration that are possible. We also have a map of the density of tweets over a week for the same city, produced by Neuhaus,[29] which we show in figure 5.6(d). We will pick this up again when we begin to explore social media in a bit more depth below.

Social media has become the collective term for online interactions that are generated by individuals communicating information about themselves or about the world at large from their own devices, often mobile devices such as smartphones. Such communications involve everything from

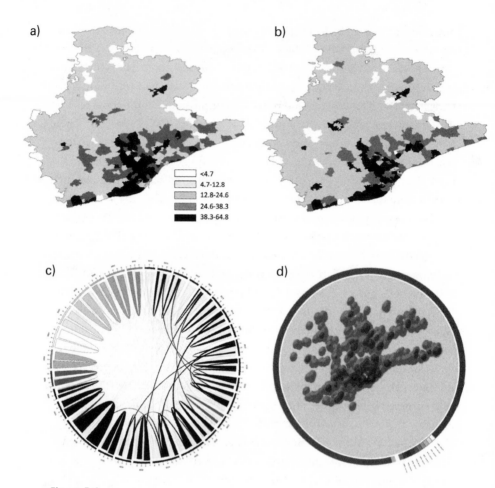

Figure 5.6
Flows of money in the city of Barcelona: (a) expenditure at the household location;
(b) revenues at the retail location; (c) money flows abstracted between the household
locations; (d) geolocated tweets across the whole city.

posting information about themselves and others as well as their opinions
on various web sites accessible by others. The various information that is
posted may not exclusively be about social issues, and an increasing proportion of social media is no longer focused on social interactions but involves
information relevant to the operation of business, government, health,
and education. For example, in the United Kingdom, hospital and medical
appointments are invariably communicated by the National Health Service
to patients through text messaging. A small proportion of this information

is geotagged by users who open their devices to geo-positioning satellites (a function which invariably needs to be activated by the user), generating data that can be visualized in space and time. In terms of generic information that can cover any subject area (within certain ethical limits), only a very small proportion is geotagged, often less than 5 percent, and usually less than 2 percent. This media is generated in real time and usually absorbed by those who are exposed to it, also in real time, as in short text messages associated with services such as Twitter.

This data is also highly biased in that the young tend to be much heavier users, with many of the portals that have been set up to log and record such interactions heavily dominated by younger rather than older adults.[30] This is partly related to the ownership and use of smart devices, laptops, and tablet computers. But unlike traditional data recorded from periodic censuses—administered so that the maximum of any sample population or total population itself is captured—it is very hard to generalize new media data with respect to its meaning for entire populations. Because meaning has to be extracted from it, often using various forms of data mining, the use of much of this data is controversial, unclear, and uncertain. These are limits to the online world that currently make it highly problematic to use such data for understanding social and economic interactions that characterize the city and display its functioning.

Where such social media data has been visualized in spatial terms, it often tends to show what we know already—a repeated criticism, of course, of all intuitively acceptable results that are explicable in hindsight. Quantity of tweets, for example, tends to co-vary with the density of different populations, although it is clear that such data also co-varies with the presence of younger people in a city, who tend to be more active during the evening than the early morning. Figure 5.7 shows the distribution of tweets over a typical week for four world cities. These "new city landscapes," as Neuhaus[31] calls them, are based on extracting tweets from one of the Twitter APIs. All the geotagged tweets for the week in question are plotted within a radius of 30 km (nearly 19 mi) of a central location in each CBD. These show an obvious correlation with population density, although we do not show these densities: we simply assume the reader has some sense that these cities have typical population densities, which decline from the core to the periphery. This is central to the standard model and is consistent with all that we will say about the spread of cities in the next chapter. However, in each case,

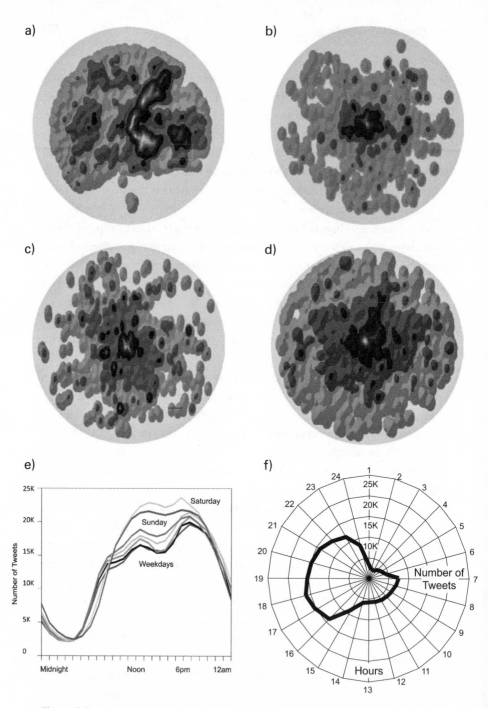

Figure 5.7

Volume of tweets in world cities: (a) New York; (b) Paris; (c) Moscow; (d) London; (e) London: daily time series; (f) London: average daily volume.

we can see differences, and we will concentrate on London in figures 5.7(d) to (f). In 5.7(d), there is much higher density to the north of the CBD in Camden, which is a retail and entertainment center. The daily profile we show in figure 5.7(e) in traditional form, and then in 5.7(f) in circle-like form. This illustrates that there is a small peak in tweets when people wake in the early morning, and a slight decline in volume as the working morning progresses, but then a rapid rise after midday that continues all the way through the afternoon, rising to a peak at about 7pm. A plateau is reached by mid-evening, which then begins a precipitous decline as people leave entertainment and other venues, preparing for sleep in the late evening.

Of course, we are guessing about what this profile means, illustrating the basic problem with all online data being routinely captured at fine temporal and spatial scales: it is impossible to tie it to independent, observable processes whose functions generate that data. We simply do not know what people are doing when they tweet, and we barely know where most of them are located. Unless there are some very dramatic changes in how we engage with media and information that captures our private behaviors, it is most unlikely we will ever be able to get much further than the illustrations we are now able to extract shown in this chapter. But inventing the future city may be as much a matter of adopting different behaviors as building new kinds of physical form that relate to the changing functions brought upon us by new technologies and changed lifestyles. In this sense, social media data such as that from Twitter potentially contains much of interest pertaining to who is contacting who about what. In short, there are a multitude of network connections embedded in such data—but the difficulty of extracting it is on a par with the difficulty of interpreting it. The best that we seem to be able to do at present is impute in some rather vague way social links based on people who retweet information targeted in some way at themselves. If a person tweeting retweets something and addresses the tweeter who wrote the first post, then this might be regarded as some sort of social link. If a tweet is sent that includes reference to somebody with a Twitter account, then this might also be regarded as a link. There may even be the possibility of extracting peoples' identities from the message itself, though this must be approached with caution.

There is enormous ambiguity in inferring such networks from data of this kind. It is not at all clear what a retweet network really means, other than the fact that some have decided the information is relevant to their contacts. The link is not necessarily reciprocal, and it probably requires an analysis of the demographics of their contacts to add any further meaning to this. This is not only relevant to Twitter, but to all social networks that involve this kind of real-time activation. If this kind of analysis is extended to sites such as Facebook, there is more content to be extracted and analyzed. It is possible social networks are then more like traditional networks, where actual contacts are measured directly. We could spend a lot longer talking about these questions, but we have to leave them unanswered. They pertain to a future that we are in the process of inventing and reinventing, and there is likely to be much more volatility in these kinds of media than in traditional physical functions, which will continue to dominate our cities in the foreseeable future.

Our last foray into this kind of data relates to data that individuals post to remote sites that record relatively unambiguous content with accurate space-time coordinates. There are now literally thousands of explorations of social media data from Twitter, Instagram, Flickr, Facebook, and so on, which have data that is encoded and temporally tagged, but little of this has been integrated in a comprehensive way. In figure 5.8(a), we show a typical map from Eric Fischer that is a visualization of tweets in London over a long period of time. At this metropolitan scale, the location of these data marks out street and railway networks. If we scale this up to the European level in figure 5.8(b), we reveal cities and urban clusters.[32] These are strongly similar to the flow maps explored in the previous chapter. In figure 5.8(c), we show maps that are extracted from the location of date- and place-stamped photographs posted to Flickr for London. Fischer has visualized both local and tourist posts from this data, to an extent showing how different kinds of posts are integrated and comparable spatially and temporally. Last but not least, we show pairs of friends globally from Facebook data visualized by Paul Butler.[33] This world map and the European map of tweets in figure 5.8(c) show the kind of global geography—or "connectography," as articulated by Parag Khanna[34]— most cities are rapidly joining. To conclude our brief foray into this digital world and the way it is changing cities and introducing new dimensions into our understanding of cities and city planning, we will conclude with a little speculation on what all this means for flux and flow in the future city.

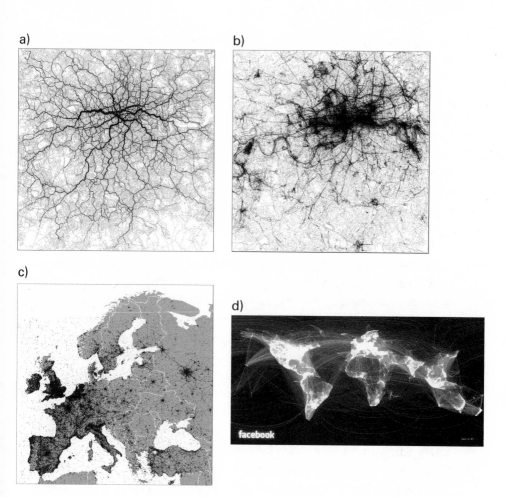

Figure 5.8
Geolocated tweets, Flickr photos, and Facebook links: (a) Fischer's London tweets; (b) Fischer's London Flickr photos; (c) Europe tweets; (d) Butler's global pairs of Facebook friends.

Future Cities, Liquid Cities

Cities connect people, but, as pointed out several times already, they do not function as machines but as organisms. People are continually connecting and disconnecting as the city grows and changes. This is very evident in all we have shown in this chapter. We have taken a tiny sample of these new kinds of digital connection that are now possible and illustrated how these vary over the day to the year. Imagine a multitude of these streams forming an enormous connected skin across the physical fabric of the city, a skin composed of many layers, continually activating and deactivating as new nodes are added to the networks, old nodes disappear, and existing nodes transform their roles. Imagine many different kinds of physical and digital infrastructure supporting these networks and changing at different rates with respect to the data pushed through their structures. The rational for such exchange is both social and economic, with different networks being used for one or the other or any combination of functions associated with how the city works as a social and economic organism. The challenge is not simply to represent such functions and channels, but to integrate them using some model of how the whole system works. Both the operation of the system, its maintenance and its quest toward optimality for its users, whoever and whatever they represent, requires a powerful theoretical framework for exploration and conditional prediction. So far, a century of effort has only produced the simplest of toy models of how urban economies and ecologies work. These are still far from the mark. The ever-growing global systems of cities is becoming more complex daily, and our existing theories, introduced albeit very crudely here, are woefully inadequate. In fact, we are running to stand still. The challenge is to make sense of all this, and quickly.

Should we be surprised by this dilemma? Probably not, because urban evolution and the cities that define it are continually changing their form and function anyway. Invention is what this is all about. Cities have been getting more complex exponentially since the dawn of history, as Jane Jacobs so persuasively argued, since tiny pockets of urbanization came to be established as far back as the Stone Age.[35] Add to this changes in technology, which in turn are part and parcel of the demographic explosion, and it is clear that we have never been able to predict what comes next. In that sense, all that actually takes place is invented by ourselves. In short, we cannot predict our inventions, and thus it is hard to know how the new digital structure of cities will play out in the next 100 years and beyond. We are all likely to be connected in a giant urban cluster by the end of this century, which will be the physical manifestation of an intricate global nervous system created by the world of information technologies we have attempted to picture here. When information is instantly available, from anywhere and anybody, at any time, things in cities begin to look different from their historic past. Cities are becoming considerably faster in their responses to new information, to innovation, to physical change. Populations with more information are able to make decisions ever more coherently and at faster and faster rates. In this sense, the city manifests a new liquidity of action, a confluence of light and speed, and ultimately becomes a "liquid city": a place where physical desires, face-to-face contacts, and digital deliberations provide a new nexus of innovation. Flows, networks, and connections, rather than inert structures, dominate this physicality as infrastructure comes to represent this new liquidity built on layer upon layer of flux and flow.

As we have shown in this and the last chapter, the exemplar for understanding and representing the city is the network. The various examples shown here illustrate network structure at many levels, where hierarchy is implicit. This kind of structure reflects growth around a series of market centers and other hubs or cores in the urban landscape, but these hubs are changing as more and more human activities come to occupy the ethereal rather than just the physical space. Networks spread out to capture consumers and producers, who come together to buy and sell in markets, while the traditional function of transportation in cities is to connect people in economic exchange. Flows of people to work and to markets to produce or consume through trade and exchange are the outward manifestations of the most obvious flows of energy forming the cement that keeps the components of the city together. Networks to channel these flows cannot develop everywhere, so they spread out, tree-like. as if reaching out into the air or the soil, the way a tree grows out in search of energy to sustain it in the most economical way. To an extent, this is what Alexander argued many years ago[36] and what the idea of the city as a fractal geometry is all about.[37] The capacity of these networks increases according to the population that can be sustained by each of its nodes, and when a node reaches capacity, new ones appear, as in edge cities that are rapidly changing the dominant form of the contemporary city from monocentricity to polycentricity. The way cities fill their space is intimately related to the way we try to use space efficiently, in two and three dimensions, and the form that results is the product of many decisions that grow the urban fabric from the bottom up. We will explore this kind of space-filling in the next chapter and speculate on how this physicality is extending into the virtual world, which increasingly influences the way we behave in the physical city.

Cities are becoming their own sensors at the most elemental level, as their physical fabric is being automated in ways that enable us to monitor their performance and use. But these combined material and digital forms are also being overlain with digital skins that seek to enable populations to use the city in countless different ways, such as figuring out in real time what services are located in different places, where friends and acquaintances reside, and what physical means of transportation there are to move to distant locations. When we combine this with more basic sensors that reflect the way buildings are working, we are augmenting our reality in ways that have not hitherto been possible. At higher spatial and temporal scales, our ability to sense the city remotely offers new insights into how cities are growing or declining, how they are being used over longer periods than real time, and how we might identify problems that emerge at a global scale more associated with individuals operating in real time. All of this offers enormous opportunities for a new age of urban design that takes account of the city as a self-organizing system blending the physical with the digital and offering new opportunities for social and economic interaction. Much of what will occur in this century will disrupt the traditional city in ways we have not yet invented. In the rest of this book, our preoccupation will be on the charting the pathways along which this might happen.

6 Outward, Inward, and Upward: Suburbs to Skyscrapers

> Most old cities are now sclerotic machines that dispense known qualities in ever-greater quantities, instead of laboratories of the uncertain. Only the skyscraper offers business the wide-open spaces of a man-made Wild West, a frontier in the sky.
>
> —Rem Koolhaas, *Delirious New York: A Retroactive Manifesto for Manhattan*, 451

If you journey from Nanjing to Shanghai through Suzhou, a distance of nearly 300 km (a bit under 200 miles), you will be struck by the fact that you pass through almost continuous urban development. The countryside seems to be turning into a new kind of city—"desakota," a term Terry McGee once coined.[1] This is a mixture of town and country, an urban sprawl, peppered by many high-rise blocks in what seem to be rural areas. This is indigenous, perhaps, to China itself, but it is symptomatic of the fact that many cities all over the world are rapidly fusing into one another, destroying the old order, and making the definition of cities as independent entities no longer appropriate. As we argued in earlier chapters, this is part and parcel of the reality that by the end of this century, nearly everyone will be living in one kind of city or another, and in many cases, we will not be able to distinguish one city from another.

I made this journey for the first time in 2002, and 15 years later, I recently retraced my steps, this time traveling from Suzhou to Shanghai. Nevertheless, I remember Suzhou in 2002 as a town of perhaps 1 million, but still enough of a small town, built around canals in its core and reminiscent of the old China in the Yangtze delta region. In the intervening years, it seemed to me that Suzhou had reached 2–3 million—but I was told quite firmly that Suzhou is now 11 million and rising. Simply add that to the Shanghai municipality's population of 23 million, and you already have more people living in the region than in any of the large city agglomerations that are officially ranked number 1 in the world such as Mexico City or Tokyo (said to be about 25–30 million). In chapter 3, the JRC urban population data turned that hierarchy upside down, revealing that the biggest agglomeration is in fact in the Pearl River Delta (Guangzhou-Dongguan-Shenzhen-Hong Kong-Macao-Zuhai). Whether you are in the Shanghai or the Guangzhou urban regions, your journey will be through a remarkable urban sprawl, more a series of adjacent and linked clusters of high-rise development all running into one another, rather different from anything resembling Phoenix or Atlanta, the archetypical examples of sprawl in America.

In many senses, this is, of course, the Chinese city of the future, just as the continuous urban development we have in western Europe, at much lower densities and with very few high rises, is our future. London is no more 8 million people than Amsterdam is 1 million. The wider London region is at least 15 million, and probably nearer 25; while in the Netherlands, it is simply impossible to draw city boundaries for a total population of nearly 17 million, which in any case spreads across the border into Belgium. Cities are still growing outward very dramatically, as much through inward migration (some still from rural areas) as through cities fusing into one another. At the same time, as China shows, the quest is also to grow upward, particularly in the cores of the largest cities. Growing inward, of course, involves replacing what already exists with new forms of development, while all these modes of expansion provide a template for the city of the future. At any point, we will never know the exact mix of such growth, be it inward, outward, or upward.

We need to be crystal clear about these three foci of development. First, when cities grow outward, they tend to add population and related activities to their periphery. This occurs either through a process of simply developing available space, which is mainly around their edges or through activities that decant from the existing core or inner areas, seeking more space and lower densities, which are also usually around their edge. These imply centrifugal forces that de-agglomerate the city, thus diffusing and de-concentrating existing activity from the core. This kind of development at lower densities, which is largely dependent on fast transportation for those living at greater distances away from the traditional cores, has been somewhat pejoratively referred to as "urban sprawl" ever since the automobile began to dominate transportation in the contemporary city nearly 100 years ago. In fact, in the 1930s in Britain, this kind of sprawl was called "ribbon development" and legislated against. Our first foray into the mechanisms that determine how cities grow will focus on these outward movements, when the city has grown fastest on its periphery. This is in stark contrast to a more recent phenomenon, where the predominant style of growth is inside the already developed city, and redevelopment and regeneration are taking place by moving inward rather than outward. This is not simply a return to the city based on centripetal forces that are increasing densities, making the city more compact, and re-concentrating activities in and around the core. It is also the renewal of worn-out infrastructures, as well as the redevelopment of perfectly usable buildings and land with more purpose-built structures, which in turn release and uplift the capital value of already developed areas. This trend has become important in the last half-century, and as world population slows, it is likely to become ever more significant in the development of the future city.

Last but not least, the tendency for city development to push upward has been present since the skyscraper became possible in the late 19th century. In fact, the push for development in the third dimension has been much more constrained than might have been imagined when the first skyscrapers emerged in American cities more than 100 years ago. In general terms, such city building has been confined to the cores of the largest cities, particularly world cities, and skyscrapers continue to be dependent on the most profitable uses in business and banking for their financing. These "cathedrals of commerce," as the original Woolworth building constructed in Manhattan in 1910 was called by the Reverend Parkes Cadman, came to dominate cities in the West during the early to mid-20th century.[2] But since the 1990s, it is the Middle East and East Asia that have adopted them wholeheartedly. The quest to build high is now a significant aim in many large cities, not simply for business uses but for a variety of activities, including residential living. The little vignette introducing this chapter captures this sense of urban form: development in the Shanghai-Suzhou-Nanjing megalopolis is punctuated by ever-higher blocks within a loosely structured sprawl that contains older rural as well as newer urban development.

Wells's Proposition

In a remarkably prescient essay written in 1902, "The Probable Diffusion of Great Cities," H. G. Wells made several predictions for our own time, more than 100 years in the future. Concerning the form and functioning of cities in every age, he suggested the following proposition, which we will adopt as our fourth principle or theme of city building. In writing about urban growth and sprawl, Wells[3] said: "the general distribution of population in a country must always be directly dependent on transport facilities." Of course, the standard model incorporates this principle, but based on this proposition, Wells foresaw what has come to be the received wisdom with respect to the growth of cities in the 20th century. In essence, he argued that, prior to the railways, the area a city could occupy was governed by two limits: first, that imposed by how far we could walk comfortably—this was about 4 miles in one direction—and second, how far we could ride a horse and carriage to accomplish the same, which was about 8 miles. The railways changed all of this, Wells argued, making journeys of up to 30 miles possible and thus massively increasing the commuter hinterland. He based these estimates on how far one could travel by walking, riding a horse or carriage, or using a train in one hour. His logic presumed a kind of iron law—that we would travel no more than an hour a day in each of two directions, with the total distance one might travel thus constrained to a window of no more than two hours a day.

The largest commuting fields that could then be conceived were those based on uninterrupted, non-congested traffic associated with a communications technology like railways, which had an average speed of 30 miles per hour. Cities with a radius up to 30 miles were suddenly possible, and, indeed, London and New York were beginning to grow to these limits in the late 19th century. But Wells went much further than this. He predicted[4] that "the available area for the social equivalent for the favored season-ticket holders of to-day will have a radius of over one hundred miles," using ideas very similar terms to the arguments we mustered relating to the extent and size of cities in chapters 2 and 3. He remarked:

> Enough has been said to demonstrate that old "town" and "city" will be, in truth, terms as obsolete as "mail coach." For these new areas that will grow out of them we want a term, and the administrative "urban district" presents itself.... Practically, by a process of confluence, the whole of Great Britain south of the Highlands seems destined to become such an urban region, laced all together not only by railway and telegraph, but by novel roads ... and by a dense network of telephones, parcels delivery tubes, and the like nervous and arterial connections.[5]

This was megalopolis by any other name. Remember that Wells wrote these words at the dawn of the automobile era. There were no digital computers, barely any electricity in homes, nothing resembling interactive networks, and it would be six years before the first "Model T" rolled off the production lines in Detroit, opening up America to a car-based culture. Some prediction!

The key insight Wells thus articulated is embedded in his proposition. This is absolutely central, not only to the way cities spread and diffuse as they grow into their two-dimensional landscape, but also in how they regenerate within their existing fabric and grow upward into the third dimension. Transport technologies and communications are the key. The very obvious point is that, as we develop communications technologies enabling us to travel further and faster under the same time limits, the spaces we can reside in and engage to the same level of interaction, if not more, increases at least in direct proportion to the speed of the travel technology. As a city constructs built forms that are long-lived in terms of the building cycle, the population— since it is growing at a faster rate—can only locate around the periphery of the city, and thus cities grow through cumulative additions. Of course, densities might increase, too, but new construction, as opposed to redevelopment, is easier to engender. As such, the outward growth of cities can occur without the possibility that development leads to lower densities, or to fragmented or uncoordinated development, which are the usual characteristics of what has come to be called urban sprawl. Thus, sprawl does not imply low density.

The next transition in transport technologies pertaining to digital information began a long time ago, but only in the last twenty years has this technology become all-pervasive, with consequent impacts on the way we communicate. Some physical movements are certainly being destroyed via substitution by electronic communications, although, as we have implied already, a large proportion of digital communication is new—that is, additional to what has gone before. So far, we have not seen dramatic changes in movement patterns, whereby people choose electronic communication rather than engaging in face-to-face activities. In some senses, digital engagement has complemented traditional material transactions, adding to their variety and volume. In terms of Wells's proposition, distance has been replaced by travel time and cost as the main determinants of movement. The distortions posed now dominate flow, accessibility, and attempts to figure out how close people are to one another. We have already seen how this occurs in the standard model: the impact of a distortion in the transportation surface defining bands of like land use around the central business district (CBD)—a river, for example—is shown in figure 4.4(a) in chapter 4. Indeed, Wells himself made the point[6] when he said: "Of course, in the case of a navigable river, for example, the commercial center might be elongated into a line and the circle of the city modified into an ellipse with a long diameter." We wonder if Wells knew of von Thünen's work; we suspect not.

In a world where a multitude of communications are online and where the latency of electronic communications is very short, the city as a machine for generating locational advantages for different activities disappears. Think of reducing travel times to zero, in the case of the physical city. The patterns that would then emerge in this fictional world would no longer accord to the standard model. But, of course, the future will always be a mix of the digital and the physical, and thus such a fictional world is not very likely. To a large extent, this future—which we have barely yet discussed and will only explore toward the end of this book—is woven into the great transition. Much of this depends on the roles of place and space in the future city, along with globalization, which is intrinsic to the uses of new information technologies and the separation of functions on a world scale. This separation is something that will clearly be reflected in the way we use space and location in the future, for it represents the ultimate uncoupling of form from function. In some respects, this is already reflected in the suburbanization of the contemporary city and the extent to which the city sprawls far beyond its traditional hard edge. But before we begin our speculations, we need to explore what suburbanization and sprawl mean in the context of how cities grow outward.

Growing Outward: Urban Sprawl

By the end of the second world war, in the 1950s, it was possible to look back on urban growth during the 20th century and realize for the first time that the automobile and rising living standards in the developed world were generating rapid, low-density residential growth on the edge of cities. Bolstering the trend toward suburbanization, more space was available at lower prices at greater distances away from the core, while increasing traffic congestion at the center and in inner areas of typical cities in western Europe and North America reinforced the demand for lower density and less congested living. The realization that cities were growing in this way led to many negative reactions. For example, the editor of *Fortune* magazine, William Holly Whyte, gathered together an eminent group of commentators on cities to critique the way in which urban development was taking place at ever-lower densities in more and more remote locations, while taking aim at the way the city core was degenerating as it lost its functions to suburban locations. The book he edited, *The Exploding Metropolis*,[7] was a strident attack on car culture in the United States but also a missive against the decline of downtown. This echoed Jane Jacobs's views—she was a contributor to the volume, and in it she emphasized her own attack on the demise of the traditional American city in the face of freeway building and the replacement of old, high-density, low-rise neighborhood housing with high towers arranged as regimented, uniformly desolate structures.[8]

Urban sprawl is the term that defines the worst aspects of this kind of suburban growth. In part, it has been viewed in a pejorative way because those who believed in much more closed, compact, perhaps walled, and certainly smaller towns and cities prior to the Industrial Revolution looked back with nostalgia on these earlier times. In 1822, the journalist William Cobbett, in *Rural Rides*, declared[9] that when riding west from London, "all Middlesex is ugly"—a sprawl of "showy, tea-garden-like houses." Although he did not use the word sprawl explicitly, he was the first in a long line of commentators who spoke critically of the way London—then referred to pejoratively as "the great wen"—grew during the 19th century, culminating in William Morris's diatribe[10] in 1883. In a lecture, Morris declared: "Need I speak to you of the wretched suburbs that sprawl all round our fairest and most ancient cities? Must I speak to you of the degradation that has so speedily befallen this city, still the most beautiful of them all?" Even Patrick Geddes, in *Cities in Evolution*, published in 1915, mirrored the sentiment when he wrote:[11] "Towns must now cease to spread like expanding ink-stains and grease-spots: once in true development, they will repeat the star-like opening of the flower, with green leaves set in alternation with its golden rays." He even attempted to portray this as a diagram of forces, shown in figure 6.1, reflecting the tension between centripetal and centrifugal pressures. With respect to these views, every generation looks back on what appears to them to be a more stable, perhaps more comprehensible time. It is certain we will do the same in this century, despite the trenchant criticisms made of urban and suburban growth during the last.

As we have noted, suburbanization is an inevitable consequence of urban growth when growth is faster than any possible increase in density within the existing city and when growth is still largely dependent on functions in the core city. But problems emerge when such growth is uncoordinated and fragmented and competes with valuable agricultural land on the

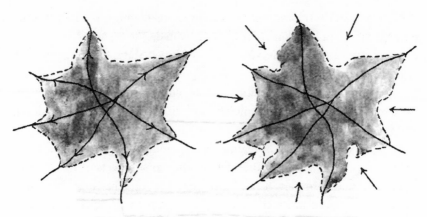

Fig. 20.—Town→Country : Country→Town.

Figure 6.1

Geddes's idea of sprawl: town → country: country → town, his caption indicating outward (centrifugal) and inward (centripetal) forces.

periphery of the city, which usually provides important produce for the city itself. Such growth increases transportation costs more than proportionately as compared to more compact growth around the city's periphery, and thereby impacts adversely on nonrenewable resources. Ewing characterizes such growth as low density, scattered, composed of strip (or ribbon) development, and homogeneous, with little variety in terms of land use mix.[12] In general, such growth is also primarily residential, often with poor access to other urban functions. Moreover, centrifugal pressures tend to push growth out further than is necessary as wealthier populations gain a taste for residential living that consumes space of a more natural "wilderness"-like character. The images of such sprawl are widely portrayed as soulless, unattractive swathes of identical housing in the manner illustrated in figure 6.2. The first picture, 6.2(a), from *The Los Angeles Times* in 1948, is a commentary on 1930s and 40s sprawl in the LA region,[13] while 6.2(b) is Levittown, New York, the classic planned suburb from the 1950s. A comparison of both immediately reveals that this kind of sprawl is long-lived, particularly in the car-based cultures of the United States.

The key issue, and one that is still quite controversial, is that urban sprawl involves a waste of resources and that the same quality of life and aspirations could be achieved by much more coordinated growth, which is likely to be higher density and more compact. There have been many attempted

Sprawl devours the garden

Figure 6.2
Urban sprawl: (a) Los Angeles, 1930s to 1940s; (b) Levittown, New York, 1950s.

demonstrations that this is the case, but most are inconclusive since they inevitably limit the focus of discussion. Moreover, all these issues—the waste of fossil fuels, the cost of constructing low-density housing, and the increased costs of accessing basic urban functions—are controversial and hence rather volatile in their interpretation.[14] Currently, there are dramatic changes beginning to take place in automobile technology and in the way vehicles are powered. These could well change the entire monetary dynamics of the "for or against sprawl" debate. In fact, more than 50 years ago, there were arguments in favor of sprawl,[15] while more recently, Gordon and Richardson[16] have pointed to the advantages of the free market in enabling cities to grow in these ways—reinforcing, they argue, consumer preferences for space and for transport as well as enabling development to take place under conditions of low congestion and low land values.

Quite a lot of attention has been focused on the two-dimensional form of sprawling cities, but our view is that morphological patterns can be constructed to produce any form of city to meet specific measures of travel cost, density, and land use mix. In short, with a little bit of ingenuity, we can construct morphologies that can be associated with many different kinds of cost structure, and this means we cannot simply look at these patterns and know whether or not they are efficient. Moreover, in many cases, what looks scattered, fragmented, and disorganized may not be anything of the sort. The notion that very different regimes of travel and residential density can give rise to similar urban forms has been well known for many years.[17] This is the principle of equifinality, which suggests that the same forms can result from many different forces or processes combining in diverse ways to produce highly similar outcomes.

Let us look at two examples of such patterns from western Europe that reveal all of these characteristics of sprawl. London is the example par excellence of the monocentric city, in that about half the working population—around 2 million persons—works in the extended center (The City, Bloomsbury, the West End, Westminster, Victoria, and Docklands/Canary Wharf), while the other half work in more suburban locations. London has never had any competing centers in its wider hinterland, although several smaller towns are now wrapped within the metropolitan fabric as these have fused with the growing metropolis.

In figure 6.3(a), we show the density of population in London within its wider region of South East England: it is immediately clear that the core city

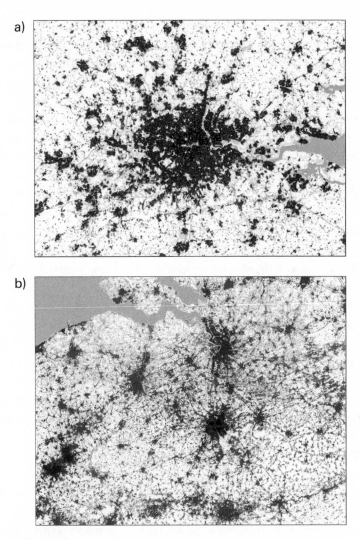

Figure 6.3
Urban growth and sprawl: (a) South East England; (b) Belgium and
northwestern France.

dominates the region, as centripetal forces have clearly pushed activity to the center. But several smaller towns in the hinterland are gradually fusing with the metropolis, and one could be forgiven for thinking of this structure as a classic polycentric system of cities with urban development on all scales. In contrast, we show urban development in central Belgium and northwest France in figure 6.3(b); here, the form looks much more scattered, and towns in general are smaller but appear to be fusing together. The big question is how much sprawl is contained in either of these systems. From these pictures it is impossible to say, for there is no clue as to how the various processes governing urban growth have worked themselves out. Even if we had pictures of how these two urban systems had grown over the last 200 years, this would not tell us the extent to which these areas have been dominated by urban sprawl. Whether towns and cities have fused together or grown incrementally, whether development has leapfrogged across greenbelts that define these systems and constrain development, or whether this growth had originated from population migration from the rural hinterland or from other regions of Europe is impossible to detect from these pictures. Very good images of how cities appear to sprawl are available from satellite pictures showing night lights (mainly available from NASA[18]), but we cannot immediately assume that what looks like explosive growth is in fact sprawl. A good example is the picture of night lights in greater Tokyo shown in figure 6.4. In short, form tells us very little unless we have much more sensitive and measurable indicators pertaining to the kinds of things Wells's proposition and the standard model indicate are important.

Urban sprawl is a reality in contemporary cities, and although there are strong moves at the present time to reverse these trends, it seems that there has been little impact on the form of cities over the last 50 or so years when such constraints have been implemented, at least in many Western cities in developed countries. Greenbelts and urban boundaries have done little to contain growth, although there is now considerable hype about populations returning to the central city, reversing a century or more of decentralization, as noted earlier in this chapter.[19] But the notion that we will all be soon living in a Jacobs-style nirvana of compact, higher-density housing in highly diverse, mixed-use environments similar to the central cities of the past seems unlikely. There is no doubt the cores of big world cities do seem to offer exciting lifestyles for the young and mobile, and currently the metropolitan as well as intellectual elite is an important demographic in such contexts.

Figure 6.4
Night lights data in greater Tokyo (from NASA).

But in most world cities, centrifugal forces still dominate, and in a world where people are still attracted to cities, either from their rural hinterland, as in the case of poorer countries, or from other cities lower down in the city-size hierarchy, suburbanization is still the dominant pattern of growth. Doubtless some of this will change, and indeed is changing a little due to new technologies of transportation, new attitudes toward travel and physical exercise, and a greater concern for a greener, more energy-efficient, conservationist world. But the notion that cities will become more rather than less compact does not seem to be one that is likely to fire urban futures. In fact, the forces distorting our traditional notions of physical mobility are holding greater and greater sway in a world where the dominant form of change will continue to be the growth of cities around their peripheries. Peripheral growth, however, is by no means the only form of development; renewal has dramatically come onto the agenda, certainly, in developed countries in the last 30 years, while the rapid rate of change in places like China is leading to much shorter lifetimes for many high-rise buildings. Thus the future will also be characterized by growth inside existing cities as well as upward into the third dimension. It is to these forces that we will now turn.

Growing Inward: Renewing Cities from Within

Cities continually renew themselves as a matter of maintenance. The life cycle of their buildings tends to be longer than our own human life cycle, although buildings are adapted at similar rates as new technologies and opportunities emerge that affect their design and use. Cities that go back to classical times, even to prehistory, have waxed and waned with respect to their size and morphology. Cities with this kind of longevity display layers of construction built on top of one another, almost as if there is a "sediment of urban living" that is a by-product of their growth. The cities of ancient Sumeria, built over millennia largely from mud-dried brick, display these layers, which are called "tells," while even more recent cities that date from the Roman era, such as London, are now some several meters (yards) or more above their level when first populated. Perhaps the most obvious change in existing cities is due to technology that, since the Industrial Revolution, has led to dramatic changes in building form and different modes of powered transport. We will examine the emergence of skyscrapers below, for cities have also begun to grow upward, but other technologies involving the use of steel frames, energy use in heating and lighting, special kinds of cladding, and so on—all of which can often be cheaper than keeping and maintaining buildings in their present form—now dominate the process of renewal.

The largest change in the form of the city has come within the last century. This is the large-scale redevelopment of the industrial city, whose form, particularly in its residential areas, was widely regarded as an unfortunate result of an Industrial Revolution that paid little attention to the needs of the growing urban population that flocked to cities during the 19th century. The quality of housing was widely regarded as substandard even with respect to the norms and values of the time, and only in the early to mid-20th century did large-scale redevelopment and renewal begin to take place. Indeed, the town planning movement, a direct consequence of these evils of urban industrialization, gave rise to the focus on mass public housing that dominated cities after World War II, particularly in Europe and North America. Similar kinds of redevelopment have recently dominated cities in East Asia, although this is a little different in that in China and India, the population has remained predominantly rural and the kinds of historic industrialization that characterized the West have not occurred. There, urbanization in the last 30 years has been generated by an industrialization based on more contemporary forms of technological change.

In fact, the redevelopment of the poorest, worst-quality slum housing was greatest in countries such as Britain, which were in the vanguard of the Industrial Revolution. It is thus instructive to briefly summarize the processes of renewal that have dominated cities there in the last 70 years. Large-scale slum clearance programs began in earnest in the late 1940s, and it was standard practice to replace only about half the residential population in the areas affected. That is, the densities of redevelopment generated much less than half of the housing replaced; prior to redevelopment, typical slum housing areas had population densities of up to 600 persons per hectare (about 250 persons per acre). It was only possible to rehouse at less than half these densities, and even that involved building what ultimately came to be an unacceptable number of high-rise blocks. The "overspill population," as it was called, was then housed in suburban locations in expanded towns, or in new towns such as the dozen or so that ring London, Manchester, and Liverpool. This kind of renewal replaced high densities with lower inside the city, but it lowered densities even further through new peripheral developments based on garden city-like principles, thus adding to suburban growth. In contrast, with respect to contemporary slums in the cities of the developing world, where there are much higher densities, the problem of redevelopment and rehousing is even more acute and cannot be considered separately from the overall context of urban growth and low-density sprawl in the wider metropolis.

Renewal from within is clearly not restricted to residential development. The massive deindustrialization that has taken place in Western cities in the last 50 years has led to vast swathes of land being cleared of old factory developments. Some new industries have developed within the existing urban fabric, but for the most part, new factories require very different configurations to contain the technological structures they need to embrace, and thus most have located in suburban areas. There has been a massive loss of manufacturing industry from the central city, while the economy itself has changed to become much more service-oriented, primarily as a result of automation. What the future holds for services and the CBDs themselves in the biggest cities is an open question due to continuing rapid automation (something we will speculate on in the final two chapters, when we discuss the role of artificial intelligence in cities of the future). Some cities, such as Detroit, have not only lost their traditional central functions and their manufacturing base in their inner areas, but have been hit by large-scale abandonment of residential housing to the point where they are beginning to "green" in their downtowns and inner areas. In terms of retailing, as noted in earlier chapters, the emergence of edge cities,[20] which have mainly been based on retail decentralization with some office development, are further evidence that renewal from within leads to significant development from without in suburban areas, thus reinforcing the tendency to urban sprawl. All this has led to strong pleas for a return to the inner city, to the point where recent policies in Britain, in particular, have steered new residential development into inner and central cities, and into brownfield—in contrast to greenfield—sites. This has led to increasing densities and more compact development in established cities during the last couple of decades, with some pointing to the very deleterious consequences on the price of housing and increasing traffic congestion that such policies appear to have caused, notwithstanding more positive benefits from compaction due to lesser costs of transport and greener, more sustainable use of land.

The process of renewal in cities is not simply one of replacing buildings, for it is intricately interwoven with the migration of different populations differentiated by social class, income, ethnicity, and so on. Chapter 3 explained how the rings of housing at different distances from the CBD were associated with different population groups in large cities like Chicago. The standard model sought to explain this in terms of the ability of different groups to pay different rents for housing, but this model was also augmented in the 1920s by the Chicago urban ecologists, who argued that the radially concentric pattern of housing types and occupancies was not fixed for all time but consisted of highly volatile "zones of transition," as noted in chapter 4. The urban ecologists[21] argued that as people became wealthier—and few disbelieved the conventional wisdom of those times that being in a big city would enable one to progress quickly up the income ladder—different ethnic and social groups would move internally within the city to optimize their quality of life. This was the process, still characteristic of many US cities, in which the rich would move ever further out, trading off nearness to the CBD for more space but incurring greater transport costs, with this process eventually filtering down to the poorest groups. At the bottom of the pile, the poorest housing would be occupied by new immigrants—invariably, in late 19th- and early 20th-century

America, arriving from overseas, usually Europe—and this would provide the driver for the growth of the city overall. Similar patterns occur in cities today, with ghettoization and gentrification specifically identified as processes that change neighborhoods. Yet it is still unclear whether such processes lead to greater overall wealth and better quality of life. As hinted in chapters 3 and 4, big cities may be more wealthy on average in per capita terms, but they may also be more unequal, with many more poor people than rich. Nevertheless, this process was originally articulated as a "benign" model of the city, in which wealth would trickle down the social hierarchy from rich to poor, notwithstanding the fairly trenchant critiques of this ideology from the wider urban studies community.

We need to introduce one last feature about how cities renew themselves from within. Most readers will not be familiar with the detailed geography of the financial district of London—called "The City"—but let me beg your indulgence, since my example of what has been and is happening there provides an excellent illustration of the thesis that most change in cities is due to renewal. Just as the human body renews itself continuously through its cells, cities continually renew their fabric as they adjust to the wider economic context, changing preferences in location and travel, and of course, technological innovation. Since the end of the Second World War, The City has undergone massive waves of building at least four times, perhaps five, coinciding with boom times and associated property speculation. Even though many buildings have been renewed through redevelopment, the overall morphology of the place has changed little—the street pattern[22] is much the same as after the Great Fire in 1666, while strict planning controls during the last century have kept the skyline low. Since the last boom began in the mid-1990s, many office buildings dating from the 1960s and 1970s have been rebuilt in situ, the center of gravity of the financial quarter has moved west from the Bank of England toward St. Paul's Cathedral, and the comparatively quiet area between The City and the eastern fringe of the West End—the shopping and entertainment core of London—has filled out and become commercially much more attractive. Within the fabric of this built environment, there has been massive change in terms of who works and lives in these areas, but little obvious change in overall physical form.

What is so interesting about this renewal is that it is not generated simply by the fact that buildings have outlived their usefulness in terms of their functional arrangement. If you currently visit Cheapside, the street linking the Bank to St. Paul's, the buildings lining the street have been replaced one by one in the last 10 years, while a new, upmarket shopping center has been built adjacent to the cathedral on the site of what was formerly a perfectly serviceable, if not rather attractive, neoclassical office quadrangle built in the 1950s. Of course, many buildings are no longer adapted to the functions for which they were originally intended, and there is always a case for redevelopment in economic terms. But property speculation and the quest for newness, style, and the lure of fashion are very significant. Moreover, perhaps the most obvious force for change is the use value that such property speculation generates. A new shopping center in that location will generate much greater profit than its existing or previous use. And of course there is the single-minded force cities, their developers, the entrepreneur capitalists required to finance projects, and even workers and residents represent as they demand to make their mark and effect change.

In understanding urban development, the focus in the past has been largely on how cities grow in terms of their morphology and economic structure, rather than the way they continually renew themselves from within: that is, the focus has been on exogenous rather than endogenous growth. This is in spite of the fact that when quite simple migration patterns are examined, they show that in most cities the internal mobility of the population on a yearly cycle in terms of housing and job changes far outstrips actual net growth of population and employment. In the United States, some 14 percent of the population move house each year, while the US population is growing at a rate 10 times less than this. In a sense, this implies that our singular focus on an urban dynamics dominated by new growth, focusing on sprawl and on ways of controlling the physical extent of cities through greenbelts and growth boundaries, can be a distraction from the key processes of urban dynamics. Much more change in cities is based on renewal and internal movements of population than on new growth, as any observation of the fine-scale urban environment will reveal. Moreover, in the last 25 years, we appear to have entered an entirely different economic regime, an era of cheap money and low interest rates where ploughing money into ever more development, particularly prestigious high-rises, has become one of the preferred asset classes. This is leading to continuous renewal in the largest cities, a trend that no longer reflects the traditional building cycle and is largely disconnected from the real economy. Whether or not such a change in the basis of the contemporary world economy is also part of the great transition represents one of the conundrums society will need to face directly in the near and medium-term future.

Seventy years or more ago, the economist Joseph Schumpeter[23] argued quite convincingly that capitalism was an incredibly efficient system precisely because of this quest for continuous renewal. He suggested that any single component of the economy—say, a firm or even an entire industry—could not withstand the deep-seated forces of competition and innovation that would eventually destroy anything that grew to dominate a market. New firms would be created on the basis of innovations established firms could never emulate, and, in this way, no firm could stay ahead of the curve.[24] Examining the earnings of the top US firms for each year over the last 50 years, only two from 1955 now remain in the top hundred, and it would appear that none of these will be in the top rank by the time this book is published. This seems to imply that the processes of "creative destruction" Schumpeter so effectively articulated are sufficiently core to the economy to reflect iron laws of social dynamics.[25] In terms of individual cities, the same kinds of creation and destruction seem to operate at a much more aggregate level. From Chandler's database,[26] introduced in chapters 2 and 3, there are no cities in the top 50 in 450 BCE remaining in that top group by 1453, and of those at the top in 1453, only six remain today. The half-life of firms in the top 100 (from the Fortune 500 list of 1955 to 1995)—years after which the number of firms reaches half the number in the initial list—is 28 years. For cities in the United States from 1790 to 2000, the equivalent is about 60 years. For the world data from 450 BCE, it is 75 years, decreasing from about 200 years two millennia ago. As we scale up from individuals to firms to cities to world populations, the dynamics becomes smoother, notwithstanding its comparative volatility. At the smallest scale, the analysis is more subjective, although far more evocative of how these processes work themselves out.

Clearly, innovations in style and technology are instrumental in creating new building forms, but so are innovations in the way property is acquired and managed against a background of raw competitive impulse. Page has picked up Schumpeter's characterization[27] in his brilliant description of the rebuilding of Manhattan during its early period of skyscraper development from the turn of the last century until the Second World War. He argues, as we have already implied, that capitalist urbanization and development is a process "not defined by simple expansion and growth but rather by a vibrant and often chaotic process of destruction and rebuilding," and that this process is central to a modernity that renews the city so that more and more profit can be extracted through the transformation of development. In this sense, these processes are central to all city building. This characterization of urban dynamics is one in which development is never complete and the city is always "provisional" in its form and function. This is pretty central to the notion that the future city can only be invented, not predicted. Page[28] summarizes this rather well when he writes:

> The "creative destruction" oxymoron suggests the tensions at the heart of urban life: between stability and change; between the notion of "place" versus undifferentiated, developable "space"; between market forces and planning controls; between economic and cultural value, and between what is considered "natural" and "unnatural" in the growth of the city.

This perspective is quite consistent with the idea that cities evolve and coevolve to outcomes that are surprising and, in this sense, show emergence. One might even say that invention is a kind of emergence, and that cities continue to surprise us in terms of their urban dynamics is quite consistent with our long-standing notion here that their future is invented. Manhattan was rebuilt during the early 20th century through an intricate combination of decisions that extracted as much profit from land development as possible, using new building technologies that enabled residential uses to be rapidly converted to commercial uses as the city grew and became more global. This process of transformation involving a hierarchy of interlocking decisions reveals change on different temporal and spatial scales, ranging from more rapid conversion of uses to new functions generated through a new built form, to slower changes in zoning ordinances and planning standards. This was a process that involved successive and diverse inventions ranging from building materials, structural designs, new business models, and a host of other, seemingly unrelated and varying factors that define how urban environments are created.

Slow processes of physical change involve major decisions that reroute movement paths in the city and occur infrequently and with great disruption. Much faster processes associated with changing the physical character of routes occur more frequently—for example, pedestrianization and other segregated areas such as bikeways, while the construction of utilities under street systems occurs as the need arises. In contrast, building redevelopments in situ vary from the simple rehabilitation and internal reconstruction of buildings to new building forms on existing sites. Comprehensive redevelopments take place much less frequently, although often more quickly than the introduction of new street and route systems. Onto this must be mapped the organizational processes reflecting the economic cycles that determine physical change. Often land is acquired, assembled, banked, and left vacant until economic conditions are judged appropriate for redevelopment, while planning and related control processes that involve many different interests can hold up development, often stopping entire schemes. In terms of new uses developed in existing built environments, open spaces and park facilities are the least likely to be defined, for most of these spaces are constructed when the city is in high-growth phases.

Growing Upward: Scraping the Sky

Chicago, rather than New York, is the crucible from which the skyscraper emerged in the late 19th century. People have always been enamored by building towers to "reach the heavens," as much for religious reasons as for economic—as witnessed, for example, in the high buildings of early medieval Italian cities such as Bologna, whose towers[29] reached over 50 meters (over 160 feet) in height. However, it was the invention of the elevator by Elisha Otis[30] in 1854, combined with the gradual development of the steel frame until it could be manufactured in sufficient production quantities, that generated the first skyscrapers, which were built in downtown Chicago from the 1880s onward. Louis Sullivan, who we have already met as the disciple of "form follows function" also became the "father" of the skyscraper: his wonderful buildings combined the elegance of the steel frame with sufficient classical ornamentation to give them real quality.[31] Among many others, the Guaranty Building in downtown Buffalo constructed in 1893 is iconic. These early buildings were very much speculative projects. They were also up to 60 meters (nearly 200 feet) in height, much like the towers of Bologna. At the time, the template for a typical high-rise building was for each story to be 3–4 meters (9–13 feet) in height, with larger stories at the base and the structure getting lighter and often slimmer as it moved from base to top.

The highest buildings are now reaching 1,000 meters (3,280 feet)—one kilometer in height—largely due to rapid advances in recent construction. But if one examines growth rates in the maximum height of skyscrapers, this falls well short of the increases in world and city populations and in the

amount of urban sprawl surrounding the biggest cities. In short, although
the quest to expand upward is unassailable, the rate of such change has not
been as great as that for urban sprawl—largely, it would appear, for technological reasons. In fact, it is hard to find comparable rates. Regulations
on heights and setbacks have also affected the ability to build high. Nevertheless, the force to build upward is partly based on the desire for more
space at the most accessible and densest points in the city, reflecting the
increasing pressure in the world's largest cities for occupying land and floor
space at the very center. The other nonquantifiable dimension is the simple
desire for high buildings. The "cathedral of commerce" (as noted earlier,
the phrase used to describe the Woolworth Building, finished in 1912
in New York City and the highest building in the world until the Chrysler
Building was constructed in 1930) typifies the preference for celebrating
success and wealth.[32] It would appear that the centripetal forces bringing
these most valued activities and people together in the center in the form of
high buildings far outweigh the centrifugal forces that are pushing less valued activities to the edge of cities. The trade-off between concentration (or
centralization) and deconcentration (or decentralization) is a complex one,
for very few individuals and even a lesser number of households demand to
live at the very center of the city, largely because it is here that the most valued activities involving business and commerce always outbid individual
populations for any amount of space other than the smallest parcel. Moreover, access to residential facilities can be quite distorted at the center in
comparison to the suburbs. Second homes have become significant in some
central locations, where high-rise development is taking place and many
new skyscrapers have been reserved for residential use, but many of these
also double as an asset class among the ownership portfolios of the rich.

The key to building upward is primarily the profit to be extracted from
the land and location, rather than the costs of tall towers, which are still
substantially greater in terms of cost per square meter/foot than those for
more conventional buildings. This largely determines the fact that high
buildings are mainly commercial in function, although in the last decade
an increasing proportion of the highest buildings are residential. Cost is an
issue, since the massive complexity of buildings up to 200 meters (over 650
feet) requires a steel core and elevator shafts as well various kinds of duct-
ing for utilities. Above this height, tall buildings require a different kind of

core support, often more than one core, and use what are, in effect, flying buttresses for structural support, in much the same way medieval cathedrals were built. Such costs are substantial, and although moving people upward rather than outward or sideways is probably cheaper in terms of mechanical transportation, the capacity of such buildings is now as much dictated by waiting times for elevators as by construction costs, per se. Nevertheless, as we will illustrate, these costs seem to be dwarfed by the profit generated by usage, particularly as most of these buildings are developed to accommodate the richest kinds of financial services. As Gilbert so presciently observed[33] at the dawn of this era, the skyscraper is "a machine that makes the land pay."

You might think it somewhat of a coincidence that urban sprawl and the building of skyscrapers began at roughly the same time—the end of the 19th century—but this is no accident in terms of the concurrent invention of industrial technologies that made these developments possible. It took almost 40 years for elevator technology to reach the point where hydraulic lifts became routine, while the automobile took much the same time to reach the point of mass production. In turn, these technologies depended initially on steam power, which emerged right at the beginning of the Industrial Revolution, a century or more before. Interestingly, no one seems to have worked out how much of the urban growth in the last 150 years can be attributed to growth outward and upward. Little, of course, has come from growth inward because most of this has been renewal. Essentially, we might say that most growth prior to 1900 was due to centripetal forces, but from that date the proportion of outward and upward growth can at least be envisaged, if not calculated. In 1900, skyscrapers like Sullivan's Guaranty Building never reached much more than 46 meters (150 feet) (13 stories) in height, but by the late 1920s, the height of the tallest buildings had reached around 320 meters (1,050 feet) (77 stories), as in the Chrysler Building, which was completed in 1930. Building heights did not get much larger until the 1970s, when the Willis Tower in Chicago was constructed. This reached nearly 450 meters (nearly 1,500 feet) (108 stories). It was not until 2010 that the breakthrough to over 800 meters (2,625 feet) occurred with the construction of the 163-story Burj Tower in Dubai. Somewhat ironically, since then a wave of tall towers have been proposed and are now under construction: the Jeddah Tower, at 1 kilometer (3,280 feet) and 170 stories, will be completed

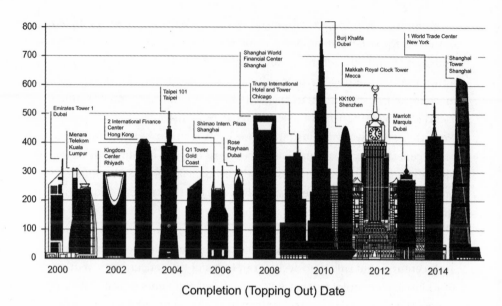

Figure 6.5
The tallest skyscrapers each year from the year 2000.

by the time you read these pages. In figure 6.5, we show a sample of the world's tall buildings. From this picture, it would appear that the skyscraper heights have grown massively in the last century, but the number of such tall buildings has not grown at anything like the same rate as outward city growth in the suburbs.

Every kind of growth—outward, inward, and upward—depends for its momentum on the state of the economy. There have, of course, been waves of publicly inspired growth, such as slum clearance in Western developed countries and mass housing in places like Hong Kong to accommodate inward migration, but most "normal" growth depends on prosperity associated with the economy. Thus the economic cycle dictates the rate and intensity at which the construction of housing, shopping malls, skyscrapers, urban renewals, and general conservation are pursued in any city. These cycles are quite distinct and of variable lengths. It appears that in the West, there are building cycles that repeat every 10–15 years; these are based on overspeculation, which is the result of high levels of liquidity and low interest rates associated with the rapid economic growth that peaks when boom turns into bust.[34] Over a much longer time period, there are the great booms and busts that are marked by world depressions and recessions. As we will see, these are highly correlated with periods of intense skyscraper speculation and building, at least in the West. There has, however, been a sea change in such building. By the 1980s, momentum had begun to move to the newly developing world in Asia Pacific, particularly Singapore and Hong Kong—which traditionally have built high in their role as world financial centers—as well as, then and now, to China. About 70 percent of all high buildings greater than 200 meters (656 feet) are now located in Chinese cities. Another economic marker, however, now dominates this development. We are still living in the shadow of the Great Recession, which hit in 2007, but economic policy has acted quite differently from previous eras: there has now been a long period of very low interest rates, which has generated a vast amount of capital for speculation in land and property. Speculative skyscraper building has been a major recipient of these funds. Unlike the last Depression in the 1930s, skyscraper building did not stop with the Great Recession, but in fact seems to have accelerated.

We will have a look at skyscraper heights for all high buildings over 200 meters (656 feet) worldwide, and then for New York City: these represent the obvious signals of cities growing upward. There are three quite accessible databases, from Emporis, the Skyscraper Page, and the Skyscraper Center.[35] We will use the latter, from which we can download data on the largest number of such high buildings. There is much we can say about such data, but to start, the total number of buildings over 200 meters (656 feet) is some 1,765, of which some 609, or 34 percent, are under construction and will be completed by 2023. This is an enormous proportion, which indicates that the biggest cities are accelerating in their construction of skyscrapers. Far from these world cities just spreading outward, which they are, this quest for building upward is being fueled by prestige projects, newer construction techniques, and of course anticipated profit margins. In fact, the percent under construction, if we look at all buildings over 150 meters (492 feet) and then 100 meters (328 feet) (which total about 2,000 and 4,000 buildings, respectively), is much smaller than for the highest buildings, at around 20 percent, revealing the intense competitive effects to push for the very highest buildings possible. An interesting but speculative debate is whether this trend will continue or, rather, there will be a return during this century to city cores with much lower-rise buildings. Currently it would seem not, since the cities with the lowest building heights in their

CBDs, like London and Paris, are now subject to enormous pressure to construct high towers.

In 1999, Andrew Lawrence, half tongue in cheek (for he began his paper with reference the British Sitcom *Faulty Towers*), proposed what he called a "skyscraper index." In this measure for predicting a major recession, he argued that the signal such a recession would begin was a rapid building boom in which skyscraper heights were pushed ever upward.[36] Mark Thornton, who has written about the business cycle and such building booms, following Lawrence, predicted that the boom would come to an end with the construction of the Burj Tower in the UAE, planned in 2007, and indeed this marked the beginning of the great recession.[37] We show these patterns in figure 6.6(a), where we graph the maximum height of skyscrapers greater than 200 meters (656 feet) built each year since 1900. This gives an impression of how the average height of tall buildings has changed over the last 100 years. To get a better picture, we have plotted the maximum height of new buildings constructed by year, along with the number of buildings greater than 200 meters (656 feet) in each of these years, in figure 6.6(b); this complements our picture of high buildings in figure 6.5. It is easy to see the booms and busts marked by the point when each recession began. Although this is hardly a rigorous demonstration that skyscraper growth is one of the best indicators of boom, thence bust, these graphs do bear out the economic history of the last century and the modern day. In fact, since the Great Recession began in 2007, which unlike any other recession heralded a long era of pump-priming—quantitative easing so called—and cheap money, skyscraper building has boomed in a way that is hardly consistent with Lawrence's index. It is entirely possible that, in economic terms, "this time is different"—this is perhaps borne out in these patterns of high-rise urban development, as well as all the other great transitions that are dominating the global economy, which we will pick up in greater detail in the final chapters.

In chapter 2, we raised one of the great conundrums in thinking about future cities: the size big cities will ultimately become and the space they use. As the size distribution of cities is largely undefined because of definitional limits, particularly for the smallest cities, we hazarded a very preliminary guess as to the total number of cities by examining size distributions and interpolating for the smallest cities, which are the hardest to observe, define, and measure. We can do the same for skyscrapers, which is even

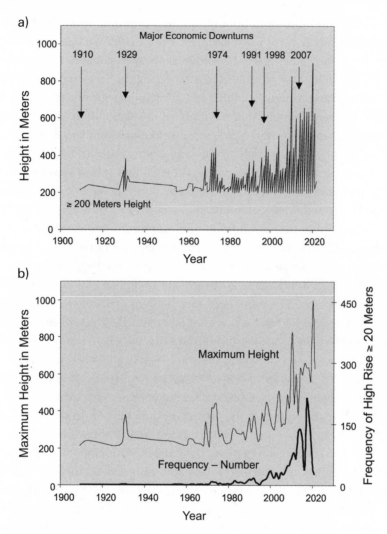

Figure 6.6
The evolution of the tallest skyscrapers from 1900: (a) heights; (b) frequencies against year of construction.

more important, because although we do have some sense of the land area cities actually occupy (for example, from the JRC data), we have little idea about how much space the world's skyscrapers contain. In fact, if we have a good link between the number and height of skyscrapers, this can be extended to all high buildings and all buildings greater than, say, 20 meters (66 feet). To probe this, if we look at the distribution of skyscrapers by height, these follow the typical size distributions popularized by Zipf as rank-size plots,[38] which apply to cities, as demonstrated in figures 2.6 and 2.7 in chapter 2. When skyscraper height is plotted against rank, as we do for all buildings greater than 200 meters (656 feet) in figure 6.7(a), we find a very strong and robust relationship. From this we can simply extend the link to heights that are much lower than 200 meters (656 feet), generating the rank, and hence the number of all buildings greater than a given height. We think a reasonable starting point is 20 meters (66 feet)—a building of some five to six stories; this shows there are 90 million buildings greater or equal to this limit. The number of such buildings falls as we increase the rank. By the time we reach a height of 50 meters (164 feet) or more, there are 1.2 million; this is the size of Sullivan's Guaranty Building in Buffalo. At 100 (328 feet) meters in height, there are 46,000, and when we reach the lower limit of our observations—200 meters (656 feet)—we predict there are 1,280 buildings. In fact, our database shows there are some 1,765: not too bad a prediction (but of the present, not the future!). In fact, although this relationship looks pretty robust, it is less so than we might imagine, so we show the relationship between the frequency (number of skyscrapers) and their heights in figure 6.7(b). This not only confirms the relationship, but gives us a check on the numbers generated. We will not repeat these, for our intention here is not a statistical analysis but simply to give some indication that we may be able to generate another measure for the size of cities.

This sort of analysis does give us a handle on how we might begin to work out the total size of buildings worldwide. Although we have not shown these, we can produce quite robust relationships between the number of stories and heights of tall buildings and, using estimates and some observations of the floor area of tall buildings, we can guess the volume of usable space associated with each. Multiplying these estimates with the numbers of high buildings from the above analysis and throwing in some noise to provide limits to the accuracy of our calculations, we begin to get an idea

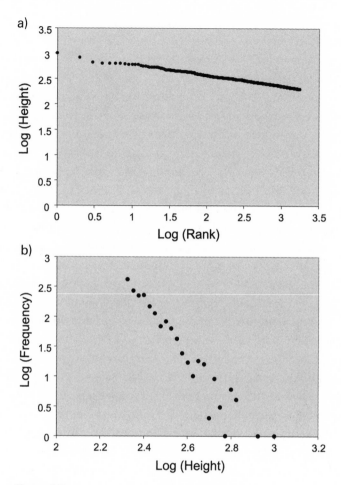

Figure 6.7
The size distribution of skyscraper heights: (a) rank-size distribution; (b) frequency distribution.

of the space used. It has never been the purpose of this book to elaborate research into these questions, but simply to point the way—for there is much to be done with respect to working out how much space is occupied for various uses. So many questions of sustainability, density, compactness, and sprawl depend on the way space is used and the way buildings are constructed. We can say little about the energy use in cities unless we know the spaces affected, and a proper discussion of the idea of compactness needs really good data on space used. We can, of course, produce better estimates at the level of cities. To conclude this chapter, let us look once again at the place that has dominated skyscraper construction—New York City—so that we can get some idea how to explore these questions for individual cities dominated by tall buildings.

What the various databases have recorded in terms of the properties of high buildings—heights and stories, land use, and construction materials—tends to be incomplete below 150 meters (492 feet) in height. Thus, for New York City, we have restricted our analysis to that limit. There are 274 buildings in this data set; we have plotted their rank size for height versus rank and stories versus rank in figure 6.8(a). The height data is almost a perfect straight line, but there is much more variation in the story ranks. Figure 6.8(b) graphs the number of stories against heights, where it is clear that the noise is substantial, implying that the variance in stories against heights gets much greater for smaller buildings. This is a complex issue, but an important one if we want to find out total space enclosed by skyscrapers, which is some combination of the number of stories and heights. We can also look at the rank-size distribution of residential and office towers from this data, where both of these are very close to one another and simply confirm the robustness and quality of the relation shown in figure 6.8(a). In fact, the land use makes little difference to the scaling. We repeat the relationships between the construction of skyscrapers and their heights over time, showing all the building heights for all 274 buildings in figure 6.8(c), where it is very easy to see the booms and busts in this profile. The great Panic of 1913 is clearly observable, as is the Great Depression, while there is a long period over the World War II where there was little high building until it took off again in the 1960s. The oil crisis of 1973–1974 and the 1990s recession are clearly visible, but the Great Recession of 2007–2008 is harder to identify. As elsewhere in the world, we seem to have entered an entirely new era of skyscraper building in the last decade. Just possibly, this time is indeed different! To complete the picture, we show Barr's map of Manhattan[39] in figure 6.8(d), where it is clear that the majority of skyscrapers cluster in midtown and downtown. But, as Barr clearly reveals, there are local issues relating to the construction of high buildings that also determine what gets built, and when and where.

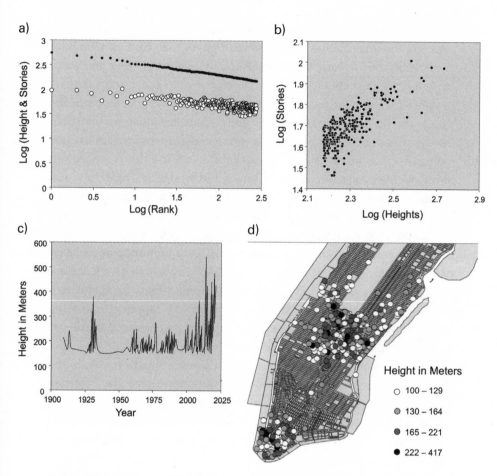

Figure 6.8
Skyscrapers in New York City: (a) rank-size distributions; (b) correlation between stories and heights; (c) heights over time; (d) clustering of skyscrapers in Manhattan.

Where Do We Go Next?

The approach to cities that we have adopted here is sometimes called "physicalism," a kind of materialism, or even positivism. This is the notion that we can understand the most significant processes determining the fundamental economic and social structure of cities in terms of the physical form associated with the way they function. It is an approach that has dominated the planning of cities since institutionalized interventions began in the late 19th century in the name of improving quality of life in cities, particularly to resolve overcrowding and poor health—the problems of rapid industrialization and urbanization. Yet this kind of physical determinism has been critiqued for many years, since it tends to privilege the physical and visual over all other viewpoints. It suggests that better cities come from rearranging physical components and is quite clearly a limited perception of the variety and diversity city life enables. The physical has also been translated into the "spatial," and much of what we have discussed so far in this book represents cities on this physical-spatial continuum; to an extent, these two terms are interchangeable. Much of urban studies, skeptical of the physical tradition, focuses on ideas that do not emphasize the spatial—sometimes referred to as a-spatial—while there are many nonspatial approaches to cities that do not consider cities as being physical or spatial whatsoever. These treat cities as the outcome of consequences of a multitude of processes that play out in many ways other than in terms of the way cities look and are arranged. Such are perspectives on cities that reflect their social and, to a lesser extent, their economic structure. Whatever the approach, however, all imply that the city at some point is a physical artifact, and in the last analysis, needs to be treated accordingly.

There is a rapidly emerging exception, however, to this tradition: the change in cities that is being forced upon us by the digital age. There are many new processes of communication that are now intrinsic to the way we function in cities, yet, in general, as we have been at pains to point out so far, these processes are far from being understood. The impact, for example, of email on how activities and groups locate in cities is by and large opaque to us, since most of this kind of activity is personalized. Even if it is available to some central authority, there is very little analysis of its content with respect to how different communications lead to different patterns of location in cities. These processes are essentially invisible compared to material flows of the kind we have traditionally seen as embodying economic and social functions in cities through physical networks. These have always been key to the way cities have formed, and we have at least been able to measure some them, though not without difficulty. Scale up these processes to include all the various media that now beset us as cities function, and the prospect of an integrated understanding becomes daunting. To an extent, many processes of communication have been fairly opaque in the past due to our inability to collect data and generate the resources to track such interactions. As a result, our ability to understand the present structure of cities is still woefully inadequate. But in a world where most of the newer processes have a much greater degree of invisibility than those of the past or present, attempts at producing ideal cities with respect to physical form are likely to be even more bizarre than those dominating the past, created by visionaries such as Le Corbusier and Frank Lloyd Wright. We need to broach this future so that we can begin a discussion of the way the city is changing in the light of all this new digital media. To this end, we will explore the emergence of the smart city, which reflects many of the processes of transition we began with in chapter 1, attempting to unravel what we know, what we want to know, and what we might expect to know about the city of the future.

7 The Sixth Kondratieff:
The Age of the Smart City

Cycles are not like tonsils, separable things that might be treated by themselves, but are, like the beat of the heart, the essence of the organism that displays them.
—Joseph Schumpeter, *Business Cycles: A Theoretical, Historical, and Statistical Analysis of the Capitalist Process*, v

Nikolai Kondratieff was one of the architects of Lenin's New Economic Policy, which sought to introduce a modicum of free enterprise into the strict economic control initiated as soon as the Soviet state was established in 1917. In this role, he identified economic cycles lasting around 50 years that began and built on technological and capital-intensive developments embodying innovative and creative inventions, yet ultimately fell victim to their own success. He argued that the exploitation of significant inventions led to overproduction, thence to decline and a fall in demand—thus initiating a new wave of innovation leading to a new cycle of capital investment and expansion. He considered this reflected Marx's theories of capitalist labor. Kondratieff's mistake was to assume these ideas could be made consistent with the dictates of the more brutal post-Lenin Stalinist regime, which reinforced the idea that the capitalist system was bound to destroy itself from within. His book *The Major Economic Cycles*, published in 1925, coincided with this shift but laid out ideas about how these long waves might be taken into account in Lenin's New Economic Policy.[1] The waves he identified, despite their obvious coincidence with technological change throughout the 19th century during the early Industrial Revolution, were increasingly at odds with the rigid received economic wisdom in Soviet Russia. He fell out of favor in the mid-1920s and was reported to the Party in 1927; eventually, he was tried on bogus charges and then imprisoned in 1930. In Stalin's Great Purge of 1938, he was tried again, convicted, and executed by firing squad. So much for identifying an important way of thinking about how new technologies complement and supplant existing forms! Nevertheless, his perspective is one we will develop in this chapter as we explore ways in which the digital revolution will continue to change the nature of cities as the current century progresses.

It is unlikely we would have heard much about Kondratieff if Joseph Schumpeter had not articulated his theory of capitalism and critique of Marxism in his exploration of economic history.[2] Between 1923 and 1939, Schumpeter published the two volumes of his mammoth treatise *Business Cycles*, elaborating these phenomena via the key idea that the intrinsically competitive nature of the capitalist system was based on the notion of "creative destruction." We saw in the last chapter how redevelopment, particularly in the largest cities, is characterized by the destruction of perfectly functional capital in the form of buildings so that new forms can be constructed, which not only enable new technologies to be implemented but also increase profitability.[3] The best examples of such activities are seen in the world's financial capitals, where high-profile buildings are continually being destroyed long before they need to be with respect to the functions they contain. But just as we can conceive of cities as organisms rather than machines, Schumpeter took these cycles as evidence that changes in the economy were observations about an evolution of functions, marked by upswings and downswings that mirror the ways in which technologies and social life interact to generate particular paths of progress. This evolutionary economics is reflected in the sentiments in the opening pages of his famous book quoted at the start of this chapter.[4]

Cyclical waves of varying duration feature in many theories of economic development, and Schumpeter himself also embraced those with shorter time scales than the 50 years proposed by Kondratieff. In this chapter, we will argue that despite the evident existence of these waves, change is getting more rapid: these waves are getting shorter and shorter, perhaps more and more intense, with ever-increasing amplitude and frequency. In fact, we consider that these waves are beginning to merge or even coalesce, prompting evolutionary change in cities, in particular via new technologies that are disruptive as well as "creatively" destructive. We will speculate below on the new kinds of technologies and inequalities that these new modes of change are forcing on the restructuring of the city in the 21st century. As a prelude to this, we will sketch the key themes that have driven digital technology over the last century, from the origins of electrical power to the invention of the digital computer and thence to the information society, which is now underpinned by diverse and deep digital data, infrastructure, and interactive interfaces that define contemporary technologies.

Kondratieff himself identified three waves beginning at the start of the Industrial Revolution. First came the invention of steam power with its key innovation, the internal combustion engine; this period lasted from around 1775 to 1825. A second wave from around 1825 to 1875 inaugurated the age of rail power and large-scale manufacturing. The third wave, which was ending when Kondratieff developed his analysis, was the age of electricity: this lasted from 1875 to 1925, or perhaps a little later, to the Great Depression. Others who then took up the challenge mark the fourth wave as being dominated by the automobile, aircraft production, and early computer technologies; this wave lasted until the invention of the PC in 1975. The fifth wave, beginning in 1975 and ending now, has been defined by global communications and all-pervasive computing.[5]

There is considerable ambiguity about these time periods and their labeling in terms of dominant causes and outcomes, but in this chapter, we will argue that the sixth Kondratieff wave will be strongly associated with digital technologies applied to cities, medicine, security, and many other aspects of everyday life, notwithstanding the massive automation that will define society from now on. In fact, we will speculate that the sixth Kondratieff is the age of the smart city, as in the title of this chapter, although there may be other characterizations depending upon one's interest and perspective. On the way to this future, these waves are overlapping, intensifying, and merging, and it now appears that this century will be marked by a sequence of technological revolutions that will change our world into one of continuous invention, innovation, creative destruction, and disruption. We will take up these speculations in the final chapter. In this one, we will sketch the wider context in terms of how all cities are embracing this "smart" digital world.

Here we will sketch how the space-time continuum with respect to cities is being distorted by changes in the technologies we use to communicate, along with what we communicate. In this sense, we examine the extent to which spatial structure and distance are changing the contemporary city, elaborating and extending Wells's proposition,[6] introduced in chapter 4. To an extent, this marks one of the major features of the great transition, beginning with the first Industrial Revolution in the late 18th century and continuing apace through the revolution in information technologies. The idea that such technologies are making cities "smart" is presently in fashion. We introduced this idea implicitly in previous chapters, but here we develop it as a paradigm—a way of thinking about the city as a computable system, in which computers and communications are converging as well as pervading public space for the first time. We will then return to Kondratieff, arguing that the current sixth wave can be associated with this spread of information technologies into the city, while also highlighting how these waves are beginning to merge. As they compress, they appear as though they are converging toward a "temporal singularity" like those noted in earlier chapters.[7] This sets the scene for our last chapter, where we will speculate on what the city will look like—or rather, what we may wish it to look like—by the end of this century.

The Annihilation of Distance

From the beginning of the Industrial Revolution, first with the development of water transport through canals and then with the advent of railroads, many commentators have spoken about the way distance is progressively shortening. The time taken to travel both within and between cities and, of course, between continents, as steam power revolutionized ship technologies, was progressively compressed, thus opening up new places to live, new markets with which to trade, and new resources to exploit. Indeed, the opening up of the American West was graphic evidence of this compression of distances, in which waves of migration associated distance conquered with travel time taken. So far, in this book, we have introduced some very simple principles pertaining to the conventional wisdom regarding how we might understand the way communications, connections, and distance influence the way cities are spatially structured. Our standard model, which provided one of the baselines introduced in chapter 3, suggested that cities' activities are organized in radial concentric fashion around a market core (or central business district) according to their ability to pay for land near the center. This leads to declining densities and intensities. As one moves further and further away from the central business district using new transport technologies, the city is able to expand, embracing an exponentially increasing land area. In this sense, once new technologies emerged that could compress distance, cities were able to break out of the straightjacket that seemed to limit their size to not much more than a million people.

We have elaborated this standard model in several ways thus far. The key underlying principle, introduced in chapter 5, is ascribed to Wells. His proposition that "the general distribution of population in a country must always be directly dependent on transport facilities" is obvious in hindsight, although Wells stated his proposition in an era when the impact of technology on distance was only dimly understood.[8] As technologies for moving ourselves, the materials we use, and—more importantly in the current era—the information we transmit improve and enable us to travel further in less time, cities begin to sprawl in ways cataloged in some detail in the last chapter. But in underpinning cities with technologies that are largely invisible, it becomes harder to figure out their impact. Wells's proposition looms large in a world where cities are becoming even more complex, while their components become less visible: the role of distance is changing, but not disappearing, and it is certainly not getting any less important.

There is another principle worth noting for providing a similar but more oblique impression of how the form and function of the future city are being affected by new technologies. In a rather technical paper[9] on simulating the growth of Detroit written nearly 50 years ago, Waldo Tobler articulated what has come to be called his "first law of geography." He wrote: "Everything is related to everything else, but near things are more related than distant things." In terms of the impact of new technologies, distant things get nearer, which means that in ever-bigger cities, the range of opportunities within reach also gets greater. This compression of distance, due to technologies that enable us to move faster, seems to imply we are provided with more opportunities to increase wealth. In fact, once we are able to communicate almost instantaneously, as current digital technology allows us to through social media, email, web access, and so on, then distance is "annihilated" with respect to activities that depend entirely on digital technology. Indeed, when the web first became established in the early 1990s, Cairncross[10] resurrected the term "the death of distance" in referring to the impact of email and the web on business and social life. In fact—as Mark Twain once said about the reporting of his own demise—this "death" has been "greatly exaggerated," and Cairncross thus provides some limits on Tobler's first law in raising the prospect that in some circumstances distance no longer matters.

This involves the "paradox of the modern metropolis," attributed to Ed Glaeser in chapter 3. This suggests accessibility in any metropolitan area has become increasingly important as the cost or time of connecting over long distances has declined.[11] In short, rather than all places becoming increasingly like one another in terms of their accessibility, the biggest and densest places, such as city cores, are becoming even more important. Fifty years ago, futurists such as Alvin Toffler argued that with the falling costs of travel, activities might decentralize to remote locations and the prospect of cities built of electronic cottages where people worked remotely instead of in the densest hubs would become the order of the day.[12] E. M. Forster's novelette, "The Machine Stops," written in 1909, painted a picture of such a world, in which everyone is self-sufficient in terms of communications and thence rather isolated.[13] In fact, the world that began to emerge from the start of the Industrial Revolution to the present day has become quite the opposite. As cities have become bigger, and as we have become ever more connected, the value of face-to-face communications has become even more important. Cities do not look as though they are spreading out in the way envisaged a century or more ago by Forster and Wells.

This nexus of transformations in distance and time, which are an immediate consequence of the revolution in communications as well as their convergence with computation, has been defined as one of the key constructs for what David Harvey[14] has termed, in a book of the same name, the "condition of postmodernity." "Time-space compression" is how he describes the way space is shrinking as advances in globalization shorten physical distances through technologies that are no longer confined to land mass and to particular routes dictated by physical geography and climate. In figure 5.8(d), we showed the global pattern of contacts associated with Facebook; there are now countless depictions of such global flows. This distortion of space and time as technologies continue to develop may be very profound. As the world shrinks in this way, we need new modes of representation to visualize their meaning. As a result, our focus must move a little away from the usual "flat" map that accompanies most discussions of form and function in the contemporary city. This is largely because it is increasingly difficult to see how the massive proliferation of individual uses of information technology can be simplified into immediate geometric and geographic representations that have characterized our understanding and planning of cities hitherto. In the next chapter, when we explore how future cities might be invented, we will use these principles to construct idealizations that build on the succession of technologies leading to the digital revolution. Here, we will speculate on how cities might change if we were to collapse all distances that determine their structure in favor of an entirely liquid form where communications are instantaneous. Anybody might live anywhere in such a world, but location would still be determined by social preferences and by the importance of our most local and long-lasting experiences of place as children. It is likely that the key determinant of any kind of clustering defining cities would be based on our need to aggregate and associate with others, not for economic motives but for social companionship. The centrality of the family and the fact that as children we live in small-scale, intimate spaces could well be the cement that continues to hold the city together. We simply do not know whether this will be the case.

Before we go further, we need to explore how this digital world and the smart city have emerged since the mid-20th century, indeed perhaps from the beginnings of the Industrial Revolution. Our argument will be that the great transition is not primarily one of industrialization: instead, it is part of a much deeper and long-lasting transition from atoms to bits, from a world dominated by energy to one of information. To this end, we will begin with some original statements about computers, defined as universal machines, first spelled out 80 or more years ago by pioneers such as Alan Turing and John von Neumann.[15]

The Information Revolution

The idea of representing phenomena in elemental either-or chunks—such as zero-one, plus-minus, black-white, yes-no, on-off—is deeply embedded in human development. At various points in recorded history, the concept has surfaced, but only since the discovery of electricity has it become central to our means of representation. With the development of mechanical technologies in the first Industrial Revolution, there were serious attempts at building analog machines that could manipulate such elemental coding. Babbage's difference and analytical engines, constructed from the 1820s but never finished by the time of his death in 1871, were in the vanguard of such developments. But it was not until the notion that an electrical pulse could be used to represent such a distinction that the prospect of the digital computer appeared during the second Industrial Revolution. In review, let us note that the division of the last 250 years into four revolutions is primarily from Schwab,[16] who argues that the first was associated with mechanical steam power until about 1830, the second with electrical power until about 1920, while the third is associated with invention of computers and information technology and ended in the late 20th century. We are now in the fourth revolution, which is essentially the world of machine intelligence, the smart city, digital health care, and the massive proliferation of information devices. We note the coincidence with Kondratieff's waves below.

The ability to represent phenomena in the binary code was proposed by several people, such as Claude Shannon, but it was also supported by a prescient speculation. In the pre and post war years, Alan Turing demonstrated that the digital computer based on encoding instructions for computation using the binary system was essentially a universal machine. Vannevar Bush then sketched such a machine that intruded into every aspect of personal life, suggesting that personal computing would be the process whereby the world would become digital. Two developments enabled the computer to become all-pervasive. First came the invention of the transistor, which led to the dramatic path to miniaturization now enshrined in Moore's law.[17] For the last 50 years, this law has demonstrated that for a silicon chip, memory and processing power have doubled while costs have halved every 18 months with little sign of slowdown, and certainly no sign of stopping, as noted in chapter 2. Second, the convergence of computers with telecommunications has enabled equally dramatic access to information that is computable. Both developments have been essential to the massive proliferation and scaling-down of computing devices and their connection to one another. Without any of this, we would be unable to speak of an information society, and certainly not of a smart or automated city.

In some respects, the first and second Industrial Revolutions, associated with mechanical and electrical power, are essential for the current revolution in information processing. A plausible interpretation of industrial development over the last 250 years (or even as far back as classical times, before the birth of Christ) now seems to suggest that the great divide between the old world and the new is marked by the transition from a world of materials and energy to one of data and information. To an extent, the most visible trace of this is what we have referred to as the great transition. It is likely, then, that cities and societies in this new world will be completely unlike those in the old. This is clearly evident in the fact that cities were only able to grow, as noted above, beyond a population of a million or so once the internal combustion engine and other mechanical technologies emerged. Now, with information technologies, physical limits on size are once again being cast in a very different light.

We can summarize these various forces via several clichés, which are often referred to in the most casual sense as "laws" and which we anticipated a little in chapter 1. These are not hard, immutable physical laws, for they are clearly dependent on social context, but they do provide simple rules for gauging the past and possibly the future impacts of information technology on cities and societies. The core of this transition is, of course, miniaturization embodied in Moore's law, first articulated in 1965 and based on his observations of what happened at Intel, where he worked on the development of the integrated circuit. Moore's law is crucial to the inexorable rise in not only computer memory but also computation. There is little doubt that current developments in artificial intelligence, which depend on continuous iteration of simple rules to extract a degree of intelligence from computation, lie at the root of current predictions about massive automation of the workplace and the disappearance of many middle-ranking jobs. This process depends intrinsically on Moore's law.[18]

The picture would not be complete without an equally important law pertaining to how computers are able to communicate with one another. Metcalfe's law, named after the first developer of the Ethernet at Xerox PARC in 1974, suggests that "the value of a network is proportional to the square of the number of nodes." In short, as the number of computers increases and as they are networked together, the value of the network, measured in terms of the amount of information that it can process, increases exponentially—at least as the square of the number of computers acting as nodes in the network. This is the form Gilder gave to Metcalfe's observations, and notwithstanding that there have been some empirical criticisms of its precise form, it still conjures up the notion that a computable society is not simply about computers, per se, but about how they are connected and the economies of scale that emerge from such networks.[19] This was only barely anticipated when Turing and Bush wrote their seminal essays, and to an extent it has taken the world by surprise. Of course, in hindsight it all seems so obvious that we should connect computable devices together to extend their processing power over large distances, but this was not foreseen until it began to happen.

There are three other laws that build on network connectivity. Gilder's (2000) own law suggests that the total bandwidth of communication systems triples every twelve months. This is much faster than Moore's law, and it is yet to be fitted precisely since the data are difficult to assemble and total bandwidth is a nebulous concept. The second is Sarnoff's law. This states that the value of a broadcast network is directly proportional to its number of viewers, which might be interpreted as the lower limit of Metcalfe's law, again suggesting that the concept of value needs a clearer definition.

All of these laws are, to some extent, "convenient fictions." To conclude on an even more fanciful note, there is a fifth: Zuckerberg's law. The founder of Facebook formalized the hype surrounding his network by stating that the information people share doubles each year.[20] This is quite important, because it moves the argument away from hardware—computers and networks—to people and information, and it is this that is so critical to the all-pervasiveness of computers and computation in contemporary and probably all future societies. Data, of course, is the next frontier. It is likely that somebody will coin a series of data laws that relate to the exponential, in fact superexponential, growth that characterizes our current ability to generate data using networked computers, the numbers and speed of which are themselves increasing exponentially. In fact, all these laws would seem to be as true for past societies as for present, except that information was harder to extract in the past since it was more bound up with material transactions. In Negroponte's phraseology, bits were then harder to separate from atoms.[21]

It is now clear that an entirely networked world has almost emerged. In such a context, the kind of computation that takes place across all possible devices will determine this network's form and function. It thus depends on what is attempted and achieved using such devices, which maps directly onto the extent to which traditional functions are automated, substituted for, or complemented by these new devices and how this new digitality generates new functions that do not currently exist. We do not have a very clear idea of the impact of all this, especially when it comes to the physical form and function of the traditional city. Virtually every aspect of the city and of our activities within it are touched in some way by digital technologies, and thus many writing and commenting about the smart city resort to hyperbole, coupling lists of everything in sight that might appear to be influenced by new information technologies.

Within the last 10 years, roughly from the time when the Great Recession began, the smartphone has emerged and is increasingly being used for a range of work, home, and entertainment activities as well as multiple routine functions involving storing (banking), generating, and using money and all kinds of email and social media. Information is now being stored remotely, and with voice activation and interaction, we have rapidly transitioned to a world where information associated with various services and stored in a diverse array of archives is immediately available. Remote servers—part of the ubiquitous "cloud"—are now the norm, even for types of computation that are still strongly place-related. The traditional hardware distinctions between mainframe, supercomputer, mini, desktop and mobile device, which represent the sequence of computer technologies emerging over the last 60 years, still exist in various forms, but these distinctions are blurring even for scientific computation. The kinds of computation that now characterize contemporary society are also evolving rapidly, and the line between computers and sensors is no longer particularly distinct. Organizations—sometimes called "stacks," sometimes platforms—are emerging, expanding our computational capabilities by integrating the supply chain involving information technologies, from data to hardware and software through to applications, in very diverse domains, while also embracing everything from how information technology is powered to how it is managed. It is into this world that the smart city has appeared as the current wave of the digital revolution. Before we chart its progress further, we need good robust theory, for without theory we have little chance of making sense of an environment entirely dominated by computers, computation, and networks. To this we now turn.

Defining the Smart City

In the last 50 years, our view of cities has been turned on its head. As we have argued so far, we consider cities to be more like organisms than machines. Biology has replaced physics as the dominant metaphor. Cities grow from the bottom up, the patterns that we see emerging as the product and outcomes of millions of individually motivated decisions, and insofar as there is any top-down planning, it is usually short-lived. Although different types of collective planning designed to solve urban problems at different scales rarely have any lasting continuity, they are nonetheless critical to articulating a future we need to design. By focusing on bottom-up decision-making, we mean that when one looks at a city in its entirety, there are few physical expressions of comprehensive planning that can be seen to be manifest physically over long periods of time—decades or centuries—but cities still embrace various kinds of planning at different scales. The ideal cities noted in previous chapters were convenient fictions, visions that were hardly ever implemented, and attempts at their building were short-lived, incomplete, and eventually abandoned.

This lack of top-down planning has of course been known for a long time. Its association with the problems of rapid growth industrialization brought to cities, particularly in the 19th century, was the force that motivated comprehensive institutionalized planning in the first place. But planning added yet another layer to the increasing complexity that has clearly characterized cities since their emergence some 5,000 years ago. As new technologies are invented and new forms of behavior, often conditioned by increasing wealth, emerge through time, new forms are layered on top of old, disrupting the old but never completely replacing them. The latest digital wave of these technologies is thus shifting our concern primarily from the physical form of cities to questions of how technology is enabling better, but less visible, communications through automation. This is the so-called "smart cities movement," which is really the latest stage in the revolution in information technologies that began with the invention of the digital computer. From our vantage point here in the early 21st century, the current manifestation of computers and communications in cities is just the latest phase of a massive diffusion of digital technologies that shows no sign of stopping.

Smart cities essentially enable computers and communications to be embedded in the very fabric of the city. The first reference to the term seems to be some 25 years ago in *The Technopolis Phenomenon: Smart Cities, Fast Systems, Global Networks* by Gibson, Kozmetsky, and Smilor.[22] Other characterizations—such as intelligent cities, wired cities, virtual cities, information cities, even electric cities—have been suggested. We will use all of these interchangeably to suggest how computers are being embedded into cities' fabric in both hard and soft ways.[23] The term "smart" has long been associated with the fact that computers can be used intelligently for many purposes, while the recent wave of devices that enable us to compute as well as remotely access data lets us demonstrate such smartness through extremely fast access to ever-increasing volumes of information. By and large, the kinds of automation that currently characterize the smart city are only intelligent or smart insofar as we, ourselves, use them intelligently. It is we who must potentially be smart rather than the devices we use, although there is much speculation that various forms of artificial intelligence, combined with our own natural intelligence, could augment our behaviors quite dramatically in the near future. It is perhaps sobering that it is always in the near future. To date, however, there has been only modest progress, despite the current hype about "deep learning" and the proliferation of voice-activated devices that enable one to search the web in almost conversational mode.

If we accept the argument that cities are largely built from the bottom up, then the degree to which they might become "smarter"—as we tend to anthropomorphize their collective behavior—depends on each and all of us acting intelligently. In this sense, grand plans to make the city smart are no different from any other kinds of grand plan and are likely to be as short-lived. We may not conceive of many of our actions as grand plans, but—whatever rationality we bring to bear on the city and in whatever form we employ it, either individually or collectively—decisions that change the city are ultimately rooted in the province of the individual. Thus, our first response to asking the question "what or where is the smartest city?" is that this is a question with no lasting answer. There may be impressive strategies to automate bits of the city, and sometimes these are integrated effectively and carefully: cities such as Barcelona are a case in point. And there are entire new towns being built with extensive automation in their various sectors, such as Masdar in the UAE or Songdo in South Korea.[24] Yet these are but islands in an encroaching sea of automation. There are also long-term strategies for urban automation deeply embedded in national comprehensive planning—Singapore is one of the classic prototypes of such an informated society—but it is the use made of such automation that is key to working out the extent to which a city is becoming smart.[25] If the essence of urban development is individual action, then a city can only be as smart as its citizens. In a world where more than half the global population has smartphones, one might even state that the answer to the question of the smartest city is the one with the largest number of smartphones, either absolutely or in *per capita* terms.

It is, however, not really possible to answer this question, because the very revolution that the smart city movement is part of is a wider diffusion of digital technologies increasingly focused on the individual. As noted above, the smart cities movement is only the latest stage in the all-pervasive revolution in information processing. Its most tangible form so far has been the embedding of computer technologies and their control into physical artifacts—buildings, roads, and so on. In fact, the miniaturization of computable devices to the scale of the phone provides a very obvious means of accessing computation remotely while on the move. If most of the smartness we are associating with the city is accessible and generated by ourselves, then the number of smartphones might superficially seem a good measure of this progress. But, to an extent, this is a mirage, because the devices are mobile. In short, intelligence shifts around, making the smart city even more of a moving target.

Thus the question "what and where is the smartest city?" not only has no answer, it is also ill-defined, largely because smartness or intelligence is a process, not an artifact or product. There may be answers to questions such as "where can one find the greatest concentration of automated public services in cities?"; or "where is the most integrated organizational structure for linking different types of energy provision?"; or "where is the most effective delivery of online information for transit users?" But these are very specific, and even these kinds of achievement depend on local conditions. In some senses, anyone who has access to a smartphone with a web link and has the resources to use it is a member of the smart city, and that will probably mean "everybody" by the end of this century.[26] When voice becomes the dominant means of interacting with such technologies, it is likely that we will no longer speak of the smart city—for, by then, the smart city will already be firmly woven into the very nature of the information technologies at our disposal. The nature of the smart city then lies in the very technology that defines it. Before we chart any kind of progress, we must digress somewhat to inquire into the nature of that technology and how individualistic it has become.

Theoretical Perspectives

It is no exaggeration to suggest that there are almost as many perspectives on the nature of the city as there are persons researching their structure, managing their organization, or engaging with their design. Cities admit multiple viewpoints and multiple theories, and it is little surprise that when a new set of technologies emerge, new perspectives are fashioned to consider how such technologies can be implemented and embedded in the city and how they might change human behaviors. In the context of highly scalable computers such as handheld devices and small-scale sensors, there is also a strong force to sell such products. With the universality of such devices, the business ethic is rapidly driving the move to the smart city. This means the corporate world is often at the forefront of popularizing the smart city, with the consequence that much of the hype involves the most obvious aspects of how the city and its parts might be automated.

If you pick up one of the many reports on smart cities written by municipalities, governments, large information and communications technology companies, consultants, and so on, or examine the many conferences that energize discussion regarding the business of smart cities, you will be struck by the somewhat random nature of the topics discussed. They rarely have any strong internal ordering and invariably simply reflect the most obvious components and activities that go on in cities. Moreover, this listing of topics based on components does not really focus on the processes of automation and how these might alter the way populations behave with respect to urban markets and forms of governance. There is, however, much speculation about how such technologies might be integrated—in terms of sharing hardware, software, and the networking capabilities that serve to tie various data and computation together—and there is even fanciful talk of building entire operating systems for cities. What these might be is anybody's guess, for an operating system assumes that there is agreement about what in a city is the focus of operation. The notion of sharing is also writ large with respect to data and software and often arrayed across "platforms" that serve to tie various systems together. Much that is written about the smart city from these perspectives does not in fact propose anything that is more generic than a will to integrate and coordinate. As the history of large information and communications technology clearly reveals, integrated workable systems are few and far between. What exists so far in terms of the smart city is very largely ad hoc—more intention than actual implementation, more heat than light.[27]

The sort of areas identified in the vast majority of the literature on smart cities that largely emanates from the nonacademic sector is not based on any distinct theory of how cities function or even how they should be managed or designed. It tends to be based on locations where sensors and computers and their concomitant networks can be developed (and sold), with mobility and energy as key themes. Services delivered to citizens are also important in this mix, but invariably these range from location-based services to municipal delivery of benefits that traditionally the public sector has been mandated to deliver. Cybersecurity, which involves everything from blockchain to Bitcoin, has recently appeared as a key function of the smart city, while financial services, retailing involving online shopping, and marketing tend to be somewhere in the frame. Waste, pollution, various kinds of utilities infrastructure, and network systems also appear as candidates for automation, but there is little focus on how they might be integrated with population demand and infrastructure supply. A concern for data—particularly open data and now "big data," which is directly related to real-time streaming and operation of automated functions in the city—is also significant. But all of these elements do not add up to a comprehensive picture of how the smart city functions or will function once automation of the kind implied here becomes available (at scale). Interacting with the public through various kinds of participatory dialogue and crowdsourcing to elicit everything from opinion, personal innovation, and responses to policy to the collection of new data are also examples of the kinds of environment the smart city can bring. This sometimes dominates the debate, but all of these perspectives and foci tend to emphasize the current and routine operation of the city rather than longer-term goals for more livable and equitable environments.

These discussions tend to be set against an implicit background of continuous economic growth with little discrimination regarding what might be important, feasible, or equitable with respect to functions that might be automated. Most contributions tend to be silent on effective organizational structures that might best enable this kind of automation. There is very little discussion about how cities function in terms of the way activities are served by markets and how resources are allocated spatially with respect to transportation. There is absolutely no discussion of the many new networks appearing that communicate data and information. It is almost as though email, the web, and the myriad of other fixed wire and wireless networks, as well as GPS and related technology, do not exist in terms of their influence on the smart city. In fact, however, the smart city is only possible because of them. Academic commentaries on the smart city are equally lacking. One exception is *Smart Cities: Big Data, Civic Hackers, and the Quest for a New Utopia*, a review by Anthony Townsend,[28] which is an excellent discussion of the key issues from the point of view of the citizen, the planner, and the industry, though it has more of a historical focus than a prolegomena for action.

What the smart city debate has thrown into sharp relief is the focus it has brought to the temporal dynamics of cities, explored in chapter 5. Most approaches to cities in the past have focused on how they function and develop over years and decades rather than finer time periods such as minutes, hours, or days, although there have always been organizational and management functions that pertain to their routine functioning. It is these that are becoming automated at a rapid rate, and thus the smart cities movement has tended to emphasize short-term dynamics rather than the longer term. Most individual decisions about urban development occur in real time, although they may have implications over many time horizons. It is this mixing of time periods that highlights the need for much clearer theoretical perspectives on exploring, understanding, and predicting the impacts of automation on the city, and this requires a much more complete framework for examining automation than we have developed hitherto. In fact, there has been no strong emphasis on dynamics in understanding and planning cities hitherto, as noted earlier, largely because cities have been considered to be in equilibrium and their improvement has often been phrased in terms of idealized plans without any realistic time horizons for implementation. If there have been time horizons, these have been end-states to a future that is far away. Thus the smart cities movement has brought time onto the agenda with a vengeance, which is likely to revolutionize how and what we plan, notwithstanding the largely atheoretical context into which these ideas are being introduced.

With digital technologies spreading everywhere—all with very different degrees of automation and impact—it is not possible to provide a coherent, all-embracing theory of the smart city. However, here we can at least imply a generic approach that focuses on how individuals and groups function in cities in terms of the myriad networks that tie groups together in space and time. Cities exist to bring people together, and their linkages portray networks of many kinds, as we have been at pains to emphasize in previous chapters. Most prior to the digital age were material and transport-related, but they are now being augmented, complemented, and substituted by ethereal flows—where information is the new energy and data is the new oil. What happens in any location within the city depends on networks of people, materials, energy, and information that is transmitted to and from these places, which act as hubs. In fact, our understanding of cities must be based on unpacking locations into the spokes that tie these hubs together, for the changes that are most durable in cities depend on what is flowing into these hubs. All this is fairly obvious and repeats material we have introduced before. In some sense, the notion that cities can only be understood in terms of their networks is not a new insight; it is an obvious consequence of why cities exist. But the idea that we can only understand cities in terms of their networks, not simply their locations, has been a long time coming.[29]

This network view of cities is based on the central principle that cities evolve from the bottom up. As we implied in the first part of this chapter, top-down planning is rare compared to the myriad of decisions made by individuals acting for their immediate family or group, usually in their own self-interest. From this, we can articulate the city as being composed of layer upon layer of networks, between which there are networks linking networks. In the medieval city, these networks were simpler, but as new technologies have emerged, new and different forms of network have been invented and constructed. The history of the city is thus one of a fast-proliferating set of networks.[30] The network view of the city has always been one primarily of social networks, but as soon as mechanical technologies began to proliferate in the early Industrial Revolution, cities began to grow as the separation of functions made it possible for individuals to carry out new tasks remotely from one other. These networks have become ever more global, but until the invention of the computer and before it the telephone and related information devices, the extent to which the world could be easily charted was quite bounded. In the last 60 years, all this has changed; in fact, it is probably within the last 30 years that information networks have massively proliferated, but only in the last decade have large numbers of people become connected to them. We are now facing a world where anyone, anywhere, with a smartphone and Internet connection, can access enormous amounts of information globally and interact with many people they have never physically met. This, of course, has dramatic implications for the city. In fact, the smart city is a constellation of networks in which real change is coming from the use of these networks. When everyone is connected to everyone else, then what we will see are more and more variants of network layered on top of one another, interwoven in strange and convoluted ways. This kind of complexity is what the smart city is bringing, although we barely have a science yet to deal with its emergence.

A Paradigm for the Smart City

Some may object to establishing the smart city as a paradigm, for it perhaps gives too much credence to what are long-term forces transforming entire ways of life. But the disconnect of urban form from function that new information technologies are bringing about is sufficiently different from all that has preceded our contemporary world to suggest we need a new approach.

Some distinction needs to be made with respect to cities before, and those generated by the first and second Industrial Revolutions, as well as those that now exist within the third and fourth. We call this a paradigm to make clear we think this is a more complete way of characterizing smart cities than any of the current approaches, which tend to be without any theoretical conception of how cities function as complex entities.[1] The paradigm is really quite simple in that we begin by making the obvious distinction between the city as it exists externally to our perceptions, and our understanding of the city that is necessary to any interventions we might make to change it. This is the difference, then, between the reality of the city and our theories about it. Our theories can come from any and every perspective, but they involve some form of abstraction that makes our models of the city distinct from the city itself.

We anticipated these distinctions in chapter 5, which focused on the real-time city, exploring its various temporal dynamics. But a better picture is illustrated in the diagram in figure 7.1, which shows the reality and our abstractions from it in a closed loop, suggesting we draw data from the real city and from this manufacture our understanding. In parallel, we exercise control over the real city through management and design, thus changing the city, which in turn feeds back as changes to the data that we draw from the city. In this sense, there are at least two loops involved in this circularity: first, the scientific method in which the city is the object of study and the

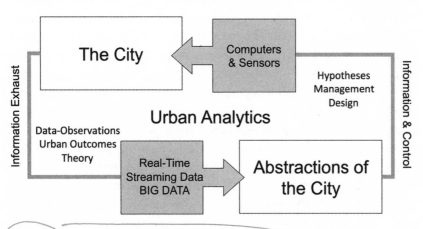

Figure 7.1
Understanding, managing, and planning the smart city.

subject of our hypotheses, hence the theories which underpin our understanding; and second, the process of management and planning, which is how we enable the city to function while at the same time changing it by design. In fact, we might separate this second loop into two—one concerned with the functioning of the real-time city, and another concerned with its design. The real-time loop is one that usually works with much shorter time horizons than the second, focusing on what we have called the "high-frequency city," in comparison with the second, the "low-frequency city." Rather than presenting three loops in figure 7.1, we show only one, but notate it to impress this threefold meaning.

A consequence of this argument is that it is difficult to date the beginnings of the smart city, and if smartness is associated more with ourselves rather than our computers, then no origins are possible. However, reflecting on the world prior to the emergence of the web in the 1990s, computation was largely associated with two sets of functions that impacted the loops in figure 7.1; first, computers were used almost from their inception to build models of complex social systems such as cities, and thus very early on became part of a loosely structured science of cities that evolved to enable a better understanding of urban problems. Such models were and are highly abstract but focus on key elements that determine how cities function. They have often been used for prediction in plan making, and indeed this was their original rationale. The second usage has been computer applications in managing complex systems or parts thereof for purposes of control. To a large extent, this involved transactions-processing, notwithstanding some early attempts at controlling and optimizing urban functions such as emergency services and utilities.[32] To a very limited extent, a third usage of computers in design has emerged, but prior to the web and the rapid increase in computer graphics capabilities, which occurred in parallel, such uses were modest and minimal. Only now is computer-aided design writ large, but most of this is not related to city planning per se.

Progress in developing computational simulations supporting understanding, management, and design was extremely slow prior to the last two decades. However, once computers came to be scaled down to the level at which personal devices could be used for interactive control and networks of sensors became robust enough to provide control in real time, the embedding of computers into the fabric of the city—rather than computers being used to understand and manage the city—became a reality. In figure 7.1, the two gray boxes indicate that once this kind of embedding began to take place as the web developed,[33] the entire picture of what is now possible in terms of the three functions—understanding through science, management and control, and thence design—is radically changed. First, the data that is available from such embedding is available in real time, and if not actually linked to real-time control, is available in a post hoc fashion for analysis and design. This data, because of its volume (and variety) is often termed "big," since in principle there is no limit to its volume as it is continuously generated.[34]

Big data tends to be associated with the very short term, whereas most traditional sources of data used to understand (and in the past even control) the city have been assembled over years, decades, or even longer. Of course, big data, assembled second by second, will also pertain to the long term when enough of it has been collected to enable long-term analysis with these new data sources. We have not quite reached the point where these new sources of data—many pertaining to transit, and some to retailing and finance—have been used for longer-term analysis, while there are also potential limits on such data due to confidentiality and ownership, and hence access. However, the nature of big data of the real-time, streamed variety is very different from traditional data sets associated with individuals and often collected through periodic censuses. Much big data is, of course, collected by streaming from mobile devices associated with individuals, but there are key problems in using this data. First, real-time data is often associated with devices that are not linked to people, and even if they are, such as via fixed sensors that an individual activates, it is rare for any attribute data to be associated with the individuals involved. If the data is individually identified, then often attribute data is simply not collected and has to be inferred. Quite frequently, that data is flawed in that it is difficult to interpret and highly biased to particular groups or cohorts. Such is the case with social media data.

What figure 7.1 does reveal, however, is that using computers in real time to control the city and engage in many traditional functions in new ways adds a new layer of complexity to traditional approaches. We have not unpacked this diagram with respect to digital versus nondigital operations and functions, but the new embedding of computers into the form and function of the city generates new kinds of networks based on information rather than material and people flows. This is where the new urban analytics we identify in figure 7.1 as a contextual backcloth is relevant. The many models, simulations, and analytical techniques grouped together under this new label are all under very rapid development at the present time due to the development of new data sources and new ideas about how the city functions in terms of information networks. None of this is yet worked out in any detail, but an enormous challenge is to devise new ways of integrating many of these perspectives and data sources as well as new forms of spatial behavior with traditional models and simulations. For this, we need new theory that embraces what we and others are calling the smart city, as well as traditional views and timeframes with respect to how cities have been understood, managed, and designed hitherto.

Kondratieff's Waves and the Emergence of Singularities

Digital technologies include hardware involving networks, switches, and sensors as well as software, dataware, and the organizational structures important to their functioning. A key point arising from our earlier history is that it is difficult to place technologies developed since the beginning of the Industrial Revolution into a distinct sequence. To an extent, mechanical preceded electrical preceded digital, and these can all be seen as part of the same processes of innovation and application, with this continuity merging one cycle, period, or wave into another. Whether anything can follow digital is an open question, although other kinds of computing (such as quantum technology and telecommunications involving voice rather than text and numbers) do define rather different technologies, at least in terms of accessing computers and data. We might think of these developments as being part of Schwab's fourth Industrial Revolution.[36] The issue with digital technologies, however, is that their development has followed Moore's law, which suggests ever-increasing rates of change. This would perhaps appear counterintuitive to our more general perception that there are distinct phases of technological development, but it appears increasingly the new reality.

The idea that development takes place in waves is also deeply ingrained in our perceptions of history, for economic theorizing and practical policy making is dominated by notions of business, credit, and other monetary cycles. These cycles seem to have more resonance than the longer waves that have been proposed for the rise and fall of civilizations, while the notion that more specific patterns such as technological change can be articulated as supercycles has gained some currency in the last 100 years. Kondratieff, who we noted earlier worked in Stalin's civil service in the 1920s, first gave form to the idea that technologies appeared to have periods of relative dominance lasting around 50 years. He pointed to the early Industrial Revolution, when the internal combustion engine was invented (from 1770 to around 1820), followed by the age of steel and steam (1820–1870), which led to the age of electricity. This was more or less finishing when Kondratieff began to theorize about all of this, though his work was short-lived due to his persecution. His ideas were quickly picked up by Schumpeter, who called these patterns Kondratieff waves (K-waves) and suggested that once a new technology has been invented, a period of consolidation and application follows.[36] Such a wave completes with a downswing characterized by falling investment in the technology, which is then superseded by a new technology, heralding the start of a new wave. These long waves were marked, said Schumpeter, by the creative destruction of the existing technology, which often appeared perfectly serviceable but was inevitably replaced by newer, shinier, and often radically different forms.

It was Kuznets who gave a clearer form to these waves, dividing each into four sequential stages, beginning with innovation, in which new technologies are first exploited (although their invention might have been much earlier), then increasingly used in a process of rising investment.[37] This is followed by steady application, during which profits gradually decline, leading to depression as the technology becomes less attractive and new tools are invented. From this emerges a period of recovery, which leads to the start of a new wave based on these new innovations. In fact, there is no definitive thinking about the length of these long waves or supercycles, nor is there any real agreement about the precise form of the stages within each cycle. But there is clearly a rise and fall, which is the mark of a wave. In some respects, the waves build on each other, and in many technologies, the earlier versions continue to be improved and are key to those that displace them, very often being used for the same applications as earlier ones.

The fourth and fifth Kondratieff waves have been characterized, respectively, as associated with automobile and digital technologies. Following the 50-year cycle, these took place between 1920 and 1970 and from 1970 to the present day. In this characterization, the sixth Kondratieff nicely fits the age of the smart city. Others suggest that the next wave will instead be an era of biotechnology, in which health moves to the fore. In some senses, this does indeed accord with the argument that the next wave of computing will be the embedding of computers into ourselves so that we might improve our health, extend our longevity, and even determine our genetic composition. However, when each of the six waves covering the time from the beginning of the Industrial Revolution are compared, they tend to be somewhat unlike one another: it would appear the first wave is invention, the next application, and so on. On this basis we are coming to the end of a wave of digital inventions, which may herald a wave of applications—in smart cities, health, space travel, and so on.

A useful interpretation of these waves has been presented by Naumer and colleagues,[38] who imply that the amplitude of each wave is getting a little greater (and perhaps the periodicity a little shorter), but their picture, shown in figure 7.2, is only one of several proposed in which the timing of the cycles differs. In fact, if these waves are getting shorter and more pronounced, this appears consistent with rapid developments in information technology, which now seem out of step with the general timing suggested a century ago by Kondratieff himself and by Schumpeter. The midpoints of each cycle are also plotted in figure 7.2 and suggest there is a much longer-term process at work, which we would argue is simply the transition from a non-mechanized, nonautomated world to our current digital one. In fact, if the waves get shorter and larger, then they will eventually coalesce to produce a singularity—an event horizon of continuous creative destruction. The meaning of such a convergence is hard to fathom, since we have no experience

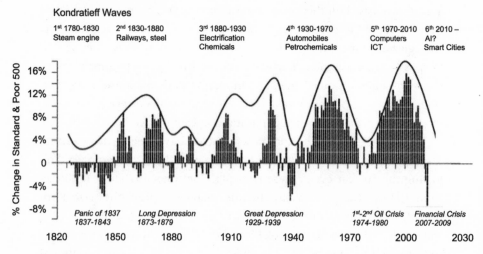

Figure 7.2
An interpretation of Kondratieff's long waves.

of such an event or environment. This is what makes it unlikely, but the prospect of continuous invention is certainly possible. It could usher in a world where everything is special and individual, something which appears to be occurring in limited contexts, particularly through social media and crowdsourced activities.

The idea of a singularity will be elaborated a little more substantively in the next chapter. In figure 7.3, we show a series of Kondratieff waves, starting at roughly 50 years in duration and decreasing at an increasing rate and growing in intensity through time (which is a proxy for the number and impact of new technologies). This shows that new inventions are becoming more rapid—that time is speeding up, as Stewart Brand so acutely observes.[39] If we then overlap these waves, we approximate the kind of superexponential rates of growth illustrated for world population growth in chapter 2. As we argued in our foray into the demography of the 21st century, the rate of change in world population reached its maximum nearly 60 years ago, and at that point it looked as though the global population would increase without bound until it reached a crisis point—a singularity—in the late 2020s. None of this could take account, however, of the fact that in the last two decades it looks as though a turning point has been reached for the world

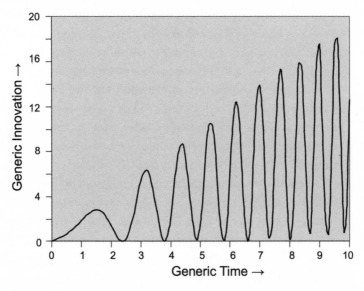

Figure 7.3
Heading toward singularity: ever-increasing and deepening Kondratieff waves.

population associated with demographic transition. But there are other massive singularities in prospect, particularly through radical advances in health care and medical interventions in the body that will prolong life, according to Kurzweil, but also in technology due to machine learning and the kind of artificial intelligence hinted at earlier.[40] This is the message preached by Brynjolfsson and McAfee, who suggest we are in a race to make sure our machines do not create an artificial intelligence that overwhelms us.[41] The rate of change in this context appears to be speeding up, not slowing down, as we pass threshold after threshold in what machines can extract from the fire hose of data now being fed to them. This we will describe and speculate on in the next and final chapter with respect to the impact it is likely to make on the city of the future.

The Future City

There is another question that cannot be answered in any definitive way, and that is: what will the city look like in the near-, medium-, or longer-term future? Our best guess is to look back and simply examine the superficiality of urban form, not function. Street patterns tend to be quite inert, while the growth of big cities is determined by culture and physiography. Of course, communications technology tends to remain familiar, and although everything looks quaint and old-fashioned in cities of the past, certainly back 100 years ago, they still appear to be "similar" to those of the present and even those, we might speculate, of the near future. It is urban functions that change, and it is very likely that the disconnect between form and function, which became evident in the 1970s, will continue full pelt until we become almost entirely connected digitally and virtually footloose locationally in terms of interacting between one place and any other. In essence, there are plenty of reasons why form may still follow function, but the disconnect is a powerful force, and it will ultimately play out when most of the functions we engage in can be operated remotely from places where they were once located.

Add to this all the very obvious automation that is in the pipeline. Many services that are currently unregulated and have emerged because of network communications—such as Uber, Airbnb and so on—do not appear to be making much impact on spatial behavior per se. Self-driving cars and related technologies that depend intrinsically on machine learning and massive historical and current data acquisition will have some effect, but the complexity of a bottom-up environment is such that this may be a lot more limited than some suggest. There is no doubt that automation in cars and connected vehicles will advance, while the substitution of renewables for fossil fuels is likely to proceed quite rapidly. Advances in construction and materials closely related to new digital technologies at all scales will make a difference to the way we design and use buildings, and the prospect of connected buildings like connected cars is on the horizon. In terms of tools we will use to explore, understand, and predict, automated physical models of cities' three-dimensional form are likely to emerge in real time, and to these will be linked various functions and flows that can also be captured almost instantaneously. Thus the notion of an immediate and continuously changing digital picture of the city is in prospect. How we interact with such tools is at issue. How we use them to produce cities that are less unequal and in which quality of life is massively improved are age-old questions. We will address some of these in our last chapter.

This list of futures is a little bit like the list of smart city technologies critiqued as being somewhat mindless earlier in this chapter, but it simply serves to show that the future is unclear—not necessarily confused, but uncertain in its detail. There is no doubt that the proliferation of digital networks—all determined by activities, many yet to be invented, and all generating data about their functioning, but most being hard to relate to individual human attributes other than the fact that individuals operate them in some way—will provide a more complex future than anything we have had to grapple with so far. In this sense, the age of the smart city is one of increasing complexity and variety, which has always been the case from the earliest cities. This makes the prospect of generating informed analysis of the future city ever more difficult. There are other significant drivers, too, we have not mentioned as yet, such as aging and climate change, that need to be factored in as well. But what is certain is that, as Haldane[42] said many years ago:

> Our only hope of understanding the universe is to look at it from as many different points of view as possible.... My own suspicion is that the universe is not only queerer than we suppose, but queerer than we can suppose.... I suspect that there are more things in heaven and earth than are dreamed of, or can be dreamed of, in any philosophy.

The limits on our ability to predict the form of future cities are largely due to the fact that we are part and parcel of their future creation and design.

8 The Inventive Century

Inventing is a lot like surfing: you have to anticipate and catch the wave at just the right time.

—Ray Kurzweil, *The Singularity Is Near*, 3

Kurzweil does not suggest his waves are like those proposed by Kondratieff and Schumpeter, but his theory of accelerating returns is built on the same premise: inventions spur innovations in technology, which take the limelight for a limited time only to be superseded by new innovations, which begin the cycle over again.[1] In fact, he suggests these waves accumulate as a succession of logistic S-shaped curves that build on one another in much the same way we might interpret Kondratieff cycles in their cumulative form. But as we discussed in the last chapter, these waves are ever increasing in intensity, getting closer and closer, crashing into one another and overlapping in such a way that they provide an impression of superexponential growth in our inventive capacities. This, Kurzweil predicts, will lead to a singularity beyond which we have no experience of what life will be like. Although we will not sketch out his vision of this new world, for it lies beyond our wilder speculations, we will explore the kinds of mechanisms that are forcing waves of technological change toward a regime of "continuous invention." In this sense, we are rapidly moving along the road to an "inventive century."

Before we discuss in more depth the kinds of future technologies that are coming to dominate the city, we will say a little more about invention, for our premise is that the future is something we invent anyway. Although we may be able to anticipate some inventions to a degree, in general, predictability is simply not possible when it comes to envisaging what the future city will be like. In fact, we might argue that the city itself is the product of our inventiveness. Although it has taken a long time—over 5,000 years—to emerge in its present form, we argued in chapters 1 and 2 that during this century, the transition from a world of "no cities" to a world of "all cities" will become complete. That is, this future marks a transition from "city 1.0" to "city 2.0" to "city ... n," as some commentators have suggested, but also a kind of clean break between a nonurban and urban world: "no city" to "city." If you have read to this point, by now you will have gathered that when we speak of inventing the future city, we do not mean establishing physical visions of the future in the manner of Frank Lloyd Wright or Le Corbusier. There is nothing wrong with these visions, for we consider them an important part of speculation. Indeed, in comparison with our inability to predict, they are useful images on which to focus when we examine the future. Freeman Dyson[2] reinforces this when he says:

> Economic forecasting makes predictions by extrapolating curves of growth from the past to the future. Science fiction makes a wild guess and leaves the judgment of its plausibility to the reader. ... For the future beyond ten years ahead, science fiction is a more useful guide than forecasting.

So these visions are still relevant, but the future we envisage must be explored using the basic principles we have established for thinking about cities in the past and the present. These are Glaeser's paradox, the standard model due to von Thünen, Well's proposition, and Tobler's first law of geography, while not forgetting our first principle—Zipf's law—which suggests that city-size distributions in the future will be much like the past, with many smaller cities than larger across many spatial and temporal scales. In this chapter, we will explore how these ideas can be used to speculate on how we might invent future cities. Before we do, however, we will return to the prospect that this century will be one of continuous invention.

In the next section, we will elaborate this idea of invention as a prelude to thinking about the city as a process rather than product. When we make this switch—which is consistent with all we have said about cities being complex systems—the focus changes from the physical and visual to the functional, enabling us to think much more clearly about questions of technology and automation in cities that we will then discuss. We need to explore the massive waves of change in automation that are currently besetting contemporary society and their effects on cities, particularly on mobility, which lies at the core of the five basic principles (associated with size, shape, and distance) we consider key to the way cities are structured. We will also embrace how these questions relate to social structure and inequality. We have said little or nothing about these questions in this book, for we do not believe we can produce a completely synoptic and synthetic view of cities: in short, we cannot produce a general theory of the city, for cities are too diverse and complex and admit a multitude, indeed an infinity, of perspectives and viewpoints. But we do need to say a little in our conclusions with respect to the big questions that dominate our time, such as climate change, aging, energy, sustainability, migration, and of course inequality. All we will do, however, is point the way, directing the reader to how to think about these problems, not suggesting solutions or even reactions, but simply ensuring some consistency with the approach to cities advocated here.

Continuous Invention

The best way to portray that we appear to moving to a time when inventions are continuous is to examine the speed at which personal communication devices have emerged over the last 200 years. Looking at the time it has taken for these devices to penetrate the population reveals a dramatic speed-up. The telegraph, invented in 1837, was hardly a personal device, but it was quite quickly taken over by the telephone, which was invented in 1876. Kurzweil tells us that it took some 40 years for the telephone to reach (be available to) one-quarter of the US population,[3] followed by the radio, first introduced in the 1900s, which took some 35 years to reach the same percentage of the population. The television, introduced in the late 1920s, took 25 years, while the personal computer, developed in the late 1970s, took 15. Next came the mobile phone, which developed by the mid-1990s. Rudimentary smartphones were first introduced only 10 years ago, but reached one-quarter of the US population in less than five. Moving on to access to networking, the World Wide Web, first popularized in the early 1990s, took about eight years. In the case of each of these inventions, their genesis goes back much further, but once they emerged with production-level quality and quantity, their penetration times have continued to shorten.

We provide a picture of this convergence in figure 8.1, where we show how the temporal trajectories of growth of these technologies are collapsing into and onto one another.[4] Of course, there has been considerable convergence between these devices. For example, the smartphone is now used much more as a generic device to access instant information of many kinds: currently, on average, these devices are used for voice communications

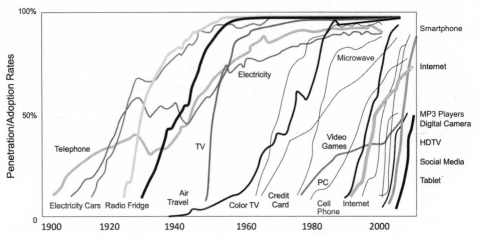

From oldest to newest, left to right, the technologies are ordered as Telephone, Electricity, Cars, Radio, Fridge, TV, Air Travel, Color TV, Credit Card, Microwave, Video Games, PC, Cell Phone, Internet, Digital Camera, MP3 Players, HDTV, Social Media, Smartphone, Tablet

Figure 8.1
The temporal penetration and diffusion of analog and digital devices.

only 20 percent of the time. Moreover, they are used as cameras, web access devices, even Wi-Fi hotspots, and they represent a convergence of palm computers from the early 1990s, mobile phones from the late 1990s, and online video and television, which dominate much of the content accessed using these devices. They are now also widely used to access location-based services and information that pertains to how we move around the city engaging in various kinds of retail purchasing, which is having an enormous impact on the location of different functions within the city. In fact, we might say these devices are disruptive of previous patterns of use in all these senses.

What happens next? What is the next device to be introduced and adopted? It may well be the already available watch/computer. But whatever it is, it is likely to involve some convergence of traditional and new devices. Electronic paper with erasable memory has been talked about for years. Simple, noninvasive digital implants might become commonplace in our bodies. But the key point of all this is to show that access to information technologies and the development of the new are speeding up. Technology is being embedded in many physical objects: in this sense, we already talk about an "Internet of Things" (IOT), which is fast being wired into the great array of objects that define our physical world. These developments in information devices, which are directly linked to Moore's law, are but the tip of the iceberg when it comes to automation. The growth of artificial intelligence (AI), machine translation, all kinds of real-time sentient data, and data generated directly by our own actions are all growing at superexponential rates.

We will briefly examine two from the many examples of how such inventions are disrupting city life, focusing on new developments in mobility. Once we have instant access to individuals through our devices, this enables massive decentralization of demand and supply for different services. If you can call up any person who can, in principle, supply a service to you almost instantly, then a system emerges where demand and supply are matched much more efficiently, since traditional systems always require physical access to some central pool. The example of personalized taxi services like Uber are a case in point: it is clear that those requiring transport can be matched to transportation much more efficiently in this system than via traditional fixed services. In short, the liquidity of the system is much enhanced by an almost instant ability to communicate. However, services like Uber do generate key problems. There is little doubt their economics disrupt the established order, but like all bottom-up activity, these services are hard to regulate, and they do require rules if standards are to be maintained and a free-for-all avoided. This is also true of all kinds of individualized digital activity, such as Twitter and Facebook, which fall foul of what traditionally have been centralized and minimal, yet widely agreed-upon, policing services. But for all their obvious disruption of existing mobility, it is unlikely that services such as Uber will make that much difference to location patterns in cities. It is possible that there may be indirect effects on other transport if this reduces demand substantially for services which can only be provided by traditional means, such as those subsidized by government, in particular. Yet overall patterns of demand are not likely to change much: demand might be high, but this is not likely to change location patterns in and of themselves.[5]

On the other hand, our second example is one in which demand and supply can exercise positive feedback on each other to change locational patterns. Postal and parcel services at the local level, which might be part of much wider systems at national and global levels, are beginning to take advantage of instant communication, particularly with respect to collecting goods and shipping them directly to those requesting them. The practice is also growing of packages that are ordered online and then delivered to some central point—like a local warehouse—where the customer picks them up. Amazon, for example, uses such a system. It is also extending work flows to solicit interest from drivers who might routinely cover an area of the city—for example, on their journey to other employment—enabling them to pick up and deliver small packages for the company, thus extending the labor market for this kind of activity. In fact, the very activity of online retailing is changing location patterns in cities. Noting again the general premises adopted in this book, changes in such interactions lead to changes in the volumes and types of activities that locate in different places.[6]

Indeed, information is so generic to the city that any new technology that enables it to be used in ways different from the past or the present has the potential to change urban form and function, with varying degrees of disruption. Currently, the impact of new information technology on the economy, social interaction, demography, and fostering economic and social inequality is gathering pace to become what might appear to be a "perfect storm." Much of what is happening is not coordinated in any way, and the sheer scale of change is likely to bring many diseconomies in its wake. The information deluge we now face is enormous, and it is entirely possible that the difficulties of building well-functioning information technology systems are leading to a long-term loss in productivity as we struggle to deal with multiple passwords and badly structured human-computer interfaces that do not enable us to search efficiently, quickly, and without bias (which is often unknown to the user), while also distorting the quest or task in hand. Moore's law is writ large in how new technologies and their embedding into the economy and the city are leading to new patterns of disruption, whose impact on form and function is as yet entirely uncertain due to its comparative invisibility.[7] The impacts, however, on the many tasks we formally engage in and that are at the base of a productive economy are at major risk of automation. Before we sketch what all this might imply for the physical form of the future city, it is worth taking time out to examine what is happening at the cutting edge of this automation.

Disruption, Automation, and Autonomy

In one sense, all change is disruptive in that it forces populations out of their existing modes of behavior and patterns of thinking, requiring them to adapt to new conditions and develop new practices. The degree of disruption, however, depends upon the proportion of people unable to adapt, and extreme disruption occurs when most of the affected population simply refuses to adopt new innovations or technologies. Moreover, the question of whether the supply of the service, or the demand, is disrupted is the problem at issue. In the case of something like Uber, the supply, which is based on existing modes of transport, might be severely disrupted by loss of jobs, while the demand by the population easily adapts, and in fact leads to a pattern that possibly acts in an overall more efficient way. To an extent, in cities, the focus is not in planning for a better quality of life by changing behaviors, but on enabling it through changes to the physical form to which people might adapt, thereby changing their actions and superficially their behavioral patterns. Disruptions in demand and supply have the power to invoke such possibilities where locational patterns might unravel.

Multiple disruptions that are largely uncoordinated, generating order effects over different regimes—first order, second order, nth order, and so on—are fast becoming the dominant scenario for future cities. Moore's law, which lies at the basis of this, has operated now for more than 50 years. Despite limits on the speed of light, which have always remained an upper bound on chip speed (and size), the law shows little sign of slowing down, as much because developments in other features of computable processes not involving raw chip technology are continually improving performance and increasing speeds. Quantum computing is on the horizon, and of course breaking up computation into sequences of tasks has always been a favorite strategy for reducing costs, increasing overall speeds of execution, and extending memory through parallel processing. Massive parallel computing—with dramatically improved memory, clock speed, storage of data, and processed results—combined with the collation of vast amounts of human behavioral data are together producing waves of change, generating a storm front that is responsible for all the hype about autonomous vehicles and machines described a little later.

These inventions ultimately affect the structure of jobs in any economy. Since prehistory, some concept of work has dominated all societies; it is only in the last 50 years that the notion we might actually need to work less has come onto the agenda. At the beginning of the Agricultural Revolution, around 10,000 BCE, mankind moved from a subsistence economy and nomadic existence to an era where most were employed in agriculture.

A decreasing proportion acted as hunter-gatherers, and agriculture continued to evolve until cities emerged around about 3,000 BCE in ancient Sumeria.[8] This period of dominant agriculture lasted until the first Industrial Revolution, although services became quite distinct in cities during these times. This then changed the structure of employment dramatically as agriculture declined in the face of automation in farming practices, while the development of various machine technologies reduced the demand for labor on the land as well as ways in which agricultural produce was packaged and marketed. In the West, the agricultural base, which traditionally had constituted more than half of all employment, fell systematically through the 19th century until it reached less than 15 percent by the early 20th century. The fact that this did not lead to mass unemployment is attributed to demand for new services, and thus tertiary industries grew to take up the shortfall. This substitution effect, of course, could only happen in an economy where such disruptions could lead to greater economic benefits. Manufacturing industries dominated until the middle of the last century, when automation really began to kick in. This marked the beginning of a period of rapid de-industrialization in the developed world, and by the end of the 20th century, manufacturing had fallen to less than 10 percent of the workforce in many Western countries. It was services and their elaboration into finance, education, and health care that grew to fill the vacuum, and once again, the economy was able to grow to support these transitions.

Many commentators speculate that we are once again facing a dramatic transition in employment as the dominant service sectors face rapid automation of their functions. This is the second Machine Age, a term introduced by Brynjolfsson and McAfee, who paint a picture of a future where many service jobs will be eliminated by a combination of two forces: first, the acquisition of smartphones and related communications devices by most of the population; and second, by AI, more specifically machine-learning methods that are generating automated ways of replacing human tasks.[9] Most populations in developed countries (excepting the poorest, oldest, or disabled) have access most of the time to devices that enable them to communicate with each other and with remote information sources. This lets those who wish to do so develop a degree of interactivity that is beginning to have disruptive effects on production and consumption. The labor market is undergoing a new form of restructuring wherein jobs are being automated faster than new ones are being created. Whether this will continue is always an open question, for in the past new forms of employ-ment have developed. One might speculate that jobs in health care, educa-tion, traditional craft industries, and niche manufacturing could fill the gap. But these jobs are being automated, too. The picture is quite unclear, and the impacts these changes will have on population and location in cities are uncertain.

Automation of communications technology relates to old communica-tions being destroyed—such as the postal service, telephone operations, and so on—while, at the same time, rendering obsolete jobs that in the past had been provided as services to the population at large, since they are now being undertaken by ourselves as individuals. Automation of many service jobs is now possible because of advances in software that enable machines to enact protocols that replace manual labor by ourselves. There is no doubt that much routine accounting can be sped up dramatically and related bureaucracies downsized by such possibilities. The extent to which such innovations will come to pass depends very largely on the degree to which tasks can be made explicit and automated. Clearly many can, but it is likely many cannot. There are fundamental limits on a variety of human decision-making tasks that will never be automated, since they involve cru-cial human choices. Automated platforms for integrating such software are on the horizon, but their widespread implementation has had a dreadful track record so far. In fact, big software projects involving thousands of agents and actors have faced many problems of integration, and although it is likely some progress will be made, their future is uncertain.

We could spend a long time agonizing over these possibilities, but it is worth saying one last word about automation, since it could well affect cities very considerably in the near future. This relates to inanimate objects, such as powered vehicles, that inhabit the city, but it also applies to any kind of physical artifact that can be endowed with "intelligence." The word intelli-gence is in quotes because the prospect of truly intelligent machines—where intelligence is defined as akin to human intelligence—is highly controversial and most unlikely. Currently, very rapid strides are being made exploring patterns in areas where data can be acquired in real time, data akin to that defined in chapter 5 as the pulse of the city. The kinds of data mining tak-ing place pertaining to human behaviors that occur in real time involve extracting fundamental patterns using powerful techniques of multivariate analysis, thus exploiting these for automating routine processes.[10]

These associated analytics are usually implemented by neural nets that simply assume many layers of variable—neurons—that are activated according to a sequential process of choosing weights that make the inputs to the process more and more consistent with the outputs. In this way, an almost perfect replication of the process of linking inputs and outputs takes place, but without any real understanding. As these weights become better representations of the process of linking inputs and outputs, the neurons are said to be "learning," and if there are many layers of these elements, this is referred to as "deep learning." It is only deep in the sense of there being many layers, not in terms of our necessarily knowing how inputs are connected to outputs—that is, in terms of explanation. In fact, face recognition has been one of the main applications for which such systems have been developed, and in that context, there is no interest in scientific explanation of how the features of a face are built up. All one is interested in is the pattern.[11] Generally, these data mining projects involve systems that are treated as black boxes where all one has is the input and the output, with no attempt to explain or even infer the meaning of the outputs with respect to the models used to connect inputs to outputs. These kinds of analysis may certainly be suitable for machine translation, as in the case of Google's translation software, or for automated robots working in an industrial context where routine tasks are fairly independent of human decision makers, but whether this kind of AI will ever replace any aspect of human decision making, design, and creation is an open question. It does not seem likely. Machines are simply different from organisms. At the level of physical function, dry is very different from wet.

In the case of systems where we interact with machines, there are many potential problems. Take an autonomous vehicle, for example—a three-body system comprising the car, the driver, and the environment in which the ensemble sits. The driver cannot be divorced from the car, but if so detached, the driver becomes the passenger, and the system reduces to a two-body problem. Even then, simply thinking about the operation of an autonomous vehicle in a noisy environment suggests that it would be near impossible to produce enough scanning equipment to sense the entire range of possibilities in and out of the car. Add the human back in, and any automated environment would require the system to resolve crucial choices involving interactions between humans in the actual environment and the car environment. And as we know, defining a system with respect to its environment is fraught with difficulty. Even by accumulating millions of miles of automated car-driver information, complete automation would not seem possible. Even linking every car to every other car globally, in a future with undreamed of information resources, it would still not seem possible to envisage all possible futures and thus avoid important dilemmas. One of our theses in this book is that the future is invented by ourselves—and self-driving cars that have nothing of this built in are unlikely to become universal. We cannot define away our ability to invent, and this means, somewhat perversely, that we cannot define away our ability to cause accidents. Therein lies the dilemma. Whether or not the case of the fatal accident associated with the iconic Tesla car in 2016 will be forgotten by the time this book is published is unclear, but even if it was driver error—whatever that is—then once again it highlights the limits of our current approach to AI. This has been reinforced by the recent accident in Arizona where an autonomous vehicle killed a pedestrian thinking that the obstacle in front of it was something to be dismissed, like a "plastic bag": further limits on what AI can do.[12]

Artificial intelligence was something Turing speculated on in the early days of digital computation. In one of his seminal papers, "Computing Machinery and Intelligence," published in 1950, he wrote:[13] "We may hope that machines will eventually compete with men in all purely intellectual fields." But the history of the field is littered with obstacles. The view now is that machines will always be different and that competition between computers and people is not an effective strategy for inventing the future. The original approach, which has been gradually abandoned, assumed that one could build rational models of mankind in order to mimic human decision making. This approach went the same way as Chomsky's linguistics, which saw formal language translation systems overtaken by massive databases in which key patterns of speech were discovered. The rule-based approach to AI was found wanting in the highly applied area of robotics, while the notion of searching for pattern in big data and then simply assuming this was the way the world worked, without explaining it, came to be the preferred strategy. In fact, there are now growing reactions to this dominant inductive approach to learning, and the rule-based approach might be beginning to reassert itself in parts of the field.[14] But whatever the approach—and it may well become a mix of both—there may still be some radical developments that will affect city and society. It is these to which we should now turn.

Idealized City Forms

Idealized cities are invariably proposed from the top down by visionaries intent on emphasizing certain principles and ideals, but usually with an intention that they might be implemented. To an extent, these are thought experiments that focus on the form of future cities. As we have already emphasized, real cities grow from the bottom up, as the product of millions of decisions made by individuals and collectives that generate great variety and heterogeneity, and which are noisy and seemingly blurred by random developments (that may in fact not be random at all, but are clearly not coordinated with one another). It is rare, however, for idealized forms to match the way cities actually grow. This disconnect is sufficient to suggest that the actual invention of the future city is a process dramatically different from the musing of visionaries, since it consists of those millions of individual decisions that in and of themselves must be treated as inventions. It is in this sense that the future city is entirely unpredictable, full of novelty and surprise. Cities are complex systems, as we have implied throughout this book.[15]

This also explains why it is so hard to be certain about the development of automation and autonomous technologies. For example, any system involving autonomous vehicles is inevitably open to the wider environment, which is full of uncoordinated decisions, and in this sense, it is quite unpredictable. It is hard enough to speculate on how new technologies and all the other features of continuous invention will impact the future form of cities in ways that influence how we locate and interact. But once we move to the nonspatial domains, the challenges for thinking about the future are dramatically magnified. Most visionaries in thinking about future cities rarely think about future behaviors, but this has and will continue to be a focus with respect to future technologies. Moreover, visionary future cities are almost entirely physical and visual in form. They stress a limited number—often only one or two—key determinants, such as density, building height, or transport geometries, in explaining their form; and they are invariably pictured as less than the full city, often being focused on single city blocks, cross-sections through a central business district (CBD) zone or neighborhood, and thus rarely illustrate how the wider set of various urban functions defining the complete city relate to its form. In an era when form is being rapidly disconnected from function in the most obvious and perhaps immediate ways, a vision for the future that does not show how form determines function, and vice versa—as our understanding of cities so far has sought to do—has little relevance to an environment where the determinants of city forms are much more complex, intricate, and indirect than they ever have been in the past.

The earliest idealizations of cities were certainly articulated in classical times, but the line between the ideal and the real becomes increasingly blurred as one goes back in time. The Roman camp (or *castrum*) was an ideal model that had great rigidity but also could be implemented quickly as armies advanced in the quest to conquer and exploit territory they had gained. In ancient Athens, Plato and Socrates alike (as noted in chapter 4) discussed the form of the ideal city, but mainly in terms of its size, organization, and government rather than its spatial extent. By and large, these early examples, when illustrated by real cities such as Miletus, a Greek colonial city on the coast of Asia Minor shown in figure 4.2(a) in chapter 4, reveal a highly geometric grid pattern with some semblance of a center or CBD around the agora and forum, but no real structure that resembles the standard model. In short, as many of the principles of city form and function were not invented until the Industrial Revolution—partly as a consequence of the rise of the industrial city anyway—it is not surprising that these are not completely reflected in early idealized city plans or in the earliest cities.

The rediscovery of the classical world in 15th century Europe through the Renaissance led to a spate of ideal cities,[16] most with quite well-defined CBDs or market forums; sectors of differing activities radiating out from the center like spokes of a wheel; and well-defined, crenelated boundaries for defensive purposes. Typical idealizations are shown in figure 8.2(a). Some of these were actually built, such as Naarden[17] in the Netherlands, shown in figure 8.2(b), and Palmanova in Italy, illustrated in figure 4.3(d). But it was the emergence of the industrial city that really brought clear structure to spatial form as reflected in the standard model, in which concentric rings of activities, radial transport routes, and a well-defined CBD stand out. As the 19th century wore on and various reactions against the conditions of the industrial city gathered pace, the idea of cities organized to reduce densities, with open space liberally scattered around and with clear neighborhood structure, came to be partly reflected in proposals for the ideal city. In figures 8.3(a) to 8.3(c), we show again parts of Howard's late 19th-century plan for the garden city, which has much-reduced densities, building on the idea that the city is like a suburb within a garden.[18]

a)

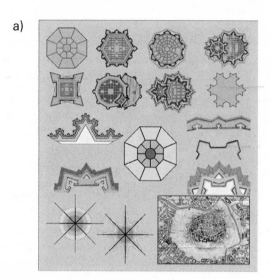

b)

Figure 8.2
Idealized Renaissance town plans: (a) a sample of idealized plans; b) Naarden, built in
Holland from the 14th century.

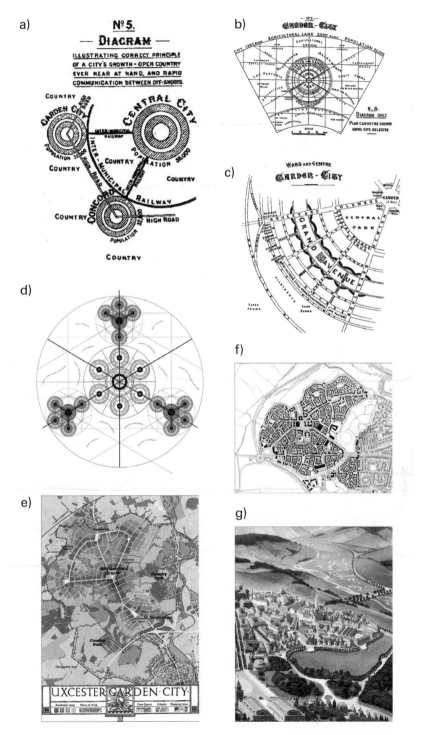

Figure 8.3
Old and new garden cities: (a–c) Howard's 1898 Plan; (d–e) the New Garden City Plan 2015 for "Uxcester"; (f–g) New Urbanism at Poundbury.

Howard's idealization, however, is only superficially like the city structures we observe in reality. The concepts of neighborhood and center are clear, but their size and distribution are based on very simplistic thinking, without any consideration of functional dependence in terms of what can be sustained. The distribution of functions in cities follows Zipf's law, and all the other properties and activities we know about real cities in terms of density and distribution follow what are now well-defined physical-spatial functions. The mismatch with observable spatial distributions is true of virtually all ideal cities, for their progenitors are rarely versed in the kinds of ideas that come from sustained study of the size and shape of the city.[19] Indeed, the late 19th century, when many of these ideas were spawned, was the beginning of the statistical study of the city.

The interest in ideal cities has waxed and waned over the last two millennia. In classical times, there was some interest, but it was largely confined to the efficiency of the grid. The reawakening of ideal city forms had to wait for the Renaissance and, following it, the Enlightenment in Europe, when a flowering of such ideas began. The great industrialist-philanthropists of the late 19th century began another wave of interest, and during the first half of the 20th century, this wave was excited by the prospect of urban renewal after World War II. But ideal cities fell out of fashion in the last half of the 20th century; only now is there a revival of interest. In fact, these idealizations have become related to real cities through time. In figures 8.3(d) and (e) we show the proposal for an ideal and sustainable city in the Oxford region developed by Urbed[20] to compare it with Howard's 1898 plan. Interestingly, Urbed's current plan contains much of the diversity and randomness that one sees in most real cities. Although it is a virtual certainty that the architects and planners who worked on this proposal did not really consider any of the formal principles of size, shape, and distribution that define all cities,[21] they knew enough about this informally to be able to inject a modicum of such thinking into the plan itself. In figures 8.3(f) and (g), we show an example of the new urbanism, which has so captured recent American thinking about self-sufficient and sustainable communities, designed by the architect Leon Krier[22] for the village of Poundbury in the United Kingdom.

There is a class of idealized cities that are determined according to their transportation. The notion of the linear city, in contrast to the compact, radially concentric city such as that proposed by Howard, has found some favor. These proposals privilege one dimension—transport—against all others. One of the first proposals, for example—by Arturo Soria y Mata, shown in figure 8.4(a)—is arrayed along a fast railway link, which arguably produces much more accessible transportation.[23] The MARS Plan for London, shown in figure 8.4(b), also transforms a large city such as London, with its radial structure, into a grid of north-south corridors.[24] This bizarre construction is even more remarkable given that the dominant structures in terms of transportation in London are east-west. The plan for a car-dominated city in Milton Keynes (the last of the British new towns), produced by Llewelyn-Davies, Weeks, Forestier-Walker, and Bor[25] and shown in figure 8.4(c), now looks strangely dated, since public transport has been slowly introduced to compensate for the fact that by no means everyone drives a car or is able to walk to work along roads with no sidewalks. Last but not least, there have been countless experiments with hexagonal networks, presumably because they look "good" from the air. Two bizarre constructions are those by Rudolf Mueller in his proposal for The City of the Future,[26] which develops the notion that the city should be arranged as hexagons for purposes of accessibility, while Charles Lamb's City Plan has streets intersect the hexagonal cells.[27] The hexagon is interesting as a neighborhood unit due to its geometric properties, but at the end of the day, this is an ideal type, notwithstanding that it maps nicely onto Christaller's system of central places,[28] which gives a strong economic rationale to the geometry of the city. These hexagonal structures are shown in figures 8.4(d) to 8.4(f).

It is easy to critique these ideal types on the basis that their authors do not relate their form to what we observe in the various ways cities have evolved, but much of this science has taken a long time coming, and there is by no means widespread agreement about what constitutes fundamental laws governing the structure of cities. To an extent, these visions belong to a bygone age, although those who speculate on the future of cities often express their ideas in the most obvious form, which is visual, in two dimensions as in the map or plan or in three dimensions when it comes to buildings. Many populate these visions with ideas about future technologies, mainly mechanical, for the invisibility of digital technologies makes it hard to present future cities in terms of the new patterns of interaction we have introduced in this and previous chapters. It would be interesting to take all these visions of future city forms and subject them to a sustained analysis with the various principles identified here involving Zipf's law, Glaeser's paradox, von Thünen's

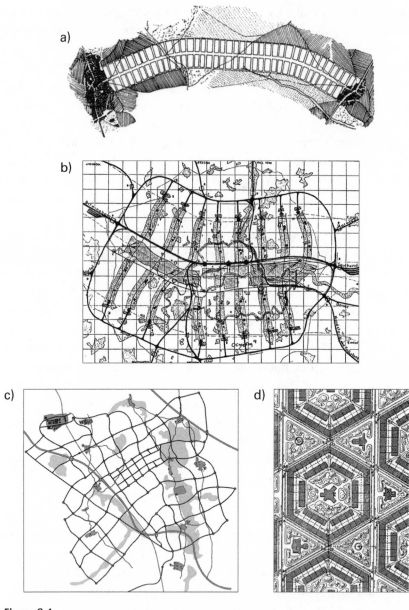

Figure 8.4
20th-century idealized city plans: (a) Ciudad Lineal, 1882; (b) MARS Plan for London, 1933–1942; (c) Milton Keynes, New Town, 1969; (d) Mueller's City of the Future, 1908; (e) Lamb's City Plan, 1904; (f) Christaller's idealized central places; (g) Christaller's realized central places, 1933.

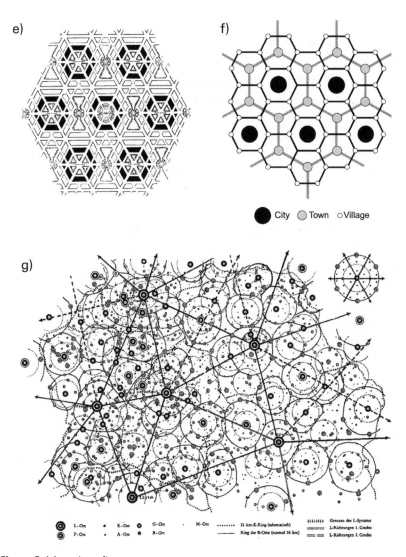

e)

f)

City   Town   Village

g)

L-Ort   K-Ort   G-Ort   M-Ort   ········ 21 km-K-Ring (schematisch)   ++++++++ Grenzen der L-Systeme
P-Ort   A-Ort   B-Ort   Ring der B-Orte (normal 36 km)   L-Richtungen 1. Grades
                                                                                        L-Richtungen 2. Grades

Figure 8.4 (continued)

standard model, Wells's proposition, and Tobler's first law of geography. But it is not possible to do this systematically, because these visions are not rich enough in analytical terms to unpack in this way. Indeed, although some of those who have made such proposals certainly believe they could be implemented, they remain first and foremost thought experiments, ideas that we can use in helping us set up a dialogue about the future city, not proposals that should be turned into a future reality. Their focus on simple principles may help us clarify our discussion of the future, but these will not provide us with ready-made inventions that, in any event, must emerge from the bottom up.

Social Restructuring: Spatial Inequalities in the City

There are a million and one things to consider when we think about cities, and so far in this book we have studiously avoided the social dimension. Here we are not able to do much more than point to the directions in which we think the arguments we espouse might be taken forward with respect to social structure in cities, but we can easily suggest how the physical form adapts to reinforce or reduce social inequalities in which persons of different status (however they be defined) segregate themselves in cities. We have already seen an example of this in our standard model, introduced in chapter 4, which showed that the bands of similar land use at increasing radial distances from the core of the city could be associated with different income and ethnic groups. The archetypal example is Chicago, illustrated in figure 4.4(b) in chapter 4. In this process, one group might invade a neighborhood, thereby instituting a succession in which another group would filter themselves out to more distant places with a better quality of life. This happens because groups of richer and probably more dominant ethnicity are able to purchase more space and afford the transportation to more distant locations away from the CBD. This releases already developed housing for less wealthy groups and, if the process continues in this way, there is a sea change when either distance from the city becomes too great for further sprawl around its edge, or travel costs to the central location increase more than proportionately, canceling out any profit in location. In an already developed city, this is invasion by one group, and its succession to the location of a displaced group, in which the bands of residential land they occupy diffuse regularly until growth stops or the physical limits of the city are reached. In this case, there may well be a return to the city, with the poorest being displaced by richer groups who out-bid them closer to the center. This process has been called gentrification, and we can envisage all these transitions generating a series of waves of growth that switch back and forth on themselves as the city fills up.

The main driver for these changes is population growth. If the growth of a city were to stop and decline set in, then processes of invasion and succession would also stop and be replaced by abandonment, as has happened in some large US cities like Detroit. It is never as simple as this, of course, because the drivers of the local economy are also key to where people live and work, but only when the city is growing does this process assert itself, with the rich pre-ferring new locations around the edge and the poor replacing the rich where they once lived. In fact, even if a city stops growing and decline begins, richer groups can still abandon the inner part of the city for the suburbs and beyond, again as in the case of Detroit. Within the spatial envelopes that contain these processes, there is also a filtering that depends on positive feed-backs that enable different social groups to reinforce the location and growth of their own kind. For example, if a niche opens for a new social group to find an acceptable location, this may herald a process of attracting like groups to the emergent cluster, which, as it grows, becomes ever more attractive to that group, thus reinforcing the position of the group within the city. This may be accompanied by a flight of those who are already established in that location, the classic example being "white flight" in US cities as black neighborhoods become established. This is not necessarily ghettoization; it may be. but it applies to any two or more groups who are competing for space in the city, with one gradually becoming more dominant due to relative preference for the neighborhood in question.

There is a particularly clever demonstration of this effect originally devel-oped by Thomas Schelling.[29] Imagine a grid of locations populated evenly by two different social groups. The disposition of these groups is that on the first row of the grid, an individual from group 1 locates in the first square on the left, from group 2 in the second square, from group 1 in the third square and so on. In the second row, the first square is an individual from group 2, the second from group 1, the third from group 2 and so on. In this way, the land-scape is a checkerboard pattern of individuals from group 1 alternating with group 2. Now let us assume these two groups have a mild preference for living among their own kind, but they are quite content to live in this checker-board existence where an individual is surrounded by four neighbors of their own group and four of the second group. Thus they live in harmony and nothing changes. However, if one of them changes their allegiance to their group—from 1 to 2, say, then at each adjacent location, the balance changes, with the individual at the adjacent cell being surrounded by three of their own kind or five of the other—or vice versa. This imbalance then sets off a process of individuals changing their group affiliations. If you are surrounded by five of your own kind and three of another kind, you are quite satisfied, but if the other way around, you are not, and you then consider changing affiliation. If this process continues, by a process of positive feedback, clusters or ghettos of single groups will emerge, and the checkerboard landscape will unravel into quite clearly segregated patterns. We show this picture in figures 8.5(a) and (b). In fact, it is more likely that individuals will change their locations than their group affiliations, but to do so, there needs to be enough space in the landscape grid. If we create such an expanded landscape, the same kind of segregated pattern emerges, with individuals moving to the nearest empty cell, say, but the pattern of segregation may be slightly less marked because of the empty space. Nevertheless, it still occurs.[30]

Just how representative is this process of the way different social groups emerge, cluster, and segregate in cities? To an extent, there is somewhat more to the process we have outlined. Positive feedback, the emergence of segregated clusters from scratch without any invasion and succession occurring, as well as different degrees of stickiness associated with the process of moving or changing one's mind all characterize this kind of segregation. Segregation often occurs immediately as the city grows: certain areas are barred from occupation by some groups, not simply because of different access to cash resources or ancient ownership rights, but because of the political and social power structure. Figure 8.5(c) shows an example of the kind of hard boundary associated with ethnic segregation in a South African city. Without going into the details of how this phenomenon happens or precisely what this is, it is sufficient to note that the only way such hard edges can occur is through political control of the use of land.[31] This often implies some form of hard discrimination, somewhat different from the softer preference bias associated with Schelling's model.[32] In figure 8.5(d), we contrast this with a rather different hard edge in which development sprawls up to a boundary imposed by either physical constraints, limits created by land ownership, or simply the mechanics of the development process.[33] Both figures 8.5(c) and

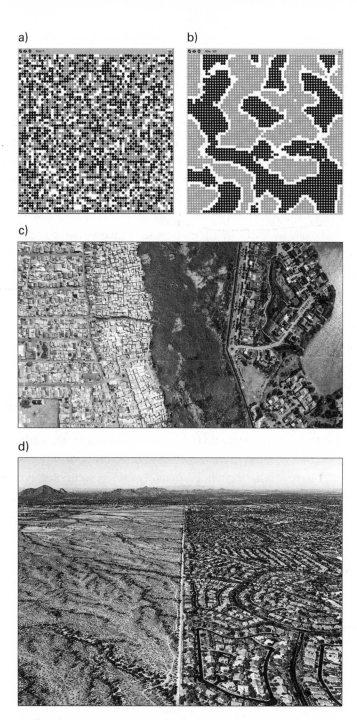

Figure 8.5
Schelling's segregation: (a) an initial landscape of two randomly positioned social groups; (b) the segregated landscape after its unraveling; (c) a real picture of segregation in South Africa; (d) the edge of sprawl in Phoenix, AZ.

(d) show how difficult it is to simply look at urban form and infer the functions that have led to it, for these latter figures could easily have been created by processes of clustering akin to those in the Schelling model.

Income, ethnic group, social class, and many other characterizations of social structure are often highly correlated. Although this may be clearly evident when one looks at cities, it is hard to unravel the processes that lead to such differences simply from the patterns—forms and functions—that we have focused upon in this book. In short, we must admit that there is little we have said here that dwells on how such income and other inequalities emerge, despite their existence within the spatial structure of cities. In general, processes of spatial competition depend on positive feedbacks that drive social and spatial inequalities and lead to segregation, although we have not been very specific in mapping out, blow by blow, the way such patterns emerge. We do not apologize for this, because the domain of cities is enormous and the entire panoply of approaches and perspectives on the city is required to form a synoptic, all-embracing view. What we have focused on here is the way in which physical interventions in the structure of cities—traditionally by manipulating their form, and more recently their functions—can lead to improvements in their quality of life, their efficiency, and the equity that marks the distribution of their populations. Our message, of course, is that this kind of physicalism is dramatically changing with respect to the form of cities, particularly as new technologies come to dominate future cities, disconnecting form from function and transforming the processes and interrelationships that provide the cement keeping the city together in first place. The challenges we have posed with respect to developing new perspectives on thinking about these questions sit within some major issues, which we will now broach in providing a wider context to the way we might invent the future city.

The Bigger Questions

How can you write a book on future cities, the reader might ask, without broaching the key questions of climate change, low carbon futures, aging, migration, and health care as well as income inequality, pollution, crime,… and the list goes on? Well, we have responded to this implicitly many times in arguing that it is our perspective upon these problems, our interpretations of how we might address them, that is the main purpose of our focus here. Yet it is worth pointing to future directions, for many of the issues pertaining to form and function are tied up with these bigger issues. So let us address these, beginning with climate change. It is not hard to understand that our interference with natural systems has led to increases in heat manifested in rising carbon levels, such as ozone in the atmosphere and pollution at more local scales. To an extent, we might speculate that the anthropomorphic effects on climate date from the time when man's footprint on earth systems really began to take off and world population began its inexorable growth. We can roughly date this to the end of the Dark Ages, but in contemporary times, of course, to the first Industrial Revolution. If the worst effects of climate change coincide with population growth—as evidenced in our early chapters—we might suppose that if population growth slows this century to something more like a steady state, then our effects on climate will diminish.

This is far from the reality, however, because at the same time, the world is getting richer and our abilities to invent new technologies that interfere with earth systems are getting stronger. In any case, some argue the damage has already been done and climate change will become ever more severe as the century wears on. Flooding will be a major consequence, but so will changes in precipitation and acceptable levels of heat. Ever more resources will need to be expended on mitigating these effects. Adapting to them is also in the frame and in terms of locations in cities, flood defenses will not change the distribution of population but simply protect existing development, while strategies for moving populations or halting development in flood-prone areas will avoid the worst consequences. In most cities that are close to the sea (and nearly two-thirds of the really big world cities are in coastal areas), flood defenses and avoidance strategies will be needed, possibly in the richest and most focal areas such as their downtowns: Manhattan, London, Shanghai, Tokyo, and so on will all require more resources to stem the tide, so to speak. The standard model applied to the world's biggest cities, pictured 100 years ago for Chicago in figure 4.4(b) in chapter 4, will still be the archetype of this future.

There are many ways we can reduce our impact on the determinants of climate, from ceasing to cut down the Amazonian rainforest to reducing our use of cars and substituting their use with walking and cycling, thus changing the resources used to power our collective modes of mobility. The whole question of energy use is tied to climate change, and the many things we might do to advance a low carbon future are key to enabling a positive and lasting response to reducing the impact of climate change. The move away from fossil fuels and the development of electric cars with ever-greater autonomy defines this space, but so does the move to alternative transport modes that use less energy and are less polluting, while a general concern with obesity and fitness also supports a shift to modes of alternative transport that are more likely to be carbon-free. Again, the consequences for the form of cities are hard to figure out. If people have the same journey times using public or private transport and the same level of service, but at lower costs, this means they can make more journeys or reduce the frequency of journeys, thus creating substantial savings in energy costs.

In the sense that Tobler[34] implied in writing "everything is related to everything else, but near things are more related than distant things," cities would then become more compact if there is energy reduction across the board. Energy-intensive objects and systems would need to adapt as well, but this is the essence of cumulative innovation, creative destruction, and continuous invention anyway. Improving energy use in transport to the point where costs converged to extremely low values compared to income would not necessarily cause everyone to run to their electronic cottages, but it would tend to distort existing travel and location patterns in ways we find hard to envisage. This might be a simple distortion, concentration, or diffusion of the existing cost surfaces for transportation, but these effects would only be of the first order. When multiplier or second-order effects are taken into account, there are possibilities of a wholescale unraveling of cities into forms that we cannot envisage, despite the fact that for the last 50 years, such changes have been in prospect. Relative unit costs of transportation have been falling, but no such unraveling has actually happened. In fact, almost the reverse has occurred, with large cities becoming ever more dominant with respect to the roles of their CBDs in attracting commercial development. In some cities, the decline of their centers is being reversed as residential populations have begun to seek more central locations, which are now deemed more attractive than the suburbs. In fact, falling energy costs appear subject to Glaeser's paradox,[35] with proximity becoming "ever more valuable as the cost of connecting across long distances has fallen."

Early in this book, we began by making a rather strong prediction that the world's population would not explode, with the ensuing dire consequences that Malthus predicted in the late 18th century. This is somewhat

counter to our argument that we are not able to predict the future, but it
is to some extent an article of faith against the idea that populations will
veer toward a singularity of unknown proportions. We argued that, if anything, stabilization will occur as the demographic transition sets in for all
the world's populations. This is due to a decline in birth rates more than an
increase in longevity or aging, notwithstanding the fact that a population
in steady state would probably continue to age as long as medical technologies continue their current progress. There is every prospect they will, and
indeed that we stand at a threshold in these terms, with dramatic medical
developments on the horizon. In such a world, our cities will still grow and
decline, but the dominant change will be growth or decline due to migration. We are already seeing major movements of peoples from less to more
privileged regions, but migration in the future will constitute many different
kinds of streams associated with all kinds of human activities, from business
and commerce reflecting ever-increasing globalization to the movement
of the world's poor toward more wealthy areas. These streams are already
having consequences in cities, with increasing tensions between different
ethnic and social groups through to increasingly competitive job markets,
which are driving wages down as much as up. The implications for the size
and shape of cities, however, are quite unclear. So far all these trends seem to
have done is reinforce Glaeser's paradox, which implies that the bigger the
city, the ever more focal it becomes in the wider scheme of things.

When we come to look more closely at the implications of an aging population, the long-term consequences are really very unclear. In an earlier
chapter, we noted that life expectancy began to increase slowly but surely
from the beginnings of the Industrial Revolution, possibly from a little earlier as Europe recovered from its Dark Ages and the Renaissance began. There
is little doubt, however, that advances in health care have come from technological innovations that have enabled much greater prosperity. This, in turn,
has led to combating disease through pharmaceutical and more direct interventions to prolong life. The prospect of really radical advances suggested by
Kurzweil[36] is still a prediction too far outside our terms here, and falls more
into the realm of our speculations concerning AI than medicine and health
care. Yet there is little doubt that as the augmentation of our own bodily
functions continues apace, which is the path on which modern medicine is
set, the kind of singularity envisaged by Kurzweil becomes ever more likely.
This is as clear a prediction as we can make, given that the future is largely

unknowable. Harari makes all this explicit in his forceful, rather dark commentary on our future history[37] when he says: "Many scholars try to predict how the world will look in 2100 or 2200. This is a waste of time. Any worthwhile prediction must take into account the ability to re-engineer human minds, and this is impossible."

An aging yet infirm population that is being augmented by medical innovation would constitute a major problem for the world's cities, as transportation and location might be massively affected. For example, China's population is aging rapidly, but unlike its near neighbor Japan, it has engendered a massive boom in high-rise housing that does not appear to be sustainable for a population with limited mobility. It may be that advances in robotics will solve such problems at the local scale, but this too is most uncertain. Referring back to chapter 6 and its discussion of skyscrapers, one consequence of our ability to build upward is that such technology is always forcing the pace. But there may be limits on such technologies, and we could well reach a hard ceiling due to unassailable technological constraints. As Harari implies in his comment on our inability to predict the future, it might appear that this future is becoming ever more unknowable—but no more so than it has ever been, as Popper so eloquently explained in the arguments in our first chapter.

There is more we might say about all these possible developments, but this would require a much more extended foray into ideas about how we should think about the future city. What is clear is that all these questions are connected to one another. The cities we see around us and that we will manufacture and invent in the future will be a synthesis of all these pressures, forces, and aspirations. The great challenge is to inquire into and inform as to what cities will look like in the most obvious physical terms in the future for, like the past and the present, they will have a strong emergent order, but an order that will be different. These differences will work themselves out from the bottom up. Thus top-down visions are essentially "thought experiments" that if implemented will work out very differently from what their progenitors expect. We can do little better than to conclude this volume with Alan Turing's own view of the future concerning the prospect for an artificial intelligence. He wrote:[38] "We can only see a short distance ahead, but we can see plenty there that needs to be done." We can say much the same for the invention of the future city.

Notes

Chapter 1

1. Karl Popper's argument that the future is inherently unpredictable was first formalized in 1934 in terms of the scientific method and published in his book *The Logic of Scientific Discovery* (London: Routledge and Kegan Paul, 1959; first German edition published in 1934). He broadened his argument to society at large in *The Poverty of Historicism* (London: Routledge and Kegan Paul, 1957).

2. Denis Gabor, *Inventing the Future* (London: Secker and Warburg, 1963), 135; and Alan Kay quoted by Deborah Wise, "Experts Speculate on Future Electronic Learning Environment," *InfoWorld* 4, no. 16 (1982): 6.

3. N. Taleb, *The Black Swan: The Impact of the Highly Improbable* (New York: Random House, 2007).

4. Bertrand Russell in *The Problems of Philosophy* (Oxford, UK: Oxford University Press, 1912) first used this example, but it is widely used in introductory expositions of the philosophy of science and scientific method; see, for example, Alan Chalmers, *What Is This Thing Called Science?*, 3rd ed. (Maidenhead, UK: The Open University Press, 1999).

5. Popper, *Scientific Discovery*.

6. In their book *Superforecasting: The Art and Science of Prediction* (New York: Random House, 2015), Tetlock and Gardner provide countless examples of situations where we can generate quite good predictions in the short term, particularly where our responses to events are immediate, almost instinctive. However, they also show that as the complexity of the phenomena in question increases, such predictability quickly disappears.

7. In *The Death and Life of Great American Cities* (Random House, New York, 1961)—one of the most prescient books about cities ever written—Jane Jacobs drew on developments in the emerging science of self-organization and complex systems to argue her case for minimal intervention in the attempt to solve cities' evident problems of congestion and poverty. Her book reflects this argument in its last chapter.

8. Jacobs was already writing in 1958 about American cities as, for example, in her journalistic work on urban sprawl. See W. H. Whyte, F. Bello, S. Freedgood, D. Seligman, and J. Jacobs, *The Exploding Metropolis* (Garden City, New York: Doubleday and Company, 1958).

9. Warren Weaver's address was given in 1947, and his paper first published as "Science and Complexity," *American Scientist* 36 (1948): 536–544.

10. Ludwig von Bertalanffy developed the idea of general system theory in the 1930s, but the best guide to the field is his *General System Theory* (Harmondsworth, UK: Penguin Books, 1972).

11. John Holland makes this point quite coherently using the example of the city in his book *Hidden Order: How Adaptation Builds Complexity* (Reading MA: Addison-Wesley, 1995), 1–2.

12. Philip Anderson, another of the founders of complexity theory and a Nobel Laureate in low-temperature physics, summarized the essence of complexity theory in the title of his paper "More Is Different," *Science,* 177, no. 4047 (1972): 393–396.

13. In John Holland, *Emergence: From Chaos to Order* (Reading, MA: Perseus Books, 1998), 1. Mies van der Rohe, the last director of the Bauhaus School, adopted the term as his cliché for minimalism in architecture. It has been used by others for simplicity in art and science: see https://en.wikipedia.org/wiki/Minimalism#Less_is _more_.28architecture.29.

14. Rittel, in an unpublished paper originally written in 1969, was inspired by an editorial written by C. West Churchman ("Wicked Problems," *Management Science* 14, no. 4 [1967]: B141–B142) in which he (Churchman) defined many problems in management as being "wicked" in the sense that obvious solutions turned out to be not so obvious, or indeed perverse. Rittel, spurred on by Melvin Webber, then generalized the argument from design to the policy and planning sciences in their paper H. W. J. Rittel and M. M. Webber, "Dilemmas in a General Theory of Planning," *Policy Sciences* 4 (1973): 155–173. Much has been written about wicked problems since this seminal paper; a good summary is contained in a 2016 special issue of *Landscape and Urban Planning* edited by Brian Head and Wei-Ning Xiang. There is a little poem by Piet Hein that sums up the dilemma those dealing with complex systems like cities will always face: "Problems worthy of attack prove their worth by fighting back" (*Grooks 1*, Doubleday and Company, New York, 1969).

15. E. Lorenz, "Predictability: Does the Flap of a Butterfly's Wings in Brazil Cause a Tornado in Texas?" Paper given to the 139th meeting of the American Association for the Advancement of Science in 1972; available at http://eaps4.mit.edu/research /Lorenz/Butterfly_1972.pdf.

16. C. Alexander, *Notes on the Synthesis of Form* (Cambridge, MA: Harvard University Press, 1962). This was his PhD thesis, and it was highly resonant with the arguments

used by Jacobs in her famous book *The Death and Life of Great American Cities*. But it is not clear that Alexander was aware of her work when he wrote his thesis. In essence, they are both saying the same thing about how cities should be developed and designed: slowly, surely, adapting to their context, and avoiding the kind of disruptions that occur when large-scale redevelopment and renewal take place or when new development at a mega-scale destroys a well-adapted system that has evolved into a stable state or niche.

17. Le Corbusier coined the phrase in 1927 in the original edition of his book *Towards a New Architecture* (New York: Dover, 1985).

18. In the following chapters, we will informally introduce five principles attributed to those who first introduced these ideas, namely Zipf in 1949; Glaeser in 2012; von Thünen in 1826; Wells in 1902; and Tobler in 1970. The principles all relate to size, flow, interaction, density, and transport. They are not necessarily all inclusive of everything we know about the structure and dynamics of cities, and others have spelled these principles out in related ways. But they provide some minimal structuring of our argument for how past as well as future cities have and will evolve; see my own book, *The New Science of Cities* (Cambridge, MA: MIT Press, 2013); and Marc Barthelemy's 2016 book *The Structure and Dynamics of Cities* (Cambridge, UK: Cambridge University Press).

19. Reported by Pascal-Emmanuel Gobry in 2011 in "Facebook Investor Wants Flying Cars, Not 140 Characters," *Business Insider*, July 30, 2011, http://www.businessinsider .com/founders-fund-the-future-2011-7?IR-T.

20. George Kingsley Zipf first formalized, and to an extent popularized, the "law" that bears his name in his 1949 book *Human Behavior and the Principle of Least Effort* (Cambridge, MA: Addison-Wesley). Others before him, however, observed that in many different systems, the objects that comprise them are ordered regularly from a single largest object to many small objects, the order being formalized as a "power law." Zipf's law has since been applied to many different social, natural, and physical systems. This prompted the Nobel Laureate Paul Krugman in 1996 (in his paper "Confronting the Mystery of Urban Hierarchy," *Journal of the Japanese and International Economies* 10: 399–418) to say: "The usual complaint about economic theory is that our models are oversimplified—that they offer excessively neat views of complex, messy reality ... in one important case, the reverse is true: we have complex, messy models, yet reality is startlingly neat and simple" (399). He points to Zipf's law for cities as containing an "astonishing empirical regularity," almost an iron law for the social sciences.

21. George Gilder, the author of many futures-oriented books on information technology such as *Telecosm: The World After Bandwidth Abundance* (New York: Simon and Schuster, 2000), is quoted in 1995 by Rich Karlgaard and Michael Malone in "City vs. Country: Tom Peters and George Gilder Debate the Impact of Technology on Location," *Forbes ASAP*, February 27, 1995: 56–61.

22. This paradox is spelled out rather clearly by Edward Glaeser in his 2012 book *Triumph of the City: How Our Greatest Invention Makes Us Richer, Smarter, Greener, Healthier, and Happier* (New York: Penguin Books). This in many ways is an early 21st century equivalent of Jacobs's *Death and Life of Great American Cities*, but incorporates many of the insights derived from urban economics and regional science developed during the last half-century.

23. L. H. Sullivan, "The Tall Office Building Artistically Considered," *Lippincott's Magazine*, March 23, 1896, 403–409.

24. Johann Heinrich von Thünen articulated his theory from his reflections about the organization of different land uses with respect to the market for the agricultural goods he produced on his estate in Mecklenburg. The essence of his theory is that those who value nearness to the market more than other producers will outbid those producers for the right to use land near the market. The market will thus clear when the trade-offs between the rents paid and the transport costs to the market are zero for all producers. This idealization of an economic market became the basis for the development of urban economics in the 1960s, almost 150 years after von Thünen had published his theory in 1826 in his book *Der Isolierte Staat*; the basic theory is contained in volume I. Peter Hall acted as editor to a translation of the volume by Carla M. Wartenberg in 1966, which appeared as *Von Thünen's Isolated State* (Oxford, UK: Pergamon Press).

25. Our flirtation with the notion that cities evolve from the bottom up rather than being planned from the top down is reflected in books from the time of Patrick Geddes, who in 1915 published *Cities in Evolution* (London: Norgate and Williams), all the way to my own recent contribution in *The New Science of Cities*.

26. H. G. Wells wrote a long essay in 1902 called *The Probable Diffusion of Great Cities*, in which he speculated how all of England would become one sprawling mass as population diffused from London. On this he based his proposition that the location of population and the means of transportation are entirely interdependent. This essay is included in his book *Anticipations*, which is online at http://www.gutenberg .org/ebooks/19229.

27. In 1970, in an almost throwaway line, Waldo Tobler wrote: "I invoke the first law of geography: everything is related to everything else, but near things are more related than distant things." This is from his paper "A Computer Movie Simulating Urban Growth in the Detroit Region," *Economic Geography*, 46, supplement, 234–240.

28. Frances Cairncross is generally acknowledged as being the popularizer of the phrase "the death of distance," from the title of her *Economist* article, which she turned into her book *The Death of Distance: How the Communications Revolution Is Changing Our Lives* (Cambridge, MA: Harvard Business Review Press, 2001). But the phrase has been used in various guises by a succession of scholars who have commented on the annihilation of distance by new transport technologies since the invention of the railway, the telegraph, and telephones in the late 18th to late 19th centuries.

29. Nicholas Negroponte characterizes the great transition as a transformation from a society based on "atoms" to one based on "bits"; see his 1995 book *Being Digital* (New York: Alfred A. Knopf). This transformation is akin to that from mechanical to electrical, non-digital to digital, no city to city, energy to information, and a host of other dichotomies that divide the old world from the new.

Chapter 2

1. Hawking's 1998 speech, "Science in the Next Millennium," deals with exponential population growth. But it is clear that his view of the future nearly 20 years ago was not informed by the fact that world population growth was slowing massively and just beginning to show all the features of logistic or S-shaped growth, moving to saturation by the end of the 21st century; see https://clintonwhitehouse4.archives.gov/Initiatives/Millennium/shawking.html.

2. The demographic transition occurs when a society moves from a condition where high birth rates and high death rates dominate and where the average lifespan is low—around 30 years (as for most societies prior to the Industrial Revolution)—to one characterized by low birth and death rates. This appears to occur when the society becomes richer and more technologically advanced. Several scholars drew attention to this feature of Western industrialized society about a century ago, but the term is usually attributed to Warren Thompson; see his 1929 article "Population," *American Journal of Sociology* 34, no. 6: 959–975.

3. Hawking, "Science in the Next Millennium."

4. Negroponte, *Being Digital.*

5. In 1798, in *An Essay on the Principle of Population,* Thomas Malthus speculated that we were headed for catastrophe. In the late 18th century, the population was growing exponentially, while the supply of food, he reasoned, could only grow linearly. He did not anticipate the Industrial Revolution, although he was in its vanguard. Denis Meadows and a team from the Sloan School at MIT, influenced very much by Jay Forrester's models of system dynamics, speculated on a similar future in 1972 in their book *The Limits to Growth: A Report for the Club of Rome's Project on the Predicament of Mankind* (New York: Universe Books). The MIT team, like Malthus before it, did not anticipate developments in information and related technologies, for the microprocessor had only just been invented when they published. These are legendary examples of the limits to our abilities to predict the future, especially when we are so close to it!

6. Heinz von Foerster and his colleagues examined world population growth and suggested that the best-fitting equation for the last 2,000 years was of the form $P(t) \propto T^{-1}$, where $P(t)$ is the population at time t and T is the difference between the time when the population of the world becomes infinite t_d and the current time t; that is, $T = t_d - t$. When we plot the data for $P(t)$ against t, as in figure 2.2, this enables us to

predict "Doomsday," when the world's population effectively becomes infinite. In fact, figure 2.2 shows the reciprocal of population $1/P(t)$ plotted against T, from which it is easier to see when Doomsday occurs; for a detailed explanation, see H. von Foerster, P. M. Mora, and L. W. Amiot, "Doomsday: Friday, 13 November, A.D. 2026," *Science* 132, no. 3436 (1960): 1291–1295.

7. The data set we have used is culled from the UN Population Division data, along with the ancient cities databases developed by Tertius Chandler in 1989 and George Modelski in 2003.

8. In figure 2.8, below, we show what has been happening to the forecast year of von Foerster's Doomsday during in the last 50 years. Using much better 2017 data from the UN Population Division ("World Population Prospects: The 2017 Revision"), by the year 2000, Doomsday is predicted to be 2044, by 2015 to be 2120, and so on. The curve marking out this transition to a world of zero population growth is the reciprocal of total population until 2015 and beyond. It shows how ever more improbable is the existence of such an event horizon.

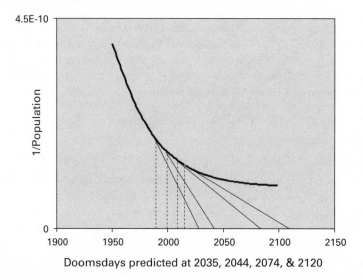

Doomsdays predicted at 2035, 2044, 2074, & 2120

9. Ray Kurzweil has written many papers and books on the "singularity." He defines 2029 as

> the consistent date I have predicted for when an AI [artificial intelligence] will pass a valid Turing test and therefore achieve human levels of intelligence. I have set the date 2045 for the "Singularity" which is when we will multiply our effective intelligence a billion fold by merging with the intelligence we have created.

This is taken from https://futurism.com/kurzweil-claims-that-the-singularity-will -happen-by-2045, and elaborated in his most popular book, *The Singularity Is Near* (New York: Viking Press, 2005).

10. Popper, *Poverty of Historicism* and *Scientific Discovery*.

11. The UN Population Division update their estimates of future population yearly; their latest report at the time of writing is "World Population Prospects: The 2017 Revision." See volume I, Comprehensive Tables, available at https://esa.un.org/unpd /wpp/Publications/Files/WPP2017_Volume-I_Comprehensive-Tables.pdf.

12. Following Henri Lefebvre's work on defining cities as urban places in his *Writings on Cities* (Oxford UK: Blackwell, 1996), Neil Brenner has collected a series of useful articles on new ways of thinking about urban agglomerations and the definition of cities in his edited volume *Implosions/Explosions: Towards a Study of Planetary Urbanization* (Berlin: Jovis Verlag, 2014).

13. Peter Hall, who wrote the first book in 1966 with the title *The World Cities* (London: Weidenfeld and Nicolson), did not coin the phrase. The origin appears to have been Patrick Geddes in his 1915 *Cities in Evolution*. It is likely, however, that the word came into use a little earlier—but not, of course, before the new world was discovered, and probably sometime in the 19th century.

14. Reba, M., Reitsma, F., and Seto, K. C. (2016) Spatializing 6,000 Years of Global Urbanization from 3700 BC to AD 2000, *Scientific Data*, 3, 160034, doi:10.1038/ sdata.2016.34.

15. This database has been constructed from a synthesis of remotely sensed data, local land use coverages, and population data from administrative units. For details and applications, see L. Dijkstra and H. Poelman, "A Harmonised Definition of Cities and Rural Areas: The New Degree of Urbanisation," Regional Working Paper 01/2014 (2014), European Commission Directorate-General for Regional and Urban Policy; and M. Pesaresi and S. Freire, "GHS Settlement grid following the REGIO model 2014 in application to GHSL Landsat and CIESIN GPW v4-Multitemporal (1975–1990–2000–2015)," European Commission, Joint Research Centre (2016), http://data.europa.eu/89h/jrc-ghsl-ghs_smod_pop_globe_r2016a.

16. R. Cura et al., "The Old and the New: Qualifying City Systems in the World with Classical Models and New Data," *Geographical Analysis* 49, no. 4 (2017): 363–386.

17. P. E. Gerland et al., "World Population Stabilization Unlikely This Century," *Science* 346, no. 6206 (2014): 234–237.

18. Karlgaard and Malone, "City vs. Country."

19. Although the distribution of city sizes in the United States and elsewhere has remained stable for over 200 years, cities move up and down the rank order quite rapidly. This is a real puzzle, in that it would appear the distribution of cities is highly stable, thus reflecting a competitive equilibrium. But in reality, this is not the case, for cities of different sizes always appear to be jostling for pride of place: see Paul Krugman, *The Self-Organizing Economy* (Boston: Blackwell, 1996); and M. Batty, "Rank Clocks," *Nature* 444 (2006): 592–596.

20. Nordpil, "World Database of Large Urban Areas, 1950–2050," Stockholm Resilience Center, Stockholm University, Stockholm, https://nordpil.com/resources /world-database-of-large-cities.

21. Zipf first introduced his law for the rank order of word frequencies in *Human Behavior and the Principle of Least Effort*. Only later in this book did he explore the notion that the frequency distribution of objects that followed his law were best graphed in terms of their rank and size. The rank, in fact, is the counter-cumulative distribution, which is formed by accumulating the frequencies from largest to smallest.

22. Batty, *New Science*.

23. In 1931, Robert Gibrat examined the statistical properties of skewed frequency distributions in his book *Les Inégalités Économiques* (Paris: Recueil Sirey). More recently, his work has been linked to scaling laws, particularly Zipf's law. Despite a very large number of articles on such laws, the field is still somewhat inchoate, in that good, consistent explanations of how and why such distributions emerge, remain stable in aggregate, and yet exhibit volatility in terms of their disaggregates, are lacking; see M. Cristelli, M. Batty, and L. Pietronero, "There Is More than a Power Law in Zipf," *Scientific Reports* 2, no. 812 (2012), doi:10.1038/srep00812.

24. We have chosen 10 billion as the upper limit. Gerland et al. forecast 9 million, while the current UN estimate (from their "World Population Prospects: 2017 Revision") is 11 billion. To work out these estimates, we simply scale the rank-size curve in figure 2.7 upward assuming the same shape. Assuming that the smallest cities are of order 1,000 population, we then figure how the intervals for each city size add to a total of 10 billion to preserve the shape of the observed rank-size distribution. This is a fairly cavalier method, however, because it assumes that there are no settlements below 1,000 persons, and we know this will never be correct. All it enables us to do is speculate about future city sizes.

25. Jane Jacobs argues in this book that, notwithstanding the move from a nomadic, tribal existence to settled agriculture some 10,000 years ago, urbanization began prior to this in small enclaves consisting of tribal members whose skills led them to specialize in producing items for their community that were beyond mere subsistence. The evidence on this is mixed, but it is consistent with what we know about early innovation and the development of agriculture; see Jacobs, *The Economy of Cities* (New York: Random House, 1969).

26. M. Batty, "Optimal Cities, Ideal Cities," *Environment and Planning B: Planning and Design* 42 (2015): 571–573.

27. Mark Jefferson coined the term "primate city" in his 1939 article "The Law of the Primate City" (*The Geographical Review* 29: 226–232), while Didier Sornette and his colleagues have extended the notion of big cities being outliers from their power laws, which they call "Dragon-Kings"; see V. F. Pisarenko and D. Sornette, "Robust

Statistical Tests of Dragon-Kings Beyond Power Law Distributions," *European Physical Journal Special Topics* 205 (2012): 95–115.

28. Eric Brynjolfsson and Andrew McAfee first argued that we are in a *Race Against The Machine*—the title of their first book, published by the Digital Frontier Press (2011). They followed this up with *The Second Machine Age: Work, Progress, and Prosperity in a Time of Brilliant Technologies* (New York: W. W. Norton & Company, 2014). The fourth Industrial Revolution is the term introduced by Karl Schwab in his book of the same name, *The Fourth Industrial Revolution* (New York: Portfolio Penguin, 2016).

Chapter 3

1. Lewis Mumford's writings about cities are particularly relevant to the perspectives developed here. The many different dimensions he uses to characterize a city are always related to how cities are structured in space and evolve over time. These he develops in several books, but his last significant writings are contained in *The City in History: Its Origins, Its Transformations, and Its Prospects* (New York: Harcourt, Brace & World, 1961). Peter Hall, in his *Cities in Civilization* (New York: Pantheon, 1998), completes the history up until the end of the 20th century, but neither author (nor many of their ilk) anticipated the dramatic changes happening with respect to the physical form of cities, now dominated by information technologies; see M. Batty, "Cities in Civilization," *Regional Studies* 51 (2017): 1282–1284.

2. The idea that cities represent hubs of innovation in the economy has become ever more important as the proportion of urbanized population has grown. As noted in chapter 2, if by the end of the 21st century most of us are living in cities, it is quite obvious that cities will be the crucible for all innovation and their applications. This is certainly alluded to by Hall and is implicit in his book, *Cities in Civilization*, but it is also key to Glaeser's arguments in *Triumph of the City*, page 10, from which the quote is taken.

3. In his *Principles of Economics*, first published in 1890, Alfred Marshall only implicitly dealt with agglomeration economies, and it was left to his successors to give his ideas substance in terms of increasing returns. The nearest he got to specifying such economies is this (book IV, chapter X, section 3):

> When an industry has thus chosen a locality for itself, it is likely to stay there long: so great are the advantages which people following the same skilled trade get from near neighborhood to one another ... if one man starts a new idea, it is taken up by others and combined with suggestions of their own; and thus it becomes the source of further new ideas. And presently subsidiary trades grow up in the neighborhood, supplying it with implements and materials, organizing its traffic, and in many ways conducing to the economy of its material.

4. Batty, *New Science*.

5. Robin Dunbar worked out that humans rarely have more than about 150 stable social relationships they count as acquaintances with whom they can engage easily.

He calculated this from correlations between the size of social groups and brain sizes among primates in a series of papers more than 20 years ago. See R. I. M. Dunbar, "Neocortex Size as a Constraint on Group Size in Primates," *Journal of Human Evolution* 22, no. 6 (1992): 469–493.

6. The small-world phenomenon was in fact first posed by Frigyes Karinthy, a Hungarian author who wrote about it in the 1920s, while Manfred Kochen and Ithiel de Sola Pool raised it as a formal sociological problem in the 1950s. Stanley Milgram popularized it in his paper "The Small-World Problem," from *Psychology Today* 1, no. 1 (1967): 61–67. It remained a relative curiosity until it was resurrected by Duncan Watts in his PhD thesis as part of the emerging science of networks and published in his book *Small Worlds: The Dynamics of Networks between Order and Randomness* (Princeton, NJ: Princeton University Press) in 1999.

7. Metcalfe's law was first articulated in 1980 by Bob Metcalfe, who invented the Ethernet at Xerox PARC. In fact, in its original form, he suggested that the power of a network is dependent upon the number of devices connected to it—its power varies as the square of the number of devices—and only later after George Gilder reformulated it (in *Telecosm: How Infinite Bandwidth Will Revolutionize Our World*), did it come to refer to the number of users connected to the network; see R. Metcalfe, "Metcalfe's Law after 40 Years of Ethernet," *Computer* 46 (2013): 26–31.

8. Herbert Simon defines the logic of hierarchy as the process whereby system elements can be aggregated together to produce a resilient system. The gist of it is as follows: resilient systems can only be assembled from a set of basic elemental components in a strict or overlapping hierarchy. In the case where one of these basic elements might fail, it only affects the subsystem that this component relates to, so the whole structure does not fall apart. Simon developed this idea using his parable of two Swiss watchmakers, one of whom built watches hierarchically and whose watches remained intact and workable; and another who built them all of one piece whose watches often fell apart. See H. A. Simon, "The Architecture of Complexity," *Proceedings of the American Philosophical Society* 106 (1962): 467–482.

9. Christopher Alexander observed that, in many city plans, neighborhoods were organized in very simple nested forms: see his papers "A City Is Not a Tree (Part I)" *Architectural Forum* 122, no. 1 (April 1965): 58–62; and, for part II, *Architectural Forum* 122, no. 2 (May 1965): 58–62. He showed that such simple hierarchies could not generate the kind of diversity Jane Jacobs spoke about in *The Death and Life of Great American Cities* (New York: Random House, 1961), yet he was well aware of the logic of hierarchies as laid out by Herbert Simon in his seminal paper ("Architecture of Complexity"). In fact, his argument is that neighborhoods, cities, and regions are structured as much more complex forms of overlapping hierarchies or lattices. His paper has resonated down the years, to the point where its influence on the field has recently been celebrated; see M. W. Mehaffy, ed., *A City Is Not a Tree*, 50th anniversary edition (Portland, OR: Sustasis Press in association with The Center for Environmental Structure, 2016).

10. Jacobs, *American Cities*; and Glaeser, *Triumph of the City*.

11. W. Christaller, *Die Zentralen Orte in Siiddeutschland* (Jena, Germany: Gustav Fischer Verlag, 1933). Published in English as *Central Places in Southern Germany*, trans. C. W. Baskin (Englewood Cliffs, NJ: Prentice Hall, 1966).

12. Patrick Geddes and Max Weber are two of several scholars who in the early 20th century articulated notions about how we might classify cities of different scales and sizes. They develop these ideas in their books: Geddes's *Cities in Evolution* and Weber's *The City* (Glencoe, NY: The Free Press, 1966), originally published in 1921. It is worth noting, however, that Adna Weber (no relation) wrote a much more technical book in 1899 called *The Growth of Cities in the Nineteenth Century* (New York: Columbia University Press), which complements these better-known works.

13. Geddes, *Cities in Evolution*, 34, 5.

14. Mumford's views about the future of cities, which became ever more pessimistic as the 20th century wore on, are best captured in his book *The Culture of Cities* (New York: Harcourt Brace and Company), published in 1938. He was castigated for these by Jacobs in her own seminal book (*American Cities*, 20–21), which offered a much more optimistic picture of the future of cities.

15. Although Geddes defined the term megalopolis, Jean Gottmann popularized it in 1966 in his book *Megalopolis: The Urbanized Northeastern Seaboard of the United States* (New York: The Twentieth Century Fund).

16. Doxiadis's 1975 article, "Action for Human Settlements" (*Ekistics* 40, no. 241: 405–448), contains his speculations about the size and scale of future cities, but it is worth looking at his more expansive writings: see C. A. Doxiadis, *Ekistics: An Introduction to the Science of Human Settlements* (New York: Oxford University Press, 1968). Some perspective on what might now seem to be extreme forecasts about a future world population is necessary, since Doxiadis was writing at a time when the net growth rate of the world's population was the greatest it had been in modern times. Since then, as demonstrated in chapter 2, the great transition has begun.

17. R. Burdett and D. Sudjic, eds., *The Endless City* (London: Phaidon Press, 2007).

18. N. Brenner and C. Schmid, "Toward a New Epistemology of the Urban?," *City* 19, no. 2–3 (2015): 151–182.

19. C. Cottineau, E. Hatna, E. Arcaute, and M. Batty, "Diverse Cities or the Systematic Paradox of Urban Scaling Laws," *Computers, Environment and Urban Systems* 63 (2017): 80–94.

20. Organisation for Economic Co-operation and Development, "Definition of Functional Urban Areas (FUA) for the OECD Metropolitan Database," 2013, https://www.oecd.org/cfe/regional-policy/Definition-of-Functional-Urban-Areas-for-the-OECD-metropolitan-database.pdf.

21. One of the most comprehensive books on network science is that by A.-L. Barabási and M. Pósfai, *Network Science* (Cambridge, UK: Cambridge University Press, 2016). The development of network science with respect to cities is key to the monograph by M. Barthelemy, *The Structure and Dynamics of Cities* (Cambridge, UK: Cambridge University Press, 2016); and to M. Batty, *New Science*.

22. Open Street Map was originally conceived by Steve Coast when he was an intern at the Centre for Advanced Spatial Analysis and in the Bartlett School of Architecture at University College London. It is one of the most exciting and innovative methods of crowdsourcing in the spatial domain. For developed countries, the maps produced are as good if not better than those from their equivalent national mapping agencies.

23. Batty, *New Science*.

24. E. Arcaute et al., "Cities and Regions in Britain through Hierarchical Percolation," *Royal Society Open Science* 3, no. 150691 (2016), doi:10.1098/rsos.150691.

25. C. Molineros, E. Arcaute, D. Smith, and M. Batty, "The Fractured Nature of British Politics" (2015), arXiv:1505.00217.

26. Jacobs, *American Cities*.

27. Alexander, "City Is Not a Tree."

28. T. C. Schelling, *Micromotives and Macrobehavior* (New York: W. W. Norton, 1978).

29. J. Cary, *Survey of the High Roads from London to Hampton Court ... Richmond* (Arundel Street Strand, London: John Carey, 1790).

30. Patrick Abercrombie's iconic diagram of London neighborhoods was but one of the key ideas in his *Greater London Plan 1944* (London: His Majesty's Stationery Office), published in 1945. The plan also introduced various ideas that are still part of the current plan, namely greenbelts, various transport corridors, and retail hubs.

31. We introduced the paradox earlier in this and in the first chapter. It is our second principle, which pertains to the way distance and time are being distorted by current information and related transportation technologies. The quote is taken from Glaeser, *Triumph of the City*, 60.

32. Cairncross, *Death of Distance*.

33. Abercrombie, "Greater London Plan."

34. Le Corbusier, *The City of Tomorrow and Its Planning* (New York: Dover Publications, 1929).

35. F. L. Wright, *When Democracy Builds* (Chicago, IL: University of Chicago Press, 1945).

Chapter 4

1. Louis Sullivan coined the phrase "form ever follows function" in 1896 in his article "The Tall Office Building Artistically Considered," *Lippincott's Magazine*, March 23, 403–409. This came to be one of the battle cries of the modern movement in art and architecture. Yet 50 years later, by mid-century, the movement was under severe scrutiny by many commentators, such as Reyner Banham, whose *Theory and Design in the First Machine Age* is widely regarded as one of the most incisive analyses of modern architecture. In the second edition of his book, published in 1980, he argued: "The Modern movement, too, is finally in disrepute.... Every now and again the Machine Aesthetic will produce a burst of creative speed, but in general this grand old vehicle is nowadays just spluttering its way to the junkyard" (9–10).

2. J. W. von Goethe, *Zur Morphologie* (Stuttgart, Germany: J. G. Cotta Publishers, 1817), 201.

3. Almost as soon as town planning emerged in the late 19th century as an institution of the state in many developed countries, transport planning came to be dominated by engineers, while land use planning and urban design were dominated by architects. Transport planning was considered quite separate from land use planning in the early years of the last century, reflecting a tension between engineering and aesthetics. But by the 1950s, a succession of calls urged integrating these two domains; this is still a major quest. See, for example, R. B. Mitchell and C. Rapkin, *Urban Traffic: A Function of Land Use* (New York: Columbia University Press, 1954).

4. C. S. Fischer, *America Calling: A Social History of the Telephone to 1940* (Berkeley, CA: University of California Press, 1994). Fischer also wrote extensively on social networks; see, for example, C. S. Fischer, *To Dwell Among Friends: Personal Networks in Town and City* (Chicago IL: University of Chicago Press, 1982). But there has been little work on the detailed processes that underpin these kinds of social networks, with the exception of work by Anna Lee Saxenian; for example, see her 1996 book, *Regional Advantage: Culture and Competition in Silicon Valley and Route 128* (Cambridge, MA: Harvard University Press).

5. One of the earliest and most influential explorations of the new networked global economy with respect to cities—in fact, long before the Internet was invented—were articles on non-place urban realms by Melvin Webber. His chapter "The Urban Place and the Non-Place Urban Realm," published in 1964 in M. M. Webber et al., eds., *Explorations into Urban Structure* (Philadelphia: University of Pennsylvania Press), is one of the most prescient speculations about the contemporary functioning of our global urban world.

6. For a thorough review, see J. Hanson, "Order and Structure in Urban Design: The Plans for the Rebuilding of London after the Great Fire of 1666," *Ekistics* 56, no. 334–335 (1989): 22–42.

7. Jacobs pictured this kind of diversity in her 1961 book *The Death and Life of Great American Cities*, in which she describes the great variety of the city as a sidewalk ballet. She wrote:

> Under the seeming disorder of the old city, wherever the old city is working successfully, is a marvelous order for maintaining the safety of the streets and the freedom of the city. It is a complex order. Its essence is intricacy of sidewalk use.…The ballet of the good city sidewalk never repeats itself from place to place, and in any one place is always replete with improvisations.…The stretch of Hudson Street where I live is each day the scene of an intricate sidewalk ballet. (201)

8. There are many sources that map ancient cities from the classical and pre-classical eras. Tony Morris's *History of Urban Form: Before the Industrial Revolutions* (3rd ed., London: Longman, 1994) is a good summary, but a more extensive set of examples is contained in two books, both published in 1999, by Spiro Kostof: *The City Shaped: Urban Patterns and Meanings Through History*, and *The City Assembled: The Elements of Urban Form Through History* (London: Thames and Hudson).

9. A selection of Renaissance plans is contained in Helen Rosenau's book *The Ideal City: Its Architectural Evolution* (London: Studio Vista, 1974).

10. Von Thünen, *Isolated State*.

11. R. E. Park and E. W. Burgess, *The City* (Chicago, IL: The University of Chicago Press, 1925).

12. The von Thünen model was rediscovered by those who started the field of regional science in the late 1950s. An early paper by the astrophysicist Martin Beckman remained unpublished for a number of years; see M. J. Beckman, "On the Distribution of Urban Rent and Residential Density," *Journal of Economic Theory* 1 (1969): 60–67. It was, however, Bill Alonso in his PhD thesis at the University of Pennsylvania who embedded the model in a demand-based microeconomic framework, establishing a partial spatial equilibrium that defined densities and rents in the way von Thünen had originally suggested. Alonso's 1964 book *Location and Land Use: Toward a General Theory of Land Rent* (Cambridge, MA: Harvard University Press) opened these ideas to the wider world and established a line of research referred to as new urban economics that attracted various high-profile mathematical economists in the 1970s and 1980s. The field had lost much of its momentum by the 1990s as it became embedded in urban economic growth theory, trade analysis, and urban econometrics, and as many of its theoretical constructs came to be viewed as simplistic and unrealistic.

13. R. Florida, *The New Urban Crisis* (New York: Basic Books, 2017).

14. Park and Burgess, *The City*; these social ecologists established the idea of the zone of transition, an inner area in the industrial city between what they called the factory zone and the residential zone associated with the working class.

15. Glaeser, *Triumph of the City*.

16. Paul Krugman's 1996 book, *The Self-Organizing Economy*, deals with various location theories a little beyond the traditions of urban economics. The quote in question is from page 13.

17. Joel Garreau, *Edge City: Life on the New Frontier* (New York: Doubleday, 1991).

18. Richard Meier, in a remarkably prescient but largely unknown book, anticipated much of what now preoccupies our concern for information and networks in cities in his *A Communications Theory of Urban Growth* (Cambridge, MA: MIT Press, 1962).

19. One of the main themes in my book *The New Science of Cities* is the notion that it is interactions, not actions—flows between locations—that constitute the key way of understanding the contemporary city. This is a big switch from the way we have thought about cities during the last half-century.

20. The selection of abstracted city networks is taken from John Cary's *Survey of the High Roads*; Johann Kohl's *Der Verkehr und die Ansiedelung der Menschen in ihrer Abhangigkeit uon der Gestaltung der Eudoberflache* (Leipzig, Germany: Arnoldische Buchhandlung, 1841); Charles Minard's *Des Tableaux Graphiques et des Cartes Figuratives* (Paris: E. Thunot et Cie, 1861); R. Unwin, *Town Planning in Practice: An Introduction to the Art of Designing Cities and Suburbs* (London: T. F. Unwin, 1909); and Alasdair Rae's 2017 work journey flow visualizations, available at http://www.undertheraedar.com/2010/09/flow-map-layout.html.

21. Analogies between the human body and the city appear everywhere in the literature on cities, the earliest references to which go back to antiquity. Richard Sennett's *Flesh and Stone: The Body and the City in Western Civilization* (London: Faber and Faber, 1994) provides a detailed historical account, while the analogy has been pursued by many practicing architect-planners, as portrayed in Victor Gruen's 1965 book *The Heart of Our Cities: The Urban Crisis, Diagnosis and Cure* (London: Thames and Hudson).

22. E. G. Ravenstein, "The Laws of Migration," *Journal of the Statistical Society of London* 48, no. 2 (1885): 167–235.

23. There is some dispute about who is originally responsible for this phrase, Plato or Heraclitus: see https://en.wikiquote.org/wiki/Heraclitus. Leonardo da Vinci's *Notebooks*, published in 1955 and translated and arranged by Edward MacCurdy (New York: Braziller), are available at https://archive.org/details/noteboo00leon.

24. Benton MacKaye published very little, but in 1928 his book *The New Exploration* (New York: Harcourt and Brace) was one of the most influential statements about the philosophy of regional planning. It gained the attention of Patrick Geddes in later life, who advised MacKaye to call the field he was pioneering "geotechnics"; see B. MacKaye, *From Geography to Geotechnics* (Urbana, IL: University of Illinois Press, 1968).

25. M. Lenormand et al., "Influence of Sociodemographic Characteristics on Human Mobility," *Scientific Reports* 5 (2015): 10075, doi:10.1038/srep10075; and H. Barbosa-Filho et al., "Human Mobility: Models and Applications," 2017, arXiv:1710.00004v1.

26. D'Arcy Wentworth Thompson's seminal book, published in 1917, *On Growth and Form* (Cambridge, UK: Cambridge University Press), introduced biology to formal mechanisms of morphogenesis (qualitative change as the size and scale of an organism evolve through growth). His work implicitly introduced us to allometry. Haldane and Huxley took this further during the period when the new genetics was being discovered; see J. B. S. Haldane, "On Being the Right Size," *Harper's Magazine*, March 1926, 424–427; and J. S. Huxley's 1932 *Problems of Relative Growth* (Baltimore, MD: Johns Hopkins University Press, 1993).

27. Thompson's "diagram of forces" was devised to show how morphologies emerged. He said one must study not only finished forms, but also the forces that molded them: "The form of an object is a 'diagram of forces,' in this sense, at least, that from it we can judge of or deduce the forces that are acting or have acted upon it." *Growth and Form*, 11.

28. Ibid., 14.

29. Patrick Geddes wrote extensively about urban form and the processes of evolution, focusing on urban spread and sprawl, in his book *Cities in Evolution* (for quotation, see page 26). Thompson wrote about the same kinds of processes in the evolution of biological systems (*Growth and Form*, 132–133). Neither author referred to the other; this is somewhat of a mystery, as they were colleagues for 30 years in the same university and both, 100 years later, are feted for their insights into the morphology of cities and analogous physical systems.

30. In the 1990s, Geoffrey West was instrumental in developing a theory of scale based on allometry, linking branching patterns in animal and plant populations using ideas from the physics of scaling. He has since extended these ideas to cities and corporations. All are included in his grand synthesis, his 2017 book *Scale: The Universal Laws of Life and Death in Organisms, Cities and Companies* (London: Weidenfeld and Nicolson).

31. Barthelemy, *Structure and Dynamics of Cities*.

32. M. Batty and P. Ferguson, "Defining Density," *Environment and Planning B* 38 (2011): 753–756.

33. Bettencourt and his colleagues have written many papers illustrating that from conventional city definitions based on administrative units, incomes appear to scale superlinearly with respect to population size; their original paper is L. M. Bettencourt et al., "Growth, Innovation, Scaling, and the Pace of Life in Cities," *Proceedings of the National Academy of Sciences USA* 104, no. 17 (2007): 7301–7306.

34. M. Gonzalez-Navarro and M. A. Turner, "Subways and Urban Growth: Evidence from Earth, Spatial Economics Research Centre," SERC Discussion Paper No. 195 (2016), London School of Economics; and C. Roth, S. M. Kang, M. Batty, and M. Barthelemy, "A Long-Time Limit for World Subway Networks," *Journal of the Royal Society Interface* 9, no. 75 (2012): 2540–2550, doi:10.1098/rsif.2012.0259.

35. Dunbar, "Neocortex Size."

36. Marshall, *Principles*; and Bettencourt et al., "Growth, Innovation, Scaling."

37. E. Arcaute et al., "Constructing Cities, Deconstructing Scaling Laws," *Journal of the Royal Society Interface* 12 (2015): 20140745.

38. Le Corbusier, *City of Tomorrow*.

39. G. B. Dantzig and T. L. Saaty, *Compact City: A Plan for a Liveable Urban Environment* (San Francisco: W. H. Freeman and Company, 1973); Y. Charbit, "The Platonic City: History and Utopia," *Population* 57, no. 2 (2002): 207–235; and E. Howard, *To-morrow: A Peaceful Path to Real Reform* (London: Routledge, 2009), first published in 1898.

40. Frank Lloyd Wright describes Broadacre City in his 1932 book *The Disappearing City* (New York: William Farquhar Payson). For his 1955 Illinois Building, see https://en.wikipedia.org/wiki/The_Illinois; and his 1957 book *A Testament* (New York: Horizon Press).

41. Alexander, "City Is Not a Tree."

42. W. Alonso, "The Economics of Urban Size," *Papers and Proceedings of the Regional Science Association* 26 (1971): 67–83.

43. H. W. Richardson, *The Economics of Urban Size* (Farnborough, UK: Saxon House, 1973).

Chapter 5

1. Geoffrey West's recent book *Scale* is the best survey of allometry in physical and social systems there is. For the longevity of humankind, the history of the average lifespan is complicated, but a good overview is at https://en.wikipedia.org/wiki/Life_expectancy.

2. The basic paper demonstrating the superlinearity between incomes and population was summarized in Bettencourt et al., "Growth, Innovation, Scaling." Departures from superlinearity are key to the results for UK cities in Arcaute et al., "Constructing Cities." Accessibility rather than income appears to scale superlinearly with population size for UK cities; see M. Batty, "A Theory of City Size (Perspectives)," *Science* 340, no. 6139 (2013): 1418–1419.

3. M. Bornstein and H. Bornstein, "The Pace of Life," *Nature* 259, no. 19 (February 1976): 557–558.

4. J. D. Walmsley and G. J. Lewis, "The Pace of Pedestrian Flows in Cities," *Environment and Behavior* 21, no. 2 (1989): 123–150.

5. S. Milgram, "The Experience of Living in Cities," *Science* 167, no. 3924 (1970): 1461–1468.

6. Morris, "History of Urban Form."

7. S. A. Thompson, "Which Cities Get the Most Sleep?" *Wall Street Journal*, August 15, 2015, http://graphics.wsj.com/how-we-sleep.

8. Formal studies of the high-frequency city, whose rhythms vary over minutes, hours, and days, do not appear to have been carried out prior to Chapin and Stewart's 1953 "Population Densities around the Clock," reprinted in 1959 in H. H. Mayer and C. F. Kohn, eds., *Readings in Urban Geography*, (Chicago: University of Chicago Press), 180–182. In fact, the wider literature on cities from antiquity is full of anecdotal descriptions of how people interact with one another in real time.

9. We noted Richard Meier's 1962 book in the last chapter. It is probably the only serious attempt at thinking about a framework for the real-time, high-frequency city ever written to date, written during a period when our thinking about cities was just beginning to break out of its physicalist, architectural past and move beyond the Machine Age.

10. For the last 200 years, cities and economies have been conceived as if they are always in a static equilibrium. In the last 25 years, complexity theory, experimental economics, and the wider role of cognition in studies of human behavior have directly challenged this paradigm of equilibrium, and it is no longer the cornerstone of social science it was once perceived to be. There are many commentaries on this, but for cities, see my essay, "Cities in Disequilibrium," in J. Johnson et al., eds., *Non-Equilibrium Social Science and Policy: Introduction and Essays on New and Changing Paradigms in Socioeconomic Thinking* (New York: Springer, 2017), 81–96.

11. Yochai Benkler's *The Wealth of Networks* (New Haven, CN: Yale University Press), published in 2006, is a comprehensive treatment of network effects in economics, while Eric Beinhocker's *The Origin of Wealth: Evolution, Complexity, and the Radical Remaking of Economics* (Boston: Harvard Business School Press), published in 2006, sets these network effects within the wider context of complexity theory.

12. Tom Standage's book *The Victorian Internet: The Remarkable Story of the Telegraph and the Nineteenth Century's On-line Pioneers* (London: Bloomsbury), published in 1998, provides a wonderful speculation that the first Industrial Revolution had its own Internet—essentially, the telegraph. In a way, his thesis marks out the pre-industrial from the post-industrial age, with global networks providing the essential

difference. Andrew Blum's 2012 book *Tubes: A Journey to the Center of the Internet* (London: Ecco Press) brings the evolution of global networks up to date, but with a focus on the hardware of the computer-communications revolution.

13. There are many sources: for example, the number of Google searches can be gleaned from http://www.internetlivestats.com/google-search-statistics, while the total global number of emails is from https://www.radicati.com/wp/wp-content/uploads/2015/02/Email-Statistics-Report-2015-2019-Executive-Summary.pdf.

14. M. Batty, "New Ways of Looking at Cities," *Nature* 377 (1995): 574.

15. Torsten Hägerstrand introduced the notion of space-time trajectories for individuals, which could be plotted in three-dimensional space, during the development of behavioral geography in the 1960s. The x and y dimensions locate the individual in space, while the z dimension records time (during the 24-hour day, or over whatever period the activity took place). An individual's space-time path can thus be plotted, and clusters of such paths identified and associated with different individuals and different activities. See T. Hägerstrand, "What about People in Regional Science?" *Papers of the Regional Science Association* 24 (1970): 7–21.

16. A. Greenfield, *Radical Technologies: The Design of Everyday Life* (London: Verso, 2017).

17. Meier, *Communications Theory*, 1.

18. The term "quantified self" has been associated with Gary Wolf and Kevin Kelly since their founding of the movement in 2007; see the Quantified Self Institute in Groningen, The Netherlands (https://qsinstitute.com/about/what-is-quantified-self).

19. S. Gray, O. O'Brien, and S. Hügel, "Collecting and Visualizing Real-Time Urban Data through City Dashboards," *Built Environment* 42, no. 3 (2016): 498–509.

20. Dashboards with extended analytics are being developed by Rob Kitchin's group at the National University of Irelands at Maynooth; see http://dashboards.maynoothuniversity.ie and their Dublin dashboard at http://www.dublindashboard.ie. Also see R. Kitchin, T. Lauriault, and G. McArdle, "Knowing and Governing Cities through Urban Indicators, City Benchmarking and Real-Time Dashboards," *Regional Studies, Regional Science* 2 (2015): 1–28; and R. Kitchin, T. Lauriault, and G. McArdle, eds. *Data and the City* (London: Routledge, 2017).

21. IBM, "Watson Marketing: 10 Key Marketing Trends for 2017," https://www-01.ibm.com/common/ssi/cgi-bin/ssialias?htmlfid=WRL12345USEN.

22. See C. Zhong, M. Batty, E. Manley, and J. Wang, "Variability in Regularity: A Comparative Study of Urban Mobility Patterns in London, Singapore and Beijing Using Smart-Card Data," *PLoS ONE*, 2016, doi:10.1371/journal.pone.0149222; and J. Reades, C. Zhong, E. Manley, R. Milton, and M. Batty, "Finding Pearls in London's Oysters," *Built Environment* 42, no. 3 (2016): 365–381.

23. R. Milton, Geospatial Computing: Fundamental Architectures and Algorithms, unpublished PhD thesis, Centre for Advanced Spatial Analysis, University College London, 2017.

24. Jon Reades has pieced together the flows on all the segments of the London tube by minute and location for three months' worth of Oyster card data from the summer of 2012. This produces a synthetic week of flow data, which when animated resembles blood flow; see https://vimeo.com/41760845.

25. Pedro Miguel Cruz produced an earlier animation of traffic flow in Lisbon in analogy to blood flow as part of his work with MIT's Senseable Cities Laboratory; see the movie at https://vimeo.com/31031656) and http://pmcruz.com/information-visualization/lisbons-blood-vessels.

26. Reades et al., "Finding Pearls."

27. Carlo Ratti and his partners in the MIT Senseable Cities Lab have produced a fascinating visualization of credit card flows for Spain from this data. View the movie at https://www.youtube.com/watch?v=8J3T3UjHbrE.

28. J. Serras et al., "Retail Model Performance Using Transaction Card Data," (presented at the EUNOIA Final Review, Madrid, November 2014, http://eunoia-project.eu/doc/finalevent/; available from joan@prospective.io).

29. F. Neuhaus, Urban Rhythms: Habitus and Emergent Spatio-Temporal Dimensions of the City, unpublished PhD thesis, Centre for Advanced Spatial Analysis, University College London, 2012.

30. P. A. Longley and M. Adnan, "Geo-temporal Twitter Demographics," *International Journal of Geographical Information Science* 30, no. 2 (2016): 369–389.

31. Neuhaus, "Urban Rhythms."

32. Leticia Roncero, "Eric Fischer's Marvelous Maps," May 14, 2015, Flickr Blog, http://blog.flickr.net/en/2015/05/14/eric-fischers-marvelous-maps.

33. Paul Butler visualized this data in "Visualizing Friendships," December 13, 2010, at https://www.facebook.com/notes/facebook-engineering/visualizingfriendships/469716398919 and http://www.notcot.com/archives/2010/12/a-world-mapped-by-friends.php.

34. P. Khanna, *Connectography: Mapping the Future of Global Civilization* (New York: Random House, 2016).

35. In her second book, *The Economy of Cities*, Jacobs defied the conventional wisdom of that time by suggesting that pockets of urbanization—embryonic cities, if you like—existed even in nomadic times, and both urbanization and the Agricultural Revolution went hand in hand in moving the world away from tribal existence. We note her work in this regard in earlier chapters, particularly chapter 4.

36. Alexander, "City Is Not a Tree."

37. M. Batty and P. Longley, *Fractal Cities: A Geometry of Form and Function* (London: Academic Press, 1994); http://www.fractalcities.org.

Chapter 6

1. Terry McGee coined the word "desakota" (from the Indonesian *desa*, "village," and *kota*, "city") from his extensive observations of rapid urban development in southeast Asia. See T. McGee, "Urbanisasi or Kotadesasi? Evolving Patterns of Urbanization in Asia," in F. J. Costa, A. K. Dutt, L. J. C. Ma, and A. G. Noble, eds., *Urbanization in Asia* (Honolulu: University of Hawaii Press, 1989), 93–108; and https://en.wikipedia.org/wiki/Desakota.

2. The Reverend Parkes Cadman so defined the skyscraper in 1916 with specific reference to the Woolworth Building. See his foreword in Edwin Cochrane's *The Cathedral of Commerce* (New York: Broadway Park Place Company, 1916), archived at http://archive.org/stream/thecathedralofco00cochiala#page/28/mode/2up; and Philip Sutton's blog post in 2013, https://www.nypl.org/blog/2013/04/22/woolworth-building-cathedral-commerce.

3. Bertie Wells (always referred to as H. G.) in his 1902 book *Anticipations*, 36.

4. Ibid., 47.

5. Ibid., 61.

6. Ibid., 43. Wells was an intellectual whose scientific and literary contributions linked fact to fiction. He studied under Thomas Huxley, Darwin's bulldog, and in this context met Patrick Geddes, whose ideas about the evolution of cities are entirely consistent with Wells's proposition. Although, like von Thünen, Wells hardly referred to Geddes's work on cities in his writings, and although there was some mutual respect between them, there was clearly a competitive edge to their association; see Alex Law's paper in 2015, "The Ghost of Patrick Geddes: Civics As Applied Sociology," *Sociological Research Online* 10, no. 2, http://www.socresonline.org.uk/10/2/law.html.

7. William Whyte was the chief editor of the book *The Exploding Metropolis* (with Bello, Freedgood, Seligman, and Jacobs).

8. Jacobs spelled out these ideas in her contribution to Whyte et al., *Exploding Metropolis*, 157–185, as well as in her first book, *Great American Cities*.

9. The 19th century was full of strident, usually negative statements about the process of urbanization. William Cobbett led the assault with his 1821 book *Rural Rides* (London: T. Nelson and Company; p. 144), available at http://www.gutenberg.org/files/34238/34238-h/34238-h.htm.

10. William Morris's diatribe is from his lecture to University College Oxford on November 7, 1883, "Lectures on Socialism: Art Under Plutocracy," reproduced by A. H. R. Ball, *Selections from the Prose Works of William Morris* (Cambridge, UK: Cambridge University Press, 1931), 108–110; available at https://www.marxists.org /archive/morris/works/1883/pluto.htm.

11. Geddes, *Cities in Evolution*, 97.

12. Reid Ewing has written several authoritative papers on suburbanization, primarily in the United States; see R. Ewing, "Is Los Angeles-Style Sprawl Desirable?" *Journal of the American Planning Association* 66, no. 1 (1997): 107–126.

13. Reproduced from M. Davies, *Ecology of Fear: Los Angeles and the Imagination of Disaster* (New York: Vintage Books, 1999).

14. There is an extensive literature on urban sprawl. An early review grounded in contemporary theory is Kenneth T. Jackson's *Crabgrass Frontier: The Suburbanization of the United States* (New York: Oxford University Press, 1985); a more recent comprehensive review is Karyn Lacy's "The New Sociology of Suburbs: A Research Agenda for Analysis of Emerging Trends," *Annual Review of Sociology* 42 (2016): 369–384.

15. J. Lessinger, "The Case for Scatteration: Some Reflections on the National Capital Region Plan for the Year 2000," *Journal of the American Institute of Planners* 38, no. 2 (1962): 159–169.

16. P. Gordon and H. W. Richardson, "Are Compact Cities a Desirable Planning Goal?" *Journal of the American Planning Association* 66, no. 1 (1997): 95–106.

17. Equifinality in the context of urban form is touched upon by Batty and Longley in *Fractal Cities* and explored in more formal terms by M. Batty, "Cities as Complex Systems: Scaling, Interactions, Networks, Dynamics and Urban Morphologies," in R. Meyers, ed., *Encyclopedia of Complexity and Systems Science*, vol. 1 (Berlin: Springer, 2009), 1041–1071.

18. NASA is continually improving its night lights data, which monitors energy pulses from human settlements globally; see https://www.nasa.gov/feature/goddard /2017/new-night-lights-maps-open-up-possible-real-time-applications; for the Tokyo map, see the NASA resource https://earthobservatory.nasa.gov/Features/CitiesAtNight.

19. Glaeser's *Triumph of the City* focuses on the return to the central city, while, more recently, Florida in his 2017 book *The New Urban Crisis* suggests (in chapters 4 and 5) that these reverse migrations are more complex than it might, at first glance, appear.

20. In his 1991 book, *Edge City*, Garreau first popularized the term. The Merriam-Webster online dictionary suggests "edge city" was first used in 1988, defining it as "a suburb that has developed its own political, economic, and commercial base independent of the central city"; see https://www.merriam-webster.com/dictionary /edge%20city.

21. The idea that wealth "trickles down" the income spectrum from rich to poor, together with the notion that in such an economy a "rising tide (of wealth) raises all boats," is deeply embedded in traditional economic theory. The Chicago social ecologists adopted it implicitly in their model of how a Western industrialized city is structured (see Park and Burgess, *The City*), but it has been widely questioned in the last 50 years by many economists and politicians; see Gerald M. Meier and Joseph E. Stiglitz, eds., *Frontiers of Development Economics: The Future in Perspective* (Washington, DC: World Bank Publications, 2001).

22. Hanson, "Order and Structure."

23. Joseph Schumpeter wrote about creative destruction and long waves from the 1920s on, but did not publish a fully comprehensive analysis until 1938 in his *Capitalism, Socialism and Democracy* (London: George Allen and Unwin Ltd).

24. R. Foster and S. Kaplan, *Creative Destruction: Why Companies That Are Built to Last Underperform the Market and How to Successfully Transform Them* (New York: Doubleday, 2001).

25. Applied to the relative economic size of firms, these dynamics are discussed in M. Batty, "Visualizing Creative Destruction," Centre for Advanced Spatial Analysis, working paper 112, 2007, University College London, http://www.casa.ucl.ac.uk/workingpapers/paper112.pdf.

26. Chandler, *Urban Growth*.

27. Max Page has applied the generic notions of creative destruction associated with Schumpeter to the development of Manhattan during its first skyscraper phase in his 1999 book, *The Creative Destruction of Manhattan: 1900–1940* (Chicago: University of Chicago Press), 2.

28. Ibid., 3.

29. During the 12th and 13th centuries, there were up to 180 towers constructed in Bologna, possibly for defensive purposes, but their precise purpose is unknown. Towers up to 100 meters (328 feet) were constructed, though most had been demolished by the 20th century, with less than 20 now standing; see https://en.wikipedia.org/wiki/Towers_of_Bologna.

30. Elisha Otis invented the mechanism that stopped an elevator falling if the cable was broken, but his company took off only after his relatively early death in 1861. It is one of the few companies from that era that is still a major force in construction.

31. It was Louis Sullivan and his associate Dankmar Adler who designed the Guaranty Building (now the Prudential Building) in downtown Buffalo. This is one of the best examples of early skyscraper design, as well as the execution of Sullivan's own mantra "form follows function" discussed in chapter 4.

32. See the Reverend Parkes Cadman, "Cathedral of Commerce."

33. C. Gilbert, "The Financial Importance of Rapid Building," *Engineering Record* 41 (1900), no. 623, quoted in J. Barr and J. Cohen, "Why are Skyscrapers So Tall? Land Use and the Spatial Location of Buildings in New York," 2010, available at https://www.aeaweb.org/conference/2011/retrieve.php?pdfid=352.

34. Homer Hoyt was one of the first economists to formally discuss such cycles in his 1933 book *One Hundred Years of Land Values in Chicago* (New York: Arno Press, reprinted 1970); more recently, Richard Barras has explored this kind of urban dynamics in his 2009 book *Building Cycles: Growth and Instability* (London: Wiley-Blackwell).

35. For the databases used, see Emporis (http://www.emporis.com), the Skyscraper Page (https://skyscraperpage.com), and the Skyscraper Center (http://www.skyscrapercenter .com).

36. Andrew Lawrence first presented his index in 1999 in his paper "The Curse Bites: Skyscraper Index Strikes," Property Report, Dresdner Kleinwort. Benson Research.

37. Mark Thornton's analysis in 2005 in his paper "Skyscrapers and Business Cycles" (*The Quarterly Journal of Austrian Economics* 8, no. 1: 51–74) assumed that the boom was coming to an end. A more recent analysis of the Great Recession with a focus on building is in E. Boyle, L. Engelhardt, and M. Thornton, "Is There such a Thing as a Skyscraper Curse?" *The Quarterly Journal of Austrian Economics* 19, no. 2 (2012): 149–168.

38. We have referred to Zipf and his rank-size methods of analysis several times, particularly in chapter 2. We use the same methods for examining the size of skyscrapers that we used for cities in chapter 2; see Zipf, *Human Behavior*.

39. The most comprehensive analysis of any city with respect to skyscrapers and the economics of their development has been made by Jason M. Barr in *Building the Skyline: The Birth and Growth of Manhattan's Skyscrapers* (New York: Oxford University Press, 2016).

Chapter 7

1. Kondratieff first presented his ideas in 1925 in his book *The Major Economic Cycles*, republished as *The Long Wave Cycle*, translated by G. Daniels (New York: E. P. Dutton, 1984). It was Schumpeter who named the waves after Kondratieff, but Kondratieff himself called them long waves in his original article in 1926; see N. D. Kondratieff, "The Long Waves in Economic Life," *The Review of Economics and Statistics* 17 (1926, 1935): 105–115, translated by W. F. Stolper. His Wikipedia entry provides a full account of his short but significant contribution and his subsequent persecution, a direct consequence of his continued support for Lenin's New Economic Policy; see https://en.wikipedia.org/wiki/Nikolai_Kondratiev.

2. J. Schumpeter, *Business Cycles: A Theoretical, Historical, and Statistical Analysis of the Capitalist Process* (1923; reprint, New York: McGraw-Hill, 1939).

3. See Page, *Creative Destruction of Manhattan*, and M. Batty, "The Creative Destruction of Cities," *Environment and Planning B* 34 (2007): 1–4.

4. Schumpeter, "Business Cycles."

5. P. Hall, "The Geography of the Fifth Kondratieff Cycle," *New Society* 26 (March 1981): 535–537; and P. Hall and P. Preston, *The Carrier Wave: New Information Technology and the Geography of Innovation 1846–2003* (London: Unwin Hyman, 1988).

6. Wells, *Anticipations*.

7. R. Kurzweil, *The Singularity Is Near* (New York: Viking Press, 2005), and H. von Foerster, P. M. Mora, and L. W. Amiot, "Doomsday: Friday, November 13, AD 2026," *Science* 132 (1960): 1291–1295.

8. Wells, *Anticipations*.

9. I do not believe Tobler ever thought of this first law of geography as being his when he described it in the paper "A Computer Movie Simulating Urban Growth in the Detroit Region" (236), but it acquired this status over the subsequent years. There was never a second or third law, although Tobler, after his first law became well known, himself suggested a second law that relates to the wider environment of the system within which the first law holds; see https://en.wikipedia.org/wiki/Waldo_R._Tobler.

10. Her article in *The Economist*, "The Death of Distance" (September 30, 1995, 5–28), which introduced this special issue, was a timely and highly focused discussion of the annihilation of distance by new digital communications. She elaborated on the article in the book *The Death of Distance*.

11. Glaeser, *Triumph of the City*.

12. A. Toffler, *Future Shock* (New York: Bantam Books, 1970).

13. E. M. Forster, *The Machine Stops* (1909; reprint, London: Penguin Classics, 2017).

14. David Harvey, particularly in his 1989 book *The Condition of Postmodernity: An Enquiry into the Origins of Cultural Change* (Oxford, UK: Blackwell; 284–307), made this kind of transformation one of his central points in his interpretations of the great transition that we are living through.

15. Turing's original papers essentially involved the logic of the algorithm. His associated philosophy of calculation quickly led to him defining such logics as universal machines. Von Neumann took a very different view that was eminently more practical, but nevertheless exploited the idea of universality in computation. Both did much of their pioneering work at Princeton's Institute for Advanced Study between

1935 and 1948. For a comprehensive account, see George Dyson's *Turing's Cathedral: The Origins of the Digital Universe* (New York: Pantheon Books, 2012).

16. Schwab, *Fourth Industrial Revolution*.

17. The binary distinction goes back many centuries, as already pointed out, but it was George Boole in the 1840s who provided the formal basis in logic that was adopted in the notion that an electrical pulse could be used for switching a circuit on and off. Alan Turing used these ideas for representing computation, Claude Shannon associated them with electric circuitry, and Vannevar Bush speculated on where all this might lead with respect to how and what we might compute in the information age. Meanwhile, Gordon Moore articulated the law that has led to their widespread application during the early years of the transistor age, building on the microchip circuitry of John Bardeen, Walter Brattain, and William Shockley at Bell Labs during their invention of the transistor in 1948. The key articles are Claude Shannon's 1937 master's thesis at MIT, published in 1938 as "A Symbolic Analysis of Relay and Switching Circuits," *Transactions of the American Institute of Electrical Engineers* 57, no. 12: 713–723; Alan Turing's 1948 article "Intelligent Machinery," The National Physical Laboratory, http://www.alanturing.net/intelligent_machinery; Vannevar Bush's 1945 article "As We May Think," *The Atlantic Monthly*, 176, no. 1 (July), 101–108; and Gordon Moore in his 1965 article "Cramming More Components onto Integrated Circuits," *Electronics* 38, no. 8 (April 19): 114–117.

18. Moore, "Integrated Circuits"; and E. Brynjolfsson and A. McAfee, *The Second Machine Age: Work, Progress, and Prosperity in a Time of Brilliant Technologies* (New York: W. W. Norton & Company, 2014).

19. Bob Metcalfe coined his law when he worked at Xerox PARC, where he and his team invented the Ethernet, which was initially used for local networking—that is, joining clusters of PCs to basic servers; see Metcalfe, "Metcalfe's Law." It was George Gilder who first brought the world's attention to what Metcalfe articulated in the early 1990s; see his 2000 book *Telecosm: How Infinite Bandwidth Will Revolutionize Our World*.

20. There are many Internet laws, and more will be coined as the digital revolution proceeds. Besides those of Moore and Metcalfe, those by Gilder, Sarnoff, and Zuckerberg are all accredited with generalizations that appear to have some validity with respect to the Internet: see https://www.netlingo.com/word/gilders-law.php (Gilder); https://techcrunch.com/2011/07/06/mark-zuckerberg-explains-his-law-of-social-sharing-video (Zuckerberg); and http://protocoldigital.com/blog/sarnoffs-law/ (Sarnoff);.

21. In chapter 1, we noted Nicholas Negroponte's distinction between a world based on atoms and one based on bits, which we loosely associate with our great transition between a world of no cities and one of cities; see Negroponte, *Being Digital*.

22. This is the earliest reference to the term "smart city" we have come across; see D. V. Gibson, G. Kozmetsky, and R. W. Smilor, *The Technopolis Phenomenon: Smart*

Cities, Fast Systems, Global Networks (Lanham, MD: Rowman and Littlefield Publishers, 1992). In the 1980s and early 1990s, the terms "wired city" and "information city" were being more widely used; see W. H. Dutton, Blumler, J. G., and Kraemer, K. L., eds., *Wired Cities: Shaping the Future of Communications* (New York: MacMillan, 1987); and M. Castells, *The Informational City: Economic Restructuring and Urban Development* (New York: John Wiley and Sons, 1991).

23. M. Batty, "The Computable City," *International Planning Studies* 2 (1997): 155–173.

24. See Lucy Williamson's article in 2013, "Tomorrow's Cities: Just How Smart Is Songdo?", *BBC News Technology*, September 2, http://www.bbc.co.uk/news/technology -23757738; and Jane Wakefield's article in 2013, "Tomorrow's Cities: Do You Want to Live in a Smart City?," *BBC News Technology*, August 19, http://www.bbc.co.uk /news/technology-22538561.

25. Singapore has pioneered plans for informating and automating their society and city-state since their 1980s Intelligent Island program; see M. Batty, "Technology Highs," *The Guardian*, June 22, 1989; and http://smartisland.com/singapore-the -smart-island-smart-nation.

26. There are currently (as of the end of 2017) some 2.32 billion smartphones in a world population of 7.59 billion; that is, some 30 percent own such phones. This is projected to rise 2.87 billion by 2020; see https://www.statista.com/statistics/330695 /number-of-smartphone-users-worldwide.

27. Attempts to automate routine functions in cities, such as policing and emergency services, have a long and somewhat checkered history. A summary of the key attempts from the 1960s on and an interpretation of the experience is given in M. Batty, "Commentary. Can It Happen Again? Planning Support, Lee's Requiem and the Rise of the Smart Cities Movement," *Environment and Planning B* 41 (2014): 388–391.

28. Anthony Townsend's book deals with several dimensions of the smart cities movement, which also incorporates the development of systems and complexity approaches to cities and urban policy; see Townsend, *Smart Cities: Big Data, Civic Hackers, and the Quest for a New Utopia* (New York: W. W. Norton and Company, 2013).

29. M. Batty, "Cities as Systems of Networks and Flows," in T. Haas and H. Westlund, eds., *In The Post-Urban World: Emergent Transformation of Cities and Regions in the Innovative Global Economy* (London: Routledge, 2017), 56–69.

30. West, *Scale*.

31. The term paradigm is used similarly to Thomas Kuhn's 1962 book *The Structure of Scientific Revolutions* (Chicago: University of Chicago Press). In essence, a paradigm can be defined as a major shift in the way a body of scientists approach a phenomenon after widespread agreement that the old ways are no longer appropriate and the new are able to resolve outstanding problems. In terms of science, these are

usually major changes in world view, but in the social sciences, there can be many paradigms all competing with one another at different scales and embodying different ideologies. It is in this context that we are using the term.

32. Batty, "Can It Happen Again?"; Townsend, *Smart Cities*.

33. Batty, *Computable City*.

34. M. Batty, "Big Data and the City," *Built Environment* 42, no. 3 (2016): 321–337.

35. Schwab, *Fourth Industrial Revolution*.

36. Kondratieff, " Long Waves in Economic Life"; Schumpeter, *Business Cycles*.

37. S. S. Kuznets, *Economic Change: Selected Essays in Business Cycles, National Income, and Economic Growth* (New York: W. W. Norton, 1953).

38. H. J. Naumer, D. Nacken, and S. Scheurer, *The Sixth Kondratieff—Long Waves of Prosperity*, Allianz Global Investors, 2010, Frankfurt am Main, Germany.

39. It is worth noting Stewart Brand's *Long Now Foundation* is an organization associated with developing a long-term perspective on social and technological evolution, endowing society with a long-term collective memory; see S. Brand, *The Clock of the Long Now: Time and Responsibility* (New York: Basic Books, 1999).

40. Von Foerster et al., "Doomsday"; and Kurzweil, *Singularity*.

41. Brynjolfsson and McAfee, *Race Against the Machine*.

42. J. B. S. Haldane, *Possible Worlds and Other Essays* (London: Chatto and Windus, 1926), 285–286.

Chapter 8

1. In his 2005 book *The Singularity Is Near*, Ray Kurzweil provides a detailed account of how successive waves of new technology are mounting and thus, in his view, leading to singularity before the middle of the 21st century is reached. His law of accelerating returns can be compared to a succession of ever shorter and more intense waves of invention—that is, Kondratieff waves. See his websites for useful archives of the evidence: http://www.kurzweilai.net and http://www.singularity.com/charts.

2. Freeman Dyson in his insightful commentaries on science and the future in his 1989 book, *Infinite in All Directions* (New York: Harper), 180.

3. Kurzweil, *Singularity*.

4. Rick Reider, "The Topic We Should All Be Paying Attention to (in 3 Charts)," 2015, Blackrock Blog, https://www.blackrockblog.com/2015/12/11/economic-trends -in-charts.

5. See R. R. Clewlow and G. S. Mishra, "Disruptive Transportation: The Adoption, Utilization, and Impacts of Ride-Hailing in the United States," research report UCD-ITS-RR-17–07, 2017, Institute of Transportation Studies, University of California, Davis, and CityLab, https://www.citylab.com/transportation/2017/02/uber-lyft -transportation-network-companies-effect-on-transit-ridership-new-york-city/517932.

6. C. Jones and N. Livingstone, "The 'Online High Street' or the High Street Online? The Implications for the Urban Retail Hierarchy," *The International Review of Retail, Distribution and Consumer Research* 28, no. 1 (2018): 47–63, https://doi.org/10.1080 /09593969.2017.1393441.

7. M. Batty, "Invisible Cities," *Environment and Planning B* 17 (1990): 127–130.

8. The received wisdom has somewhat changed in the last 50 years. In her 1969 book *The Economy of Cities,* Jane Jacobs vociferously argued urban pursuits existed even in nomadic times, and that when distinct cities actually emerged in Sumeria, urban life had already become established, alongside the Agricultural Revolution that began around 10,000 BCE.

9. The "second machine age," a term used by Brynjolfsson and McAfee in their 2014 book, was actually first used by J. M. Keynes, according to John Lancaster (see https:// www.lrb.co.uk/v37/n05/john-lanchester/the-robots-are-coming). Keynes wrote about it, but only used the notion of a second age implicitly in his 1931 essay "The Economic Possibilities for our Grandchildren," in his *Essays in Persuasion* (London: Macmillan). In fact, Reyner Banham also used the term in the title of his book 1960 book *Theory and Design in the First Machine Age;* the emphasis was on much earlier technologies than those discussed by Brynjolfsson and McAfee.

10. M. Ford, *The Rise of the Robots: Technology and the Threat of Mass Unemployment* (New York: Basic Books, 2015).

11. There are many books and papers on neural nets and deep learning, but a recent basic text is Ethem Alpaydin's *Introduction to Machine Learning,* 3rd ed. (Cambridge, MA: MIT Press, 2014), which introduces the range of techniques and models that lie at the basis of contemporary AI and pattern recognition.

12. The Tesla accident has been widely reported, since it is the first involving a fatality and a car with autonomous capabilities; see https://www.theguardian .com/technology/2016/jun/30/tesla-autopilot-death-self-driving-car-elon-musk. For reporting on the accident in Phoenix, see https://www.theguardian.com/technology /2018/mar/19/uber-self-driving-car-kills-woman-arizona-tempe and https://www .technologyreview.com/the-download/611094/in-a-fatal-crash-ubers-autonomous -car-detected-a-pedestrian-but-chose-to-not/ (quote in text from latter link).

13. A. M. Turing, "Computing Machinery and Intelligence," *Mind* 59, no. 236 (1950): 460.

14. Artificial intelligence developed very rapidly from the 1950s. The general goal of programming computers was to simulate as closely as possible human decision making. However, by the 1980s, it was generally recognized that this was a fruitless task, and the field switched to considering how computers could be made to produce intelligible outputs, largely through exploiting massive databases and neural net–like algorithms to simulate structures that explained a variety of patterns. The key difference between the early days and the present is that there is no longer any quest for causal explanation. Most current activity, although using language that implies explanation like "learning," is simply based on pattern matching.

15. M. Batty, *Cities and Complexity: Understanding Cities with Cellular Automata, Agent-Based Models, and Fractals* (Cambridge, MA: The MIT Press, 2005).

16. Helen Rosenau's book provides a useful compendium of largely Renaissance ideal city plans; see Rosenau, *The Ideal City.*

17. Figure 8.2(a) is taken from various city plan forms reproduced in Morris's *History of Urban Form*. Naarden is one of the most complete fortified towns in Europe and is part of an outer defensive ring around Amsterdam. Figure 8.2(b) is taken from https://www.iamsterdam.com/en/plan-your-trip/day-trips/castles-and-gardens/naarden.

18. Ebenezer Howard's garden city was first published in 1898 as *Tomorrow: A Peaceful Path to Reform*. A revised second edition was printed in 1902 with a different title, *Garden Cities of Tomorrow.*

19. Batty, *New Science.*

20. *Uxcester Masterplan*, A Report for the Wolfson Economics Prize, Urbed, 2014, available at http://urbed.coop/projects/wolfson-economic-prize.

21. M. Batty, "The Size, Scale, and Shape of Cities," *Science* 319, no. 5864 (February 8, 2008): 769–771.

22. L. Krier, *The Architecture of Community* (Washington, DC: Island Press, 2011).

23. Arturo Soria y Mata produced his Ciudad Lineal in 1882 as an idea for controlled expansion of a city organized around a main transport artery using the example of Madrid: see http://arqui-2.blogspot.co.uk/2014/07/ciudad-lineal-la-utopia-construida-de.html.

24. J. R. Gold, "The MARS Plans for London, 1933–1942: Plurality and Experimentation in the City Plans of the Early British Modern Movement," *Town Planning Review* 66 (1995): 243–267.

25. Llewelyn-Davies, Weeks, Forestier-Walker, and Bor, Milton Keynes Planning Study, *Architects' Journal*, 1969, https://www.architectsjournal.co.uk/news/culture/aj-archive-milton-keynes-planning-study-1969/10016661.article.

26. Rudolf Müller, Osterreichische Wochenschrift fur den offentlich Baudienst, XIV, Jg. 1908. Translated by Eric M. Nay, Cornell University, 1995, http://urbanplanning .library.cornell.edu/DOCS/muller.htm.

27. Charles R. Lamb, "City Plan," *The Craftsman* 6 (1904): 3–13, http://urbanplan ning.library.cornell.edu/DOCS/lamb.htm.

28. Christaller, *Die Zentralen Orte*; and https://blogs.ethz.ch/prespecific/2013/05/01/ diagrams-christaller-central-place-theory. Various idealized central place theory (CPT) landscapes are presented in T. Akamatsu, Y. Takayama, and K. Ikeda, "Self-Organization of Hexagonal Agglomeration Patterns in New Economic Geography Models," *Journal of Economic Behavior and Organization* 99 (2014): 32–52.

29. Thomas Schelling's original article in 1969 "Models of Segregation" (*American Economic Review, Papers and Proceedings* 58: 488–493) was very much a thought experiment with hardly any reference to residential location. The model is elaborated a little more in his book *Micromotives and Macrobehavior*.

30. Batty, *Cities and Complexity*.

31. The picture in Figure 8.5(a) is from the Southern Cape Peninsula segregated communities of Masiphumelele and Lake Michelle area, 20 km (12 mi) from Cape Town, South Africa, and is available at http://unequalscenes.com/masiphumelele -lake-michelle.

32. For a comprehensive review and extensions, see W. A. V. Clark and M. Fossett, "Understanding the Social Context of the Schelling Segregation Model," *Proceedings of the National Academy of Sciences USA* 105, no. 11 (2008): 4109–4114.

33. The boundary between Scottsdale, Arizona, and the Salt River Indian Reservation, at https://www.reddit.com/r/CityPorn/comments/71c7w4/the_boundary_between _scottsdale_arizona_usa_and.

34. Tobler, "Computer Movie."

35. Glaeser, *Triumph of the City*, 60.

36. Kurzweil, *Singularity*.

37. Most commentaries on the future, whether from journalists or academics, tend to focus on making predictions. Yuval Harari's recent (2016) book *Homo Deus: A Brief History of Tomorrow* (London: Vintage) is an exception, for he is intent on demonstrating that the future is largely unknowable, as it always has been.

38. Turing, "Computing Machinery," 460.

Bibliography

Abercrombie, P. *Greater London Plan 1944*. London: His Majesty's Stationery Office, 1945.

Akamatsu, T., Y. Takayama, and K. Ikeda. Self-Organization of Hexagonal Agglomeration Patterns in New Economic Geography Models. *Journal of Economic Behavior & Organization* 99 (2014): 32–52.

Alexander, C. A City Is Not a Tree. *Architectural Forum* 122 (1+2) (1965): 58–62.

Alexander, C. *Notes on the Synthesis of Form*. Cambridge, MA: Harvard University Press, 1962.

Alonso, W. The Economics of Urban Size. *Papers and Proceedings of the Regional Science Association* 26 (1971): 67–83.

Alonso, W. *Location and Land Use: Toward a General Theory of Land Rent*. Cambridge, MA: Harvard University Press, 1964.

Alpaydin, E. *Introduction to Machine Learning*. 3rd ed. Cambridge, MA: The MIT Press, 2014.

Anderson, P. W. More Is Different. *Science* 177, no. 4047 (1972): 393–396.

Arcaute, E., E. Hatna, P. Ferguson, H. Youn, A. Johansson, and M. Batty. Constructing Cities, Deconstructing Scaling Laws. *Journal of the Royal Society, Interface* 12 (2015): 20140745.

Arcaute, E., C. Molineros, E. Hatna, R. Murcio, C. Vargas-Ruiz, A. P. Masucci, and M. Batty. Cities and Regions in Britain through Hierarchical Percolation. *Royal Society Open Science* 3 (2016): 150691. doi:10.1098/rsos.150691.

Ball, A. H. R. The Modern City. Lectures on Socialism: Art Under Plutocracy. In *Selections from the Prose Works of William Morris*, 108–110. 1931. Reprint, Cambridge, UK: Cambridge University Press, 2014. https://www.marxists.org/archive/morris/works/1883/pluto.htm.

Banham, R. *Theory and Design in the First Machine Age.* 1960. Reprint, Cambridge, MA: The MIT Press, 1980.

Barabási, A.-L., and M. Pósfai. *Network Science.* Cambridge, UK: Cambridge University Press, 2016.

Barbosa-Filho, H., M. Barthelemy, G. Ghoshal, C. R. James, M. Lenormand, T. Louail, R. Menezes, J. J., Ramasco, S. Simini, and M. Tomasini. Human Mobility: Models and Applications. Preprint, submitted September 29, 2017. arXiv:1710.00004v1.

Barr, J. M. *Building the Skyline: The Birth and Growth of Manhattan's Skyscrapers.* New York: Oxford University Press, 2016.

Barr. J., and J. Cohen. Why are Skyscrapers So Tall? Land Use and the Spatial Location of Buildings in New York. 2010. https://www.aeaweb.org/conference/2011/retrieve.php?pdfid=352.

Barras, R. *Building Cycles: Growth and Instability.* London: Wiley-Blackwell, 2009.

Barthelemy, M. *The Structure and Dynamics of Cities: Urban Data Analysis and Theoretical Modeling.* Cambridge, UK: Cambridge University Press, 2016.

Batty, M. Big Data and the City. *Built Environment* 42, no. 3 (2016): 321–337.

Batty, M. *Cities and Complexity: Understanding Cities with Cellular Automata, Agent-Based Models, and Fractals.* Cambridge, MA: The MIT Press, 2005.

Batty, M. Cities as Complex Systems: Scaling. Interactions. Networks. Dynamics and Urban Morphologies. In *Encyclopedia of Complexity and Systems Science*, vol. 1, edited by R. Meyers, 1041–1071. Berlin: Springer, 2009.

Batty, M. Cities as Systems of Networks and Flows. In *The Post-Urban World: Emergent Transformation of Cities and Regions in the Innovative Global Economy*, edited by T. Haas and H. Westlund, 56–69. London: Routledge, 2017.

Batty, M. Cities in Civilization. *Regional Studies* 51 (2017): 1282–1284.

Batty, M. Cities in Disequilibrium. In *Non-Equilibrium Social Science and Policy: Introduction and Essays on New and Changing Paradigms in Socio-Economic Thinking*, edited by J. Johnson, A. Nowak, P. Ormerod, B. Rosewell, and Y-C. Zhang, 81–96. New York: Springer, 2017.

Batty, M. Commentary. Can It Happen Again? Planning Support. Lee's Requiem and the Rise of the Smart Cities Movement. *Environment & Planning B* 41 (2014): 388–391.

Batty, M. The Computable City. *International Planning Studies* 2 (1997): 155–173.

Batty, M. The Creative Destruction of Cities. *Environment & Planning B* 34 (2007): 1–4.

Batty, M. Invisible Cities. *Environment & Planning B* 17 (1990): 127–130.

Batty, M. *The New Science of Cities*. Cambridge, MA: The MIT Press, 2013.

Batty, M. New Ways of Looking at Cities. *Nature* 377 (1995): 574.

Batty, M. Optimal Cities, Ideal Cities. *Environment and Planning B: Planning & Design* 42 (2015): 571–573.

Batty, M. Rank Clocks. *Nature* 444 (2006): 592–596.

Batty, M. The Size, Scale, and Shape of Cities. *Science* 319, no. 5864 (2008): 769–771.

Batty, M. Technology Highs. *The Guardian*, June 22, 1989, 29.

Batty, M. A Theory of City Size (Perspectives). *Science* 340 (2013), 1418–1419.

Batty, M. Visualizing Creative Destruction. Working paper 112. Centre for Advanced Spatial Analysis, University College London. 2007. https://www.ucl.ac.uk/drupal/bartlett/casa/sites/bartlett/files/migrated-files/paper112_0.pdf.

Batty, M., and P. Longley. *Fractal Cities: A Geometry of Form and Function*. London: Academic Press, 1994. http://www.fractalcities.org.

Batty, M., and P. Ferguson. Defining Density. *Environment & Planning B* 38 (2011): 753–756.

Beckman, M. J. On the Distribution of Urban Rent and Residential Density. *Journal of Economic Theory* 1 (1969): 60–67.

Beinhocker, E. D. *The Origin of Wealth: Evolution, Complexity, and the Radical Remaking of Economics*. Boston: Harvard Business School Press, 2006.

Benkler, Y. *The Wealth of Networks*. New Haven, CT: Yale University Press, 2006.

Bettencourt, L. M., J. Lobo, D. Helbing, C. Kühnert, and G. B. West. Growth, Innovation, Scaling, and the Pace of Life in Cities. *Proceedings of the National Academy of Sciences of the United States of America* 104, no. 17 (2007): 7301–7306.

Blum, A. *Tubes: A Journey to the Center of the Internet*. London: Ecco Press, 2012.

Bornstein, M., and H. Bornstein. The Pace of Life. *Nature* 259 (1976): 557–558.

Boyle, E., L. Engelhardt, and M. Thornton. Is There Such a Thing as a Skyscraper Curse? *Quarterly Journal of Austrian Economics* 19, no. 2 (2012): 149–168.

Brand, S. *The Clock of the Long Now: Time and Responsibility*. New York: Basic Books, 1999.

Brenner, N. J., ed. *Implosions/Explosions: Towards a Study of Planetary Urbanization*. Berlin: Jovis Verlag, 2014.

Brenner, N., and C. Schmid. Towards a New Epistemology of the Urban? *City* 19, no. 2–3 (2015): 151–182.

Brynjolfsson, E., and A. McAfee. *Race Against the Machine*. Lexington, MA: Digital Frontier Press, 2011.

Brynjolfsson, E., and A. McAfee. *The Second Machine Age: Work. Progress. and Prosperity in a Time of Brilliant Technologies*. New York: W. W. Norton, 2014.

Burdett, R., and D. Sudjic, eds. *The Endless City*. London: Phaidon Press, 2007.

Butler, P. *Visualizing Friendships*. December 13, 2010. https://www.facebook.com/notes/facebook-engineering/visualizingfriendships/469716398919; http://www.notcot.com/archives/2010/12/a-world-mapped-by-friends.php.

Bush, V. As We May Think. *Atlantic Monthly* 176, no. 1 (1945): 101–108.

Cairncross, F. The Death of Distance. *The Economist*, September 30, 1995, 5–28.

Cairncross, F. *The Death of Distance: How the Communications Revolution Is Changing Our Lives*. Cambridge, MA: Harvard Business Review Press, 2001.

Cary, J. *Survey of the High Roads from London to Hampton Court.... Richmond. Arundel Street, Strand*. London: John Carey, 1790.

Castells, M. *The Informational City: Economic Restructuring and Urban Development*. New York: John Wiley and Sons, 1991.

Chalmers, A. F. *What Is This Thing Called Science?* 3rd ed. Maidenhead, UK: The Open University Press, 1999.

Chandler, T. *Four Thousand Years of Urban Growth: An Historical Census*. Lampeter, UK: Edward Mellon, 1987.

Chapin, F. S., and P. H. Stewart. Population Densities around the Clock. In *Readings in Urban Geography*, edited by H. H. Mayer and C. F. Kohn, 180–182. Chicago: University of Chicago Press, 1959.

Charbit, Y. The Platonic City: History and Utopia. *Population* 57, no. 2 (2002): 207–235.

Christaller, W. *Die Zentralen Orte in Siiddeutschland*. Jena, Germany: Gustav Fischer Verlag, 1933. Published in English as *Central Places in Southern Germany*, trans. C. W. Baskin (Englewood Cliffs, NJ: Prentice Hall, 1966.

Churchman, C. West. Wicked Problems. *Management Science* 14, no. 4 (1967): B141–B142.

Clark, W. A. V., and M. Fossett. Understanding the Social Context of the Schelling Segregation Model. *Proceedings of the National Academy of Sciences of the United States of America* 105, no. 11 (2008): 4109–4114.

Clewlow, R. R., and G. S. Mishra. Disruptive Transportation: The Adoption, Utilization, and Impacts of Ride-Hailing in the United States. Research Report UCD-ITS-RR-17-07. Davis, CA: Institute of Transportation Studies. University of California, 2017.

Cobbett, W. *Rural Rides*. London: T. Nelson and Company, 1821. http://www
.gutenberg.org/files/34238/34238-h/34238-h.htm.

Cochrane, E. A. *The Cathedral of Commerce*. New York: Broadway Park Place Company,
1916. http://archive.org/stream/thecathedralofco00cochiala#page/28/mode/2up.

Corbusier, Le. *The City of Tomorrow and Its Planning*. 1929. Reprint, New York: Dover
Publications, 1987.

Corbusier, Le. *Towards a New Architecture*. 1927. Reprint, New York: Dover Publications, 1985.

Cottineau, C., E. Hatna, E. Arcaute, and M. Batty. Diverse Cities or the Systematic
Paradox of Urban Scaling Laws. *Computers, Environment and Urban Systems* 63 (2017):
80–94.

Cristelli, M., M. Batty, and L. Pietronero. There Is More than a Power Law in Zipf.
Scientific Reports 2 (2012): 812. doi:10.1038/srep00812.

Cruz, P. M. Lisbon's Blood Vessels—A Mapping Experiment. 2011. https://vimeo.com
/31031656 and http://pmcruz.com/information-visualization/lisbons-blood-vessels.

Cura, R., C. Cottineau, E. Swerts, C. Antonio Ignazzi, A. Bretagnolle, C. Vacchiani-
Marcuzzo, and D. Pumain. The Old and the New: Qualifying City Systems in the
World with Classical Models and New Data. *Geographical Analysis* 49, no. 4: 363–386
(2017). doi:10.1111/gean.12129.

Dantzig, G. B., and T. L. Saaty. *Compact City: A Plan for a Liveable Urban Environment*.
San Francisco: W. H. Freeman and Company, 1973.

Davies, M. *Ecology of Fear: Los Angeles and the Imagination of Disaster*. New York: Vintage Books, 1999.

Dijkstra, L., and H. Poelman. A Harmonised Definition of Cities and Rural Areas:
The New Degree of Urbanisation. Regional Working Paper 01/2014. Brussels: European Commission Directorate-General for Regional and Urban Policy, 2014.

Doxiadis, C. A. Action for Human Settlements. *Ekistics* 40, no. 241 (1975): 405–448.

Dunbar, R. I. M. Neocortex Size as a Constraint on Group Size in Primates. *Journal of
Human Evolution* 22, no. 6 (1992): 469–493.

Dutton, W. H., J. G. Blumler, and K. L. Kraemer, eds. *Wired Cities: Shaping the Future
of Communications*. New York: MacMillan, 1987.

Dyson, F. *Infinite in All Directions*. New York: Harper, 1989.

Dyson, G. *Turing's Cathedral: The Origins of the Digital Universe*. New York: Pantheon
Books, 2012.

Ewing, R. Is Los Angeles-Style Sprawl Desirable? *Journal of the American Planning
Association* 66, no. 1 (1997): 107–126.

Fischer, C. S. *America Calling: A Social History of the Telephone to 1940*. Berkeley, CA: University of California Press, 1994.

Fischer, C. S. *To Dwell Among Friends: Personal Networks in Town and City*. Chicago: University of Chicago Press, 1982.

Florida, R. *The New Urban Crisis*. New York: Basic Books, 2017.

Ford, M. *The Rise of the Robots: Technology and the Threat of Mass Unemployment*. New York: Basic Books, 2015.

Forster, E. M. *The Machine Stops*. 1909. Reprint, London: Penguin Classics, 2017.

Foster, R., and S. Kaplan. *Creative Destruction: Why Companies That Are Built to Last Underperform the Market and How to Successfully Transform Them*. New York: Doubleday, 2001.

Gabor, D. *Inventing the Future*. London: Secker and Warburg, 1963.

Garreau, J. *Edge City: Life on the New Frontier*. New York: Doubleday, 1991.

Geddes, P. G. *Cities in Evolution*. London: Norgate and Williams, 1915.

Gerland, P. E., A. E. Raftery, H. Ševčíková, N. Li, D. Gu, T. Spoorenberg, L. Alkema, et al. World Population Stabilization Unlikely This Century. *Science* 346, no. 6206 (2014): 234–237.

Gibrat, R. *Les Inégalités Économiques*. Paris: Recueil Sirey, 1931.

Gibson, D. V., G. Kozmetsky, and R. W. Smilor. *The Technopolis Phenomenon: Smart Cities, Fast Systems, Global Networks*. Lanham, MD: Rowman and Littlefield Publishers, 1992.

Gilbert, C. The Financial Importance of Rapid Building. *Engineering Record* 41 (1900): 643–644.

Gilder, G. Gilder's Law. 2018. https://www.netlingo.com/word/gilders-law.php.

Gilder, G. *Telecosm: How Infinite Bandwidth Will Revolutionize Our World*. Glencoe, NY: Free Press. 2000.

Glaeser, E. *Triumph of the City: How Our Greatest Invention Makes Us Richer, Smarter, Greener, Healthier, and Happier*. New York: Penguin Press, 2012.

Gobry, P.-E. Facebook Investor Wants Flying Cars, Not 140 Characters. *Business Insider*, July 30, 2011. http://www.businessinsider.com/founders-fund-the-future-2011-7?IR-T.

Goethe, J. W. von. *Zur Morphologie*. Stuttgart, Germany: J. G. Cotta Publishers, 1817.

Gold, J. R. The MARS Plans for London, 1933–1942: Plurality and Experimentation in the City Plans of the Early British Modern Movement. *Town Planning Review* 66 (1995): 243–267.

Gonzalez-Navarro, M., and M. A. Turner. Subways and Urban Growth: Evidence from Earth. Spatial Economics Research Centre. SERC Discussion Paper No. 195. London: London School of Economics, 2016.

Gordon, P., and H. W. Richardson. Are Compact Cities a Desirable Planning Goal? *Journal of the American Planning Association* 66, no. 1 (1997): 95–106.

Gottmann, J. *Megalopolis: The Urbanized Northeastern Seaboard of the United States.* New York: The Twentieth Century Fund, 1961.

Gray, S., O. O'Brien, and S. Hügel. Collecting and Visualizing Real-Time Urban Data through City Dashboards. *Built Environment* 42, no. 3 (2016): 498–509.

Greenfield, A. *Radical Technologies: The Design of Everyday Life.* London: Verso, 2017.

Gruen, V. *The Heart of Our Cities: The Urban Crisis. Diagnosis and Cure.* London: Thames and Hudson, 1965.

Hägerstrand, T. What about People in Regional Science? *Papers of the Regional Science Association* 24 (1970): 7–21.

Haldane, J. B. S. On Being the Right Size. *Harper's Magazine*, March 1926, 424–427.

Haldane, J. B. S. *Possible Worlds and Other Essays.* London: Chatto and Windus, 1926.

Hall, P. The Geography of the Fifth Kondratieff Cycle. *New Society* 26 (March 1981): 535–537.

Hall, P., and P. Preston. *The Carrier Wave: New Information Technology and the Geography of Innovation 1846–2003.* London: Unwin Hyman, 1988.

Hall, P. G. *Cities in Civilization.* New York: Pantheon, 1998.

Hall, P. G. *The World Cities.* London: Weidenfeld and Nicolson, 1966.

Hanson, J. Order and Structure in Urban Design: The Plans for the Rebuilding of London after the Great Fire of 1666. *Ekistics* 56, no. 334–335 (1989): 22–42.

Harari, Y. N. *Homo Deus: A Brief History of Tomorrow.* London: Vintage, 2016.

Harvey, D. *The Condition of Postmodernity: An Enquiry into the Origins of Cultural Change*, 284–307. Oxford, UK: Blackwell, 1989.

Hawking, S. Science in the Next Millennium. The White House Millennium Council. Washington DC. 1998. https://clintonwhitehouse4.archives.gov/Initiatives/Millennium/shawking.html.

Head, B., and W.-N. Xiang. Working with Wicked Problems in Socio-Ecological Systems: More Awareness, Greater Acceptance, and Better Adaptation. Special issue. *Landscape and Urban Planning* 154 (2016): 1–132.

Hein, P. *Grooks 1.* New York: Doubleday and Company, 1969.

Holland, J. H. *Emergence: From Chaos to Order*. Reading, MA: Perseus Books, 1998.

Holland, J. H. *Hidden Order: How Adaptation Builds Complexity*. Reading, MA: Addison-Wesley, 1995.

Howard, E. *To-morrow: A Peaceful Path to Real Reform*. 1898. Reprint, London: Routledge, 2009.

Hoyt, H. *One Hundred Years of Land Values in Chicago*. 1933. Reprint, New York: Arno Press, 1970.

Huxley, J. S. *Problems of Relative Growth*. Baltimore, MD: Johns Hopkins University Press, 1993.

IBM. Watson Marketing: 10 Key Marketing Trends for 2017. 2017, https://www-01 .ibm.com/common/ssi/cgi-bin/ssialias?htmlfid=WRL12345USEN.

Jackson, K. T. *Crabgrass Frontier: The Suburbanization of the United States*. New York: Oxford University Press, 1985.

Jacobs, J. *The Death and Life of Great American Cities*. New York: Random House, 1961.

Jacobs, J. *The Economy of Cities*. New York: Random House, 1969.

Jefferson, M. The Law of the Primate City. *Geographical Review* 29 (1939): 226–232.

Jones, C., and N. Livingstone. The 'Online High Street' or the High Street Online? The Implications for the Urban Retail Hierarchy. *The International Review of Retail Distribution and Consumer Research* 28 (2017): 47–63. https://doi.org/10.1080/09593969 .2017.1393441.

Karlgaard, R. and M. Malone. City vs. Country: Tom Peters and George Gilder Debate the Impact of Technology on Location. Technology Issue. *Forbes ASAP* 155, no. 5 (February 27, 1995): 56–61.

Keynes, J. M. *Essays in Persuasion*. London: Macmillan, 1931.

Khanna, P. *Connectography: Mapping the Future of Global Civilization*. New York: Random House, 2016.

Kitchin, R., T. P. Lauriault, and G. McArdle, eds. *Data and the City*. London: Routledge, 2017.

Kitchin, R., T. Lauriault, and G. McArdle. Knowing and Governing Cities through Urban Indicators, City Benchmarking and Real-Time Dashboards. *Regional Studies, Regional Science* 2 (2015): 1–28.

Kohl, J. *Der Verkehr und die Ansiedelung der Menschen in ihrer Abhangigkeit uon der Gestaltung der Eudoberflache*. Leipzig, Germany: Arnoldische Buchhandlung, 1841.

Kondratieff, N. D. The Long Waves in Economic Life. Translated by W. F. Stolper. First published 1926. *Review of Economics and Statistics* 17 (1935): 105–115.

Kondratieff, N. D. *The Major Economic Cycles*. First published as *The Long Wave Cycle*, translated by G. Daniels, 1925. Reprint, New York: E. P. Dutton, 1984.

Koolhaas, R. *Delirious New York: A Retroactive Manifesto for Manhattan*. 1978. Reprint, New York: Monacelli Press, 1994.

Kostof, S. *The City Assembled: The Elements of Urban Form Through History*. London: Thames and Hudson, 1999.

Kostof, S. *The City Shaped: Urban Patterns and Meanings Through History*. London: Thames and Hudson, 1999.

Krier, L. *The Architecture of Community*. Washington, DC: Island Press, 2011.

Krugman, P. A. Confronting the Mystery of Urban Hierarchy. *Journal of the Japanese and International Economies* 10 (1996): 399–418.

Krugman, P. A. *The Self-Organizing Economy*. Boston: Blackwell, 1996.

Kuhn, T. S. *The Structure of Scientific Revolutions*. Chicago: University of Chicago Press, 1962.

Kurzweil, R. *The Singularity Is Near*. New York: Viking Penguin, 2005.

Kuznets, S. S. *Economic Change: Selected Essays in Business Cycles, National Income, and Economic Growth*. New York: W. W. Norton, 1953.

Lacy, K. The New Sociology of Suburbs: A Research Agenda for Analysis of Emerging Trends. *Annual Review of Sociology* 42 (2016): 369–384.

Lamb, C. R. City Plan. *Craftsman* 6 (1904): 3–13. http://urbanplanning.library .cornell.edu/DOCS/lamb.htm.

Law, A. The Ghost of Patrick Geddes: Civics As Applied Sociology. *Sociological Research Online* 10, no. 2 (2005). http://www.socresonline.org.uk/10/2/law.html.

Lawrence, A. The Curse Bites: Skyscraper Index Strikes. Property Report, Dresdner Kleinwort. London: Benson Research, 1999.

Lefebvre, H. *Writings on Cities*. Oxford, UK: Blackwell, 1996.

Leonardo da Vinci. *Notebooks of Leonardo da Vinci 1452–1519*. Translated and arranged by E. MacCurdy. New York: Braziller, 1955. https://archive.org/details /noteboo00leon accessed 12/18/2017.

Lenormand, M., T. Louail, O. G. Cantú-Ros, M. Cornell, R. Harran, J. M. Arias, M. Barthelemy, M. San Miguel, and J. J. Aramco. Influence of Sociodemographic Characteristics on Human Mobility. *Scientific Reports* 5 (2015): 10075. doi:10.1038/srep10075.

Lessinger, J. The Case for Scatteration: Some Reflections on the National Capital Region Plan for the Year 2000. *Journal of the American Institute of Planners* 38, no. 2 (1962): 159–169.

Llewelyn-Davies, Weeks, Forestier-Walker, and Bor. Milton Keynes Planning Study. 50th anniversary edition. *Architects' Journal* (1969). https://www.architectsjournal.co .uk/news/culture/aj-archive-milton-keynes-planning-study-1969/10016661.article.

Longley, P. A., and M. Adnan. Geo-temporal Twitter Demographics. *International Journal of Geographical Information Science* 30, no. 2 (2016): 369–389.

Lorenz, E. Predictability: Does the Flap of a Butterfly's Wings in Brazil Cause a Tornado in Texas? Paper given to the 139th Meeting of the American Association for the Advancement of Science. 1972. http://eaps4.mit.edu/research/Lorenz/Butterfly_1972 .pdf.

MacKaye, B. *From Geography to Geotechnics*. Urbana, IL: University of Illinois Press, 1968.

MacKaye, B. *The New Exploration*. New York: Harcourt and Brace, 1928.

Malthus, T. R. *1798. An Essay on the Principle of Population*. Oxford, UK: Oxford University Press Edition, 2008.

Marshall, A. *Principles of Economics*. 8th ed. 1890. Reprint, London: Macmillan and Co., 1920.

McGee, T. Urbanisasi or Kotadesasi? Evolving Patterns of Urbanization in Asia. In *Urbanization in Asia*, edited by F. J. Costa, A. K. Dutt, L. J. C. Ma, and A. G. Noble, 93–108. Honolulu, HI: University of Hawaii Press, 1989.

Meadows, D. H., D. L. Meadows, J. Randers, and W. W. Behrens, III. *The Limits to Growth: A Report for the Club of Rome's Project on the Predicament of Mankind*. New York: Universe Books, 1972.

Mehaffy, M. W., ed. *A City Is Not a Tree*. 50th Anniversary Edition. Portland, OR: Sustasis Press in association with The Center for Environmental Structure, 2016.

Meier, G. M., and J. E. Stiglitz, eds. *Frontiers of Development Economics: The Future in Perspective*. Washington, DC: World Bank Publications, 2001.

Meier, R. L. *A Communications Theory of Urban Growth*. Cambridge, MA: The MIT Press, 1962.

Metcalfe, R. Metcalfe's Law after 40 Years of Ethernet. *IEEE Computer* 46, no. 12 (2013): 26–31.

Milgram, S. The Experience of Living in Cities. *Science* 167, no. 3924 (1970): 1461–1468.

Milgram, S. The Small-World Problem. *Psychology Today* 1, no. 1 (1967): 61–67.

Milton, R. Geospatial Computing: Architectures and Algorithms for Mapping Applications. Unpublished PhD thesis. University College London: Centre for Advanced Spatial Analysis, 2017.

Minard, C. *Des Tableaux Graphiques et des Cartes Figuratives.* Paris: E. Thunot et Cie, 1861.

Mitchell, R. B., and C. Rapkin. *Urban Traffic: A Function of Land Use.* New York: Columbia University Press, 1954.

Modelski, G. *World Cities: -3000 to 2000.* Washington, DC: Faros 2000, 2003.

Molineros, C., E. Arcaute, D. Smith, and M. Batty. The Fractured Nature of British Politics. Preprint, submitted May 1, 2015. arXiv:1505.00217.

Moore, G. E. Cramming More Components onto Integrated Circuits. *Electronics* 38, no. 8 (April 19, 1965): 114–117.

Morris, A. E. J. *History of Urban Form: Before the Industrial Revolutions.* 3rd ed. London: Longman, 1994.

Müller, R. Osterreichische Wochenschrift fur den offentlich Baudienst, XIV, Jg. 1908. Translated by Eric M. Nay. Cornell University, Spring 1995. http://urbanplan ning.library.cornell.edu/DOCS/muller.htm.

Mumford, L. *The Culture of Cities.* New York: Harcourt Brace and Company, 1938.

Mumford, L. *The City in History: Its Origins. Its Transformations. and Its Prospects.* New York: Harcourt Brace and Company, 1961.

Mumford, L. What Is a City? *Architectural Record* 82 (1937): 58–62.

NASA. Nightlights Data and Cities at Night. 2018. https://www.nasa.gov/feature /goddard/2017/new-night-lights-maps-open-up-possible-real-time-applications; https://earthobservatory.nasa.gov/Features/CitiesAtNight.

Naumer, H. J., D. Nacken, and S. Scheurer. The Sixth Kondratieff—Long Waves of Prosperity. Allianz Global Investors. Frankfurt am Main, Germany: Kapitalanlagegesellschaft mbH. Mainzer Landstraße. 2010.

Negroponte, N. *Being Digital.* New York: Alfred A. Knopf, 1995.

Neuhaus, F. Urban Rhythms: Habitus and Emergent Spatio-Temporal Dimensions of the City. Unpublished PhD thesis. University College London: Centre for Advanced Spatial Analysis, 2012.

Nordpil. World Database of Large Urban Areas, 1950–2050. Stockholm: Stockholm Resilience Center, Stockholm University, 2014. https://nordpil.com/resources/world -database-of-large-cities/.

Organisation for Economic Co-operation and Development. Definition of Functional Urban Areas (FUA) for the OECD Metropolitan Database. Paris: OECD, 2013. https://www.oecd.org/cfe/regional-policy/Definition-of-Functional-Urban-Areas-for -the-OECD-metropolitan-database.pdf.

Page, M. *The Creative Destruction of Manhattan: 1900–1940*. Chicago: The University of Chicago Press, 1999.

Park, R. E. and E. W. Burgess. *The City*. Chicago: The University of Chicago Press, 1925.

Pesaresi, M., and S. Freire. GHS Settlement grid following the REGIO model 2014 in application to GHSL Landsat and CIESIN GPW v4-Multitemporal 1975–1990–2000–2015. Joint Research Centre, Ispra, Italy: European Commission, 2016. http://data .jrc.ec.europa.eu/dataset/jrc-ghsl-ghs_smod_pop_globe_r2016a.

Pisarenko, V. F., and D. Sornette. Robust Statistical Tests of Dragon-Kings Beyond Power Law Distributions. *European Physical Journal Special Topics* 205 (2012): 95–115.

Popper, K. R. *The Logic of Scientific Discovery*. London: Routledge and Kegan Paul, 1959.

Popper, K. R. *The Poverty of Historicism*. London: Routledge and Kegan Paul, 1957.

Rae, A. Flow Map Layout. 2017. http://www.undertheraedar.com/2010/09/flow-map -layout.html.

Ratti, C. Spring Spree: Spending Patterns in Spain During Easter 2011. MIT Senseable Cities Laboratory, 2013. https://www.youtube.com/watch?v=8J3T3UjHbrE.

Ravenstein, E. G. The Laws of Migration. *Journal of the Statistical Society of London* 48, no. 2 (1885): 167–235.

Reades, J. Pulse of the City. 2012. https://vimeo.com/41760845.

Reades, J., C. Zhong, E. Manley, R. Milton, and M. Batty. Finding Pearls in London's Oysters. *Built Environment* 42, no. 3 (2016): 365–381.

Reba, M., F. Reitsma, and K. C. Seto. Spatializing 6.000 Years of Global Urbanization from 3700 BC to AD 2000. *Scientific Data* 3, no. 160034 (2016). doi:10.1038/ sdata.2016.34.

Reider, R. The Topic We Should All Be Paying Attention To (in 3 Charts). Blackrock Blog, 2015. https://www.blackrockblog.com/2015/12/11/economic-trends-in-charts./

Richardson, H. W. *The Economics of Urban Size. Farnborough*. Hants, UK: Saxon House, Lexington Books, 1973.

Rittel, H. W. J., and M. M. Webber. Dilemmas in a General Theory of Planning. *Policy Sciences* 4 (1973): 155–173.

Roncero, Leticia. "Eric Fischer's Marvelous Maps," May 14, 2015, Flickr Blog, http:// blog.flickr.net/en/2015/05/14/eric-fischers-marvelous-maps/.

Rosenau, H. *The Ideal City: Its Architectural Evolution*. London: Studio Vista, 1974.

Roth, C., S. M. Kang, M. Batty, and M. Barthelemy. A Long-Time Limit for World Subway Networks. *Journal of the Royal Society Interface* 9, no. 75 (2012): 2540–2550. doi:10.1098/rsif.2012.0259.

Russell, B. *The Problems of Philosophy*. Oxford, UK: University Press, 1912.

Sarnoff, D. Sarnoff's Law. 2013. http://protocoldigital.com/blog/sarnoffs-law; http://www.nytimes.com/1971/12/13/archives/david-sarnoff-of-rca-is-dead-visionary-broadcast-pioneer-david.html.

Saxenian, A. *Regional Advantage: Culture and Competition in Silicon Valley and Route 128*. Cambridge, MA: Harvard University Press, 1996.

Schelling, T. C. *Micromotives and Macrobehavior*. New York: W. W. Norton, 1978.

Schelling, T. C. Models of Segregation. *American Economic Review* 58 (1969): 488–493.

Schumpeter, J. *Business Cycles: A Theoretical. Historical. and Statistical Analysis of the Capitalist Process*. 1923. Reprint, New York: McGraw-Hill, 1939.

Schumpeter, J. A. *Capitalism. Socialism and Democracy*. London: George Allen and Unwin, 1938.

Schwab, K. *The Fourth Industrial Revolution*. New York: Portfolio Penguin, 2016.

Sennett, R. *Flesh and Stone: The Body and the City in Western Civilization*. London: Faber and Faber, 1994.

Serras, J., M. Lenormand, V. Zachariadis, R. Herranz, H. Fry, J. Ramasco, and M. Batty. Retail Model Performance Using Transaction Card Data. Presented at the EUNOIA Final Review, Madrid, November 2014. http://eunoia-project.eu/doc/finalevent/; available from joan@prospective.io.

Shannon, C. E. A Symbolic Analysis of Relay and Switching Circuits. *Transactions of the American Institute of Electrical Engineers* 57, no. 12 (1938): 713–723.

Simon, H. A. The Architecture of Complexity. *Proceedings of the American Philosophical Society* 106 (1962): 467–482.

Soria y Mata, A. *Ciudad Lineal*. 1882. http://arqui-2.blogspot.co.uk/2014/07/ciudad-lineal-la-utopia-construida-de.html.

Standage, T. *The Victorian Internet: The Remarkable Story of the Telegraph and the Nineteenth Century's On-line Pioneers*. London: Bloomsbury, 1998.

Sullivan, L. H. The Tall Office Building Artistically Considered. *Lippincott's Magazine*, March 23, 1896, 403–409.

Taleb, N. N. *The Black Swan: The Impact of the Highly Improbable*. New York: Random House, 2007.

Tetlock, P., and D. Gardner. *Superforecasting: The Art and Science of Prediction*. New York: Random House, 2015.

Thompson, D. Wentworth. *On Growth and Form*. Cambridge, UK: Cambridge University Press, 1917.

Thompson, S. A. Which Cities Get the Most Sleep? *Wall Street Journal*, August 15, 2017. http://graphics.wsj.com/how-we-sleep.

Thompson, W. Population. *American Journal of Sociology* 34, no. 6 (1929): 959–975.

Thornton, M. Skyscrapers and Business Cycles. *Quarterly Journal of Austrian Economics* 8, no. 1 (2005): 51–74.

Tobler, W. R. A Computer Movie Simulating Urban Growth in the Detroit Region. *Economic Geography* 46 Supplement (1970): 234–240.

Toffler, A. *Future Shock*. New York: Bantam Books, 1970.

Townsend, A. M. *Smart Cities: Big Data, Civic Hackers, and the Quest for a New Utopia*. New York: W. W. Norton, 2013.

Turing, A. M. Computing Machinery and Intelligence. *Mind* 59, no. 236 (1950): 433–460.

Turing, A. M. Intelligent Machinery. The National Physical Laboratory. London, 1948. http://www.alanturing.net/intelligent_machinery.

United Nations. Comprehensive Tables, vol. I. World Population Prospects: The 2017 Revision. New York: Department of Economic and Social Affairs, UN Population Division. 2017. https://esa.un.org/unpd/wpp/Publications/Files/WPP2017 _Volume-I_Comprehensive-Tables.pdf.

Unwin, R. *Town Planning in Practice: An Introduction to the Art of Designing Cities and Suburbs*. London: T. F. Unwin, 1909.

Urbed. Uxcester Masterplan: A Report for the Wolfson Economics Prize. Urbed, Manchester, UK, 2014.

Von Bertalanffy, L. *General System Theory*. Harmondsworth: Penguin Books, 1972.

Von Foerster, H., P. M. Mora, and L. W. Amiot. Doomsday: Friday. November 13. AD 2026. *Science* 132 (1960): 1291–1295.

Von Thünen, J. H. *Von Thünen's Isolated State*. Edited by P. G. Hall, translated by Carla M. Wartenberg. Oxford, UK: Pergamon Press, 1966. First published as *Der Isolierte Staat*, vol. I. Hamburg, Germany: Perthes, 1826.

Wakefield, J. Tomorrow's Cities: Do You Want to Live in a Smart City? *BBC News*, August 19, 2013. http://www.bbc.co.uk/news/technology-22538561.

Walmsley, J. D., and G. J. Lewis. The Pace of Pedestrian Flows in Cities. *Environment and Behavior* 21, no. 2 (1989): 123–150.

Watts, D. *Small Worlds: The Dynamics of Networks between Order and Randomness*. Princeton, NJ: Princeton University Press, 1999.

Weaver, W. Science and Complexity. *American Scientist* 36 (1948): 536–544.

Webber, M. M. The Urban Place and the Non-Place Urban Realm. In *Explorations into Urban Structure*, edited by M. M. Webber, J. W. Dyckman, D. L. Foley, A. Z. Guttenberg, C. W. L. Wheaton, and C. B. Wurster, 79–153. Philadelphia, PA: University of Pennsylvania Press, 1964.

Weber, A. *The Growth of Cities in the Nineteenth Century*. New York: Columbia University Press and The Macmillan Company, 1899.

Weber, M. *The City*. 1921. Reprint, Glencoe, NY: The Free Press. 1966.

Wells, H. G. *Anticipations*. London: Chapman and Hall, 1902.

West, G. *Scale: The Universal Laws of Life and Death in Organisms. Cities and Companies*. London: Weidenfeld and Nicolson, 2017.

Whyte, W. H., F. Bello, S. Freedgood, D. Seligman, and J. Jacobs. *The Exploding Metropolis*. Garden City, New York: Doubleday and Company, 1958.

Wiener, N. *Inventions*. 1954. Reprint, Cambridge, MA: The MIT Press, 1994.

Williamson, L. Tomorrow's Cities: Just How Smart Is Songdo? *BBC News*, September 2, 2013. http://www.bbc.co.uk/news/technology-23757738.

Wise, D. Experts Speculate on Future Electronic Learning Environment. *InfoWorld* 4, no. 16 (1982): 6.

Wright, F. L. *The Disappearing City*. New York: William Farquhar Payson, 1932.

Wright, F. L. *A Testament*. New York: Horizon Press, 1957.

Wright, F. L. *When Democracy Builds*. Chicago: University of Chicago Press, 1945.

Zhong, C., M. Batty, E. Manley, and J. Wang. Variability in Regularity: A Comparative Study of Urban Mobility Patterns in London. Singapore and Beijing Using Smart-Card Data. *PLoS ONE* 11, no. 2 (2016): e0149222. doi:10.1371/journal.pone.0149222.

Zipf, G. K. *Human Behavior and the Principle of Least Effort*. Cambridge, MA: Addison-Wesley, 1949.

Zuckerberg, M. Mark Zuckerberg Explains His Law of Social Sharing. *TechCrunch*, July 6, 2011. https://techcrunch.com/2011/07/06/mark-zuckerberg-explains-his-law-of-social-sharing-video.

Name Index

Subject Index